Current
Directions
in
DEVELOPMENTAL
PSYCHOLOGY

READINGS FROM THE
ASSOCIATION FOR
PSYCHOLOGICAL SCIENCE

Current
Directions
in
DEVELOPMENTAL
PSYCHOLOGY
Second Edition

EDITED BY

Lynn S. Liben

The Pennsylvania State University

Boston • New York • San Francisco
Mexico City • Montreal • Toronto • London • Madrid • Munich • Paris
Hong Kong • Singapore • Tokyo • Cape Town • Sydney

Acquisitions Editor: Michelle Limoges
Series Editorial Assistant: Christina Manfroni
Marketing Manager: Kate Mitchell
Production Editor: Patty Bergin
Editorial Production Service: TexTech International
Composition Buyer: Linda Cox
Manufacturing Buyer: JoAnne Sweeney
Electronic Composition: TexTech International
Cover Administrator: Linda Knowles

For related titles and support materials, visit our online catalog at www.ablongman.com.

Between the time website information is gathered and then published, it is not unusual for some sites to have closed. Also, the transcription of URLs can result in typographical errors. The publisher would appreciate notification where these errors occur so that they may be corrected in subsequent editions.

Library of Congress Cataloging-in-Publication Data

Current directions in developmental psychology / edited by Lynn S. Liben—2nd edition.
   p. cm.
ISBN-13: 978-0-205-59750-5
ISBN-10:   0-205-59750-5
1. Developmental psychology.   I. Liben, Lynn S.
BF713.5.C87   2008
155—dc22   2007051140

Printed in the United States of America

10 9 8 7 6 5 4 3 2 1   11 10 09 08

Contents

Introduction

Sampling and Integrating Research in Developmental Psychology

It is a daunting task to try to capture any one field with a single collection of papers. Indeed, in the case of developmental psychology it is an impossible task because the field is so broad and diverse. In a real sense, developmental psychology is as vast as psychology itself, because virtually any topic in psychology raises the fascinating question, how did it [the phenomenon under study] come to be this way?

The goal of this book, therefore, is not to provide an exhaustive review of the discipline. Instead, it is to offer a taste of some of the exciting, high quality, contemporary, and specialized research in the field that has appeared in the APS journal, *Current Directions in Psychological Science*. Given that there have been far more articles describing work of this kind than can be accommodated in a single volume, the final selections for this book were motivated by an effort to meet some more specific goals.

First, taken as a group, the articles were selected to provide a sense of the vast array of substantive topics and approaches that fall under the umbrella of developmental psychology. Specifically, they were selected to represent six topics: Biological Foundations, Infant Processes, Cognitive Development, Family Environments, Social Groups, and Cultural Contexts. Although this is not the only structure that may be used to organize the content of developmental psychology, it is one that can encompass or organize most of what is studied in the discipline. Within this substantive diversity, an effort has also been made to sample across methodologies and designs. Thus, for example, within the 30 individual articles included in the reader are those that study development using highly controlled laboratory settings and those that use ecologically valid natural settings; those that use correlational methods and those that use classic experimental methods; and those that use cross-sectional designs and those that use longitudinal designs. Collectively the articles also draw from a variety of the major theoretical approaches, including Piaget, Vygotsky, Bronfenbrenner, and Bowlby.

Second, the articles were selected to capture some of the enduring conceptual issues in developmental psychology. One issue that underlies much of the work represented in this book is what is commonly referred to as the nature/nurture controversy. Can developmental outcomes be explained by biological factors or by environmental experiences? Articles in this book demonstrate the continuing interest in this question, offering varied perspectives on how it might be answered, and, indeed, on whether it should be addressed at all. A second is the continuity/discontinuity issue. Should development be conceptualized as gradual, or is it better to think of development as discontinuous, with development progressing in distinct, qualitatively different stages? Articles bearing on this issue are those studying how behaviors or concepts at one part of life are connected to similar phenomena at another part of life. A third issue is what is known as the mind/body problem which addresses the value (or harm) in splitting mind from body in our work (also referred to as the Cartesian position of dualism). Many articles in this book are relevant to this issue insofar as they illustrate what is gained by studying behavioral and biological factors simultaneously, or by studying directional or reciprocal effects of body-related changes and mind-related changes.

Third, articles were selected to convey the importance of a lifespan perspective on development. Thus, although most of the articles concern phenomena related to infancy and childhood—the emphasis of most courses in developmental psychology—some address phenomena in adolescence, adulthood (especially adults in the role of parenting), and in later adulthood and aging. Attention to later portions of life is critical for a comprehensive approach to development.

Finally, the selection of articles was motivated by an attempt to showcase, rather than hide, theoretical and methodological controversy. Sometimes novices in a field are dismayed to discover that even the experts do not agree. They want to hear the answer, the correct answer. But science progresses through controversies. Competing perspectives on a topic or about a method can inspire ever better methods and additional data, and the debates about them often clarify (even as they often exaggerate) what the alternative positions really are.

Collectively, the articles in this book offer a window into the field of contemporary developmental psychology. They provide detailed examples of specific research programs that can be used to enrich other course material such as a comprehensive textbook. Perhaps they will also whet readers' appetites to consult the many other outstanding articles on development that have appeared in *Current Directions*, and even inspire some readers to enter the field of developmental psychology and ultimately contribute to later editions of this book.

Section 1: Biological Foundations

In 1958, Anne Anastasi published an article entitled "Heredity, Environment, and the Question 'How?'" (*Psychological Review*) in which she suggested that the "heredity-environment question" was "a dead issue." Arguing that it is fruitless to ask "which" or "how much" heredity and environment contribute to developmental outcomes, she urged that the field instead study "how," the mechanisms by which these factors work. Despite the head-nodding that followed, a half-century later, many developmental psychologists continue to be engaged in the same attempt to answer the "how much" question. Contemporary scientists have a more sophisticated set of tools with which to explore the question, but the underlying debate about whether it is even a sensible question continues.

The first two articles represent the continuing controversy about the possibility of examining the independent roles of nature and nurture. In the first article, Gilbert Gottlieb explicitly rejects the notion that one can ever separate out and measure genetic effects. He argues that the "central dogma" of molecular biology—that gene activity has a unidirectional affect on developmental outcomes—is untenable. In its place he offers a complex, multi-level view of the reciprocal influence of genes and environment—probabilistic epigenesis. He faults behavior geneticists for trying to do the impossible in separating contributions from genes and environment, and illustrates his argument by both human and nonhuman research.

As one of those behavior geneticists so critiqued, in the second article, Eric Turkheimer argues explicitly against Gottlieb's position, articulating some of the practical limitations preventing experimental manipulation of either genes or environments in humans that are promulgated by Gottlieb. Turkheimer describes the rationale for using twin studies as a means of revealing the size of genetic contributions. Further, he argues that Gottlieb's criticism of behavior geneticists' inattention to actual developmental mechanisms—while in some sense true—is equally applicable to Gottlieb's own approach.

The next two articles likewise offer a contrast, but this time one concerning differential developmental outcomes of specific prenatal environments. Janet DiPietro examines whether child outcomes are affected by maternal stress during pregnancy. Explaining the absence of direct neural connections between mother and fetus, she identifies other potential transmission mechanisms, and reviews both animal and human research whose results address the effects of stress. She concludes that maternal stress has no clear negative consequences on humans, and may even have a positive effect on later cognitive abilities.

In the article that follows, Christopher Newland and Erin Rasmussen focus on prenatal exposure to methylmercury. Again, only correlational research is possible with humans, and thus they turn to experimental research with animals in which prenatal contaminant exposure is manipulated. They present strong evidence that methylmercury disrupts neural development and provide data from behavioral measures showing sometimes subtle, but long lasting, effects of prenatal exposure. Taken together, these two articles not only offer substantive data about effects of two kinds of prenatal exposure, but also provide a clear rationale for the use of animal models in the study of human development.

The final paper in this section, by Maestripieri, addresses the role of biological factors on one of the most central constructs of the socio-emotional side of human development—attachment. A strong attachment bond between child and parent (or some other adult) is critical for the human infant's survival, just as it is for any species in which the young begin life unable to feed and protect themselves. Maestripieri highlights research in developmental psychology showing that early attachment relationships predict many aspects of later developmental outcomes, and reviews empirical work linking hormonal environments (prenatal, perinatal and postpartum periods) to bonding and attachment.

Environmental and Behavioral Influences on Gene Activity

Gilbert Gottlieb[1]

Center for Developmental Science, University of North Carolina at Chapel Hill, Chapel Hill, North Carolina

Abstract

The central dogma of molecular biology holds that "information" flows from the genes to the structure of the proteins that the genes bring about through the formula DNA $\rightarrow$ RNA $\rightarrow$ protein. In this view, a set of master genes activates the DNA necessary to produce the appropriate proteins that the organism needs during development. In contrast to this view, probabilistic epigenesis holds that necessarily there are signals from the internal and external environment that activate DNA to produce the appropriate proteins. To support this view, I review a substantial body of evidence showing that external environmental influences on gene activation are normally occurring events in a large variety of organisms, including humans. This demonstrates how genes and environments work together to produce functional organisms, thus extending the model of probabilistic epigenesis.

Keywords

central dogma; probabilistic epigenesis; predetermined epigenesis

A virtual revolution that has taken place in our knowledge of environmental and behavioral influences on gene expression has not yet seeped into the social sciences in general and the behavioral sciences in particular. Earlier, it was not recognized that environmental and behavioral influences play an important role in triggering gene activity. Paradoxically, in biology there is an explicit dogma, formulated as such, that does not permit environmental influences on gene activity: the central dogma of molecular biology, first enunciated by Crick in 1958.

Although the central dogma may seem quite remote from psychology, I think it lies behind some psychological and behavioral theories that emphasize the sheerly endogenous (internal) development of the nervous system and early behavior (e.g., Elman et al., 1996) and the "innate foundation of the psyche" (e.g., Tooby & Cosmides, 1990), independent of experience or functional considerations. Such theories follow from the essentially dichotomous view that genes and other endogenous factors construct part of the organism and environment determines other features of the organism. The present essay is an attempt to show how genes and environment necessarily cooperate in the construction of organisms, and specifically, to show how genes require environmental and behavioral inputs to function appropriately during the normal course of individual development.

THE CENTRAL DOGMA

The central dogma asserts that "information" flows in only one direction from the genes to the structure of the proteins that the genes bring about. The formula for

Genetic Activity According To Central Dogma

$$\text{DNA} \longrightarrow \text{DNA} \underset{\longleftarrow}{\overset{?}{\rightleftarrows}} \text{RNA} \longrightarrow \text{Protein}$$

Fig. 1. The central dogma of molecular biology. The right-going arrows represent the central dogma. Retroviruses (represented by the left-going arrow from RNA to DNA) were not part of the dogma, but after their discovery, Crick (1970) said they were not prohibited in the original formulation of the dogma (Crick, 1958).

this information flow is DNA → RNA → protein. (Messenger RNA, or mRNA, is the intermediary in the process of protein synthesis. In the lingo of molecular biology, the process by which RNA is formed from the DNA template is called transcription, and the process by which proteins are formed from the RNA template is called translation.) After retroviruses were discovered in the 1960s (in retroviruses, RNA reversely transcribes DNA instead of the other way around), Crick wrote a postscript to his 1958 article in which he congratulated himself for not claiming that reverse transcription was impossible: "In looking back I am struck not only by the brashness which allowed us to venture powerful statements of a very general nature, but also by the rather delicate discrimination used in selecting what statements to make" (Crick, 1970, p. 562). Any ambiguity about the controlling factors in gene expression in the central dogma was removed in a later article by Crick, in which he specifically said that the genes of higher organisms are turned on and off by other genes (Crick, 1982, p. 515). Figure 1 shows the central dogma of molecular biology in the form of a diagram.

THE GENOME ACCORDING TO CENTRAL DOGMA

The picture of the genome that emerges from the central dogma is one of (a) encapsulation, setting the genome off from influences above the genetic level (supragenetic influences), and (b) a largely feedforward (unidirectional) informational process in which the genes contain a blueprint or master plan for the construction and determination of the organism. In this view, the genome is not seen as part of the holistic, bidirectional developmental-physiological system of the organism, responsive to signals from internal cellular sources such as the cytoplasm of the cell or to extracellular influences such as hormones, and the genome is seen as certainly not responsive to influences from outside the organism, such as stimuli or signals from the external environment.

In this essay, my goal is to show that the normally occurring influences on genetic activity include influences from the external environment, that is, to demonstrate that the genome is not encapsulated and is in fact a part of the organism's general developmental-physiological adaptation to environmental stresses and signals: Genes express themselves appropriately only in responding to internally and externally generated stimulation. Further, in this holistic view, although genes participate in the making of protein, protein is also subject to other influences, and protein must be further stimulated and elaborated to become part of the nervous system (or other systems) of the organism. Thus, genes operate at the lowest level of organismic organization, and they do not, in and of themselves, produce finished traits or features of the organism. The organism is a product of epigenetic development, that is, a process that involves not only the genes but also many other supragenetic influences. Because this latter point has been the subject of numerous publications (reviewed in Gottlieb, 1992), I do not deal with it further here, but, rather, restrict this essay to documenting that the activity of genes is regulated in just the same way as the rest of the organism, being called forth by signals from the normally occurring external environment, as well as the internal environment. Although this fact is not well known in the social and behavioral sciences, it is surprising to find that it is also not widely appreciated in biology proper (Strohman, 1997). In biology, the external environment is seen as the agent of natural selection in promoting evolution, not as a crucial feature of individual development. Many biologists subscribe to the notion that "the genes are safely sequestered inside the nucleus of the cell and out of reach of ordinary environmental effects" (Wills, 1989, p. 19).

FROM CENTRAL DOGMA OF MOLECULAR BIOLOGY TO PROBABILISTIC EPIGENESIS

As can be seen in Table 1, a number of different naturally occurring environmental signals can stimulate gene expression in a large variety of organisms from nematodes to humans. To understand the findings summarized in Table 1, the nongeneticist needs to know that there are three levels of evidence of genetic activity in the right-hand column of Table 1: protein expression or synthesis, mRNA activity, and genetic activity itself. As the middle column of the table shows, there are important environmental and behavioral signals affecting genetic activity, even though the activity of the genes is quite remote from these stimuli. After proteins are made, many factors must intervene before neurons or behaviors are realized; the route from protein to neuron or behavior is not direct. The fact that normally occurring environmental events stimulate gene activity during the usual course of development in a variety of organisms means that genes and genetic activity are part of the developmental-physiological system and do not stand outside of that system.

The main purpose of this essay is to place genes and genetic activity firmly within a holistic developmental-physiological framework, one in which genes not only affect each other and mRNA but are affected by activities at other levels of the system, up to and including the external environment. This holistic developmental system of bidirectional, coacting influences is captured schematically in Figure 2. In contrast to the unidirectional and encapsulated genetic predeterminism of the central dogma, a probabilistic view of epigenesis holds that the sequence and outcomes of development are probabilistically determined by the critical operation of various stimulative events that occur both within and outside the organism.

The probabilistic-epigenetic framework presented in Figure 2 not only is based on what we now know about mechanisms of individual development at all levels of analysis, but also derives from our understanding of evolution and natural selection. Natural selection serves as a filter and preserves reproductively successful phenotypes (outcomes of development). These successful phenotypes are a product of individual development, and thus are a consequence of the adaptability of the organism to its developmental conditions. Therefore, natural

Table 1. *Normally occurring environmental and behavioral influences on gene activity*

Species	Environmental signal or stimulus	Resulting alteration
Nematodes	Absence or presence of food	Diminished or enhanced neuronal *daf-7* gene mRNA expression, inhibiting or provoking larval development
Fruit flies	Transient elevated heat stress during larval development	Presence of proteins produced by heat shock and thermotolerance (enhanced thermal regulation)
Fruit flies	Light-dark cycle	Presence of PER and TIM protein expression and circadian rhythms
Various reptiles	Incubation temperature	Sex determination
Songbirds (canaries, zebra finches)	Conspecific song	Increased forebrain mRNA
Hamsters	Light-dark cycle	Increased pituitary hormone mRNA and reproductive behavior
Mice	Acoustic stimulation	Enhanced c-*fos* expression, neuronal activity, and organization of the auditory system
Mice	Light-dark cycle	c-*fos*-induced mRNA expression in hypothalamus, circadian locomotor activity
Rats	Tactile stimulation	Enhanced c-*fos* expression and increased number of somatosensory (sense of touch) cortical neurons[a]
Rats	Learning task involving vestibular (balance) system	Change in nuclear RNA base ratios in vestibular nerve cells
Rats	Visual stimulation	Increased RNA and protein synthesis in visual cortex[a]
Rats	Environmental complexity	Increased brain RNA diversity
Rats	Prenatal nutrition	Increase in cerebral DNA (increased number of brain cells)
Rats	Infantile handling, separation from mother	Increased hypothalamic mRNAs for corticotropin-releasing hormone throughout life
Cats	Visual stimulation	Increased visual cortex[a] RNA complexity (diversity)
Humans	Academic examinations taken by medical students (psychological stress)	Reduced mRNA activity in interleukin 2 receptor (immune system response)

Note. mRNA = messenger RNA; PER and TIM are proteins arising from activity of *per* (*period*) and *tim* (*timeless*) genes; activity of c-*fos* genes leads to production of c-FOS protein. References documenting the findings listed can be found in Gottlieb (1998, Table 2).
[a]Cortex is the outer covering of the brain, or gray matter.

selection has preserved (favored) organisms that are adaptably responsive to their developmental conditions, both behaviorally and physiologically. Organisms with the same genes can develop very different phenotypes under different developmental conditions, as witness the identical twins shown in Figure 3. These men were raised in different homes and developed striking physical, behavioral, and psychological differences, despite their identical genomes.

BIDIRECTIONAL INFLUENCES

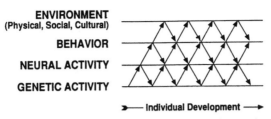

Fig. 2. The probabilistic-epigenetic framework. The diagram depicts the completely bidirectional and coactive nature of genetic, neural, behavioral, and environmental influences over the course of individual development. From *Individual Development and Evolution: The Genesis of Novel Behavior* (p. 152), by G. Gottlieb, 1992, New York: Oxford University Press. Copyright 1992 by Oxford University Press, Inc. Reprinted with permission.

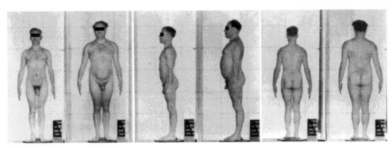

Fig. 3. Remarkable illustration of the enormous phenotypic variation that can result when monozygotic (single-egg) identical twins are reared apart in very different family environments from birth. From *Fetus Into Man* (p. 120), by J.M. Tanner, 1978, Cambridge, MA: Harvard University Press. Copyright 1978 by Harvard University Press, renewed 1989 by J.M. Tanner. Adapted with permission.

Because the probabilistic-epigenetic view presented in Figure 2 does not portray enough detail at the level of genetic activity, it is useful to flesh that out, to show how it differs from the previously described central dogma of molecular biology. As shown in Figure 4, the original central dogma explicitly posited one-way traffic—DNA → RNA → protein—and was silent about any other flows of information (Crick, 1958). The bottom of Figure 4 illustrates probabilistic epigenesis, which is inherently bidirectional in the horizontal and vertical levels (Fig. 2). Thus, this diagram has information flowing not only from RNA to DNA, but from protein to protein and from DNA to DNA. The only relationship that is not yet supported is protein → RNA, in the sense of protein altering the structure of RNA, but there are other influences of protein on RNA activity (not its structure) that would support such a directional flow. For example, a process known as *phosphorylation* can modify proteins so that they activate (or inactivate) other proteins (protein → protein), which, when activated, trigger rapid production of mRNA (protein → RNA activity). When mRNAs are transcribed by DNA, they do not necessarily become immediately active but require a further signal to do so. The consequences of phosphorylation could provide that signal

Genetic Activity According To Central Dogma

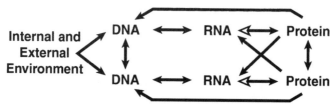

Genetic Activity According To Probabilistic Epigenesis

Fig. 4. Influences on genetic activity according to the central dogma (top) and probabilistic epigenesis (bottom). The filled arrows indicate documented sources of influence, and the open arrow from protein back to RNA indicates what remains a theoretical possibility in probabilistic epigenesis but is prohibited in the central dogma (as are protein ←—→ protein influences). Protein → protein influences occur (a) when prions (abnormally conformed proteins) transfer their abnormal conformation to other proteins and (b) when, during normal development, proteins activate or inactivate other proteins (as in the case of phosphorylation, described in the text). The filled arrows from protein to RNA represent the activation of mRNA by protein (e.g., as a consequence of phosphorylation). DNA ←—→ DNA influences are termed epistatic, referring to the modification of the expression of genes depending on the genetic background in which they are located. In the central dogma, genetic activity is dictated solely by genes (DNA → DNA), whereas in probabilistic epigenesis, internal and external environmental events activate genetic expression through proteins (protein → DNA), hormones, and other influences. To keep the diagram manageable, the fact that behavior and the external environment exert their effects on DNA through internal mediators (proteins, hormones, etc.) is not shown; nor is it shown that the protein products of some genes regulate the expression of other genes. (See the text for further discussion of this figure.)

(protein → protein → mRNA activity → protein). A process like this appears to be involved in the expression of "fragile X mental retardation protein." This protein is produced as described under normal conditions but is missing in the brain of fragile X mental retardates; thus, fragile X mental retardation represents a failure of gene (or mRNA) expression rather than a positive genetic contribution.[2]

CONCLUSIONS

The central dogma lies behind the persistent trend in biology and psychology to view genes and environment as making identifiably separate contributions to the phenotypic outcomes of development. Quantitative behavior genetics (the study of the heritability of behavior when one does not know how many or which genes are correlated with a given trait) is based on this erroneous assumption. Although genes no doubt play a constraining role in development, the actual limits of these constraints are quite wide and, most important, cannot be specified in advance of experimental manipulation or accidents of nature. There is no doubt that development is constrained at all levels of the system (Fig. 2), not only by genes and environments.

Finally, I do hope that the emphasis here on normally occurring environmental influences on gene activity does not raise the specter of a new, subtle form of "environmentalism." I do not think I would be labeled an environmentalist if I were to say organisms are often adaptably responsive to their environments. So, by calling attention to genes being adaptably responsive to their internal and external environments, I am not being an environmentalist but merely including genetic activity within the probabilistic-epigenetic framework that characterizes the organism and all of its constituent parts.

In view of the findings reviewed here, in the future it would be most important to eschew both genetic determinism and environmental determinism, as we now should understand that it is truly correct (not merely a verbalism) to say that environments and genes necessarily cooperate in bringing about any outcome of individual development.

Recommended Reading

Gottlieb, G. (1997). *Synthesizing nature-nurture: Prenatal roots of instinctive behavior.* Mahwah, NJ: Erlbaum.

Nijhout, H.F. (1990). Metaphors and the role of genes in development. *BioEssays, 12,* 441–446.

Stent, G. (1981). Strength and weakness of the genetic approach to the nervous system. *Annual Review of Neuroscience, 4,* 163–194.

Wahlsten, D., & Gottlieb, G. (1997). The invalid separation of nature and nurture: Lessons from animal experimentation. In R.J. Sternberg & E. Grigorenko (Eds.), *Intelligence, heredity, and environment* (pp. 163–192). New York: Cambridge University Press.

Acknowledgments—The author's research and scholarly activities are supported in part by National Institute of Mental Health Grant P50-MH-52429. This article is an abstract of an article that appeared in the *Psychological Review,* 1998, Vol. 105, pp. 792–802, and is reproduced here with the permission of the American Psychological Association.

Notes

1. Address correspondence to Gilbert Gottlieb, Center for Developmental Science, Campus Box 8115, University of North Carolina, Chapel Hill, NC 27599-8115.

2. "Genetic" disorders, both mental and physical, often represent biochemical deficiencies of one sort or another due to the lack of expression of the genes and mRNAs needed to produce the appropriate proteins necessary for normal development. Thus, the search for "candidate genes" in psychiatric or other disorders is most often a search for genes that are not being expressed, not for genes that are being expressed and causing the disorders. So-called cystic fibrosis genes and manic depression genes, among others, are in this category. The instances that I know of in which the presence of genes causes a problem

are Edward's syndrome and trisomy 21 (Down syndrome), wherein the presence of an extra, otherwise normal, chromosome (18 and 21, respectively) causes problems. In some cases, it is of course possible that the expression of mutated genes can be involved in a disorder, but, in my opinion, it is often the lack of expression of normal genes that is the culprit.

References

Crick, F. (1970). Central dogma of molecular biology. *Nature, 227,* 561–563.

Crick, F. (1982). DNA today. *Perspectives in Biology and Medicine, 25,* 512–517.

Crick, F.H.C. (1958). On protein synthesis. In *The biological replication of macromolecules* (Symposia of the Society for Experimental Biology No. 12., pp. 138–163). Cambridge, England: Cambridge University Press.

Elman, J.L., Bates, E.A., Johnson, M.H., Karmiloff-Smith, A., Parisi, D., & Plunkett, K. (1996). *Rethinking innateness: A connectionist perspective on development.* Cambridge, MA: MIT Press.

Gottlieb, G. (1992). *Individual development and evolution: The genesis of novel behavior.* New York: Oxford University Press.

Gottlieb, G. (1998). Normally occurring environmental and behavioral influences on gene activity: From central dogma to probabilistic epigenesis. *Psychological Review, 105,* 792–802.

Strohman, R.C. (1997). The coming Kuhnian revolution in biology. *Nature Biotechnology, 15,* 194–200.

Tanner, J.M. (1978). *Fetus into man.* Cambridge, MA: Harvard University Press.

Tooby, J., & Cosmides, L. (1990). The past explains the present: Emotional adaptations and the structure of ancestral environments. *Ethology and Sociobiology, 11,* 375–424.

Wills, C. (1989). *The wisdom of the genes: New pathways in evolution.* New York: Basic Books.

This article has been reprinted as it originally appeared in *Current Directions in Psychological Science*. Citation information for this article as originally published appears above.

Three Laws of Behavior Genetics and What They Mean

Eric Turkheimer[1]

Department of Psychology, University of Virginia, Charlottesville, Virginia

Abstract

Behavior genetics has demonstrated that genetic variance is an important component of variation for all behavioral outcomes, but variation among families is not. These results have led some critics of behavior genetics to conclude that heritability is so ubiquitous as to have few consequences for scientific understanding of development, while some behavior genetic partisans have concluded that family environment is not an important cause of developmental outcomes. Both views are incorrect. Genotype is in fact a more systematic source of variability than environment, but for reasons that are methodological rather than substantive. Development is fundamentally nonlinear, interactive, and difficult to control experimentally. Twin studies offer a useful methodological shortcut, but do not show that genes are more fundamental than environments.

Keywords

genes; environment; development; behavior genetics

The nature-nurture debate is over. The bottom line is that everything is heritable, an outcome that has taken all sides of the nature-nurture debate by surprise. Irving Gottesman and I have suggested that the universal influence of genes on behavior be enshrined as the first law of behavior genetics (Turkheimer & Gottesman, 1991), and at the risk of naming laws that I can take no credit for discovering, it is worth stating the nearly unanimous results of behavior genetics in a more formal manner.

- *First Law*. All human behavioral traits are heritable.
- *Second Law*. The effect of being raised in the same family is smaller than the effect of genes.
- *Third Law*. A substantial portion of the variation in complex human behavioral traits is not accounted for by the effects of genes or families.

It is not my purpose in this brief article to defend these three laws against the many exceptions that might be claimed. The point is that now that the empirical facts are in and no longer a matter of serious controversy, it is time to turn attention to what the three laws mean, to the implications of the genetics of behavior for an understanding of complex human behavior and its development.

VARIANCE AND CAUSATION IN BEHAVIORAL DEVELOPMENT

If the first two laws are taken literally, they seem to herald a great victory for the nature side of the old debate: Genes matter, families do not. To understand why such views are at best an oversimplification of a complex reality, it is necessary to consider the newest wave of opposition that behavior genetics has generated. These new critics, whose most articulate spokesman is Gilbert Gottlieb (1991, 1992, 1995), claim that the goal of developmental psychology is to specify the actual developmental processes that lead to complex outcomes. In lower animals, whose breeding and environment can be brought under the control of the scientist, it is possible to document such developmental processes in exquisite detail. The critics draw an unfavorable comparison between these detailed animal studies and twin studies of behavior genetics, which produce only statistical conclusions about the relative importance of genes and environment in development.

The greatest virtue of the new challenge is that it abandons the implausible environmentalist contention that important aspects of behavior will be without genetic influence. Gottlieb (1992) stated, "The present . . . viewpoint holds that genes are an inextricable component of any developmental system, and thus *genes are involved in all traits*" (p. 147). Unlike earlier critics who deplored the reductionism they attributed to behavior genetic theories of behavior, the developmental biologists take behavior genetics to task for not being mechanistic *enough*. Once vilified as the paragon of determinist accounts of human behavior, behavior genetics is now chastised for offering vague and inconclusive models of development (Gottlieb, 1995; Turkheimer, Goldsmith, & Gottesman, 1995), and judged by the standards of developmental psychobiology in lower animals, it is true enough that behavior genetic theories of complex human behavior seem woefully poorly specified. But ultimately the charge is unfair, because there is no equivalent in developmental psychobiology to the behavior genetic study of marital status or school performance. The great preponderance of the exquisite experimental science that goes into animal psychobiology is quite simply impossible to conduct in humans.

Human developmental social science is difficult—equally so for the genetically and environmentally inclined—because of the (methodologically vexing, humanistically pleasing) confluence of two conditions: (a) Behavior emerges out of complex, nonlinear developmental processes, and (b) ethical considerations prevent us from bringing most human developmental processes under effective experimental control. Figure 1 is a schematic illustration of the problem. Individual genes (Genes 1, 2, and 3) and their environments (which include other genes) interact to initiate a complex developmental process that determines adult personality. Most characteristic of this process is its interactivity: Subsequent environments to which the organism is exposed depend on its earlier states, and each new environment changes the developmental trajectory, which affects future expression of genes, and so forth. Everything is interactive, in the sense that no arrows proceed uninterrupted from cause to effect; any individual gene or environmental event produces an effect only by interacting with other genes and environments.

For the behavior geneticist, however, the quasi-experimental gift of genetically identical and nonidentical twins offers a remarkable, if deceptively simple, method to span this daunting interactive complexity. Thanks to the fact that identical twins are on average exactly twice as similar genetically as nonidentical twins, one can use straightforward statistical procedures to estimate the proportion of variability

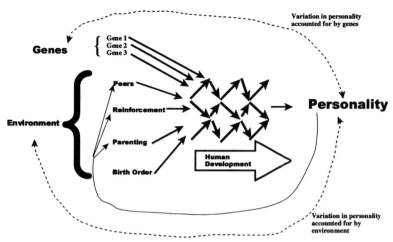

Fig. 1. Schematic diagram of contrasting roles of genes and environment in development of personality. One-headed arrows link causes to effects; two-headed arrows indicate correlations. Genes and environments are both causal inputs into an interactive developmental system (represented by the network of arrows in the center of the figure), but because people select and shape their own environments (as represented by lighter one-headed arrows from personality to environments), correlations across the developmental system (dotted two-headed arrows) are easier to detect for genes than for environments.

in complex outcomes that is associated with causally distant genes, all the while maintaining a state of near-perfect ignorance about the actual causal processes that connect genes to behavior. This methodological shortcut is not available to rivals of behavior genetics who seek to measure the effects of families on behavior. How similar was my rearing environment to that of my siblings? And how similar was it to the environment of my adopted sibling, if I have one, or to the environment of my biological sibling who was raised by someone else? The apparent victory of nature over nurture suggested by the first two laws is thus seen to be more methodological than substantive. In a world in which there were occasional occurrences of "identical environmental twins," whose experiences were exactly the same, moment by moment, and another variety who shared exactly (but randomly) 50% of their experiences, environmentalists could reproduce the precision of their rivals, and like the behavior geneticists could measure with great precision the total contribution of the environment while knowing almost nothing about the developmental processes that underlie it.

The old-fashioned nature-nurture debate was about whether or not genes influence complex behavioral outcomes, and that question has been decisively answered in the affirmative. The new question is how we can proceed from partitioning sources of variance to specifying concrete developmental processes (Turkheimer, 1998), and although critics like Gottlieb are correct that heritability per se has few implications for a scientific understanding of development, they have failed to emphasize two crucial points. First, heritability does have one certain consequence: It is no longer possible to interpret correlations among biologically related family members as prima facie evidence of sociocultural causal mechanisms. If the children of depressed mothers grow up to be depressed themselves, it does not necessarily demonstrate that being raised by a depressed mother is itself depressing. The children might have grown up equally depressed if they had been adopted and raised by different mothers, under the influence of their biological mother's genes. For every behavior geneticist who continues to report moderate heritabilities as though they were news, there is an environmentalist who reports causally ambiguous correlations between genetically related parents and children. Second, the problem the critics have uncovered extends well beyond behavior genetics: It is a rare environmentalist who has never used statistical methods to predict behavioral outcomes from earlier events, in the hope that the specific developmental mechanisms can be filled in later. The disconnect between the analysis of variance and the analysis of causes, to use Lewontin's (1974) phrase, is not a proprietary flaw in behavior genetic methodology; in fact, it is the bedrock methodological problem of contemporary social science.

NONSHARED ENVIRONMENT AND THE GLOOMY PROSPECT

Even after the effects of genes and the shared effects of families have been accounted for, around 50% of the differences among siblings is left unexplained. In recent years, scientists interested in the genetics of behavior have come to call this unexplained portion the "nonshared environment." Although according to the second law shared environment accounts for a small proportion of the variability in behavioral outcomes, according to the third law, nonshared environment usually accounts for a substantial portion. So perhaps the appropriate conclusion is not so much that the family environment does not matter for development, but rather that the part of the family environment that is shared by siblings does not matter. What does matter is the individual environments of children, their peers, and the aspects of their parenting that they do not share. Plomin and Daniels (1987) reviewed evidence of the predominance of nonshared environmental variance and posed a seminal question: Why are children in the same family so different? They proposed that siblings are different because nonshared environmental events are more potent causes of developmental outcomes than the shared environmental variables, like socioeconomic status, that have formed the traditional basis of sociocultural developmental psychology.

Plomin and Daniels's explanation involves a subtle conceptual shift, best described in terms of a distinction between the objective and effective environment (Goldsmith, 1993; Turkheimer & Waldron, 2000). What qualifies an environmental event as nonshared? There are two possibilities. The first is objective: An event is nonshared if it is experienced by only one sibling in a family, regardless of the consequences it produces. The other possibility is effective: An environmental event is nonshared if it makes siblings different rather than similar, regardless of whether it was experienced by one or both of them. Plomin and Daniels's proposal, then, is that the nonshared environment as an effectively defined variance component can be explained by objectively nonshared environmental events. The question, "Why are children in the same family so different?" is answered, "Because measurable differences in their environments make them that way."

This proposal has been enormously influential, spawning an entire area of empirical inquiry into the consequences of measured environmental differences among siblings. Ironically, that same literature has quite decisively demonstrated that the conjecture is false. A review of 43 studies that measured differences in the environments of siblings and related them to differences in the siblings' developmental outcomes (Turkheimer & Waldron, 2000) has shown that although upwards of 50% of the variance in behavioral outcomes is accounted for by the effectively defined variance component called nonshared environment, the median percentage accounted for by objectively defined nonshared events is less than 2%. What could be going on?

Plomin and Daniels (1987) almost identified the answer to this question, but dismissed it as too pessimistic:

> One gloomy prospect is that the salient environment might be unsystematic, idiosyncratic, or serendipitous events such as accidents, illnesses, or other traumas. . . . Such capricious events, however, are likely to prove a dead end for research. More interesting heuristically are possible systematic sources of differences between families. (p. 8)

The gloomy prospect is true. Nonshared environmental variability predominates not because of the systematic effects of environmental events that are not shared among siblings, but rather because of the unsystematic effects of all environmental events, compounded by the equally unsystematic processes that expose us to environmental events in the first place (Turkheimer & Gottesman, 1996).

A model of nonshared variability based on the gloomy prospect is radically different from the Plomin model based on systematic consequences of environmental differences among siblings. Most important, the two models suggest very different prospects for a genetically informed developmental psychology. Again and again, Plomin and his colleagues have emphasized that the importance of nonshared environment implies that it is time to abandon shared environmental variables as possible explanations of developmental outcomes. And although modern environmentalists might not miss coarse measures like socioeconomic status, it is quite another thing to give up on the causal efficaciousness of normal families, as Scarr (1992), Rowe (1994), and Harris (1998) have urged. If, however, nonshared environmental variability in outcome is the result of the unsystematic consequences of both shared and nonshared environmental events, the field faces formidable methodological problems—Plomin and Daniels's gloomy prospect—but need not conclude that aspects of families children share with siblings are of no causal importance.

CONCLUSION: ANTICIPATING THE GENOME PROJECT

It is now possible for behavior genetics to move beyond statistical analyses of differences between identical and nonidentical twins and identify individual genes that are related to behavioral outcomes. What should we expect from this endeavor? Behavior geneticists anticipate vindication: At long last, statistical variance components will be rooted in the actual causal consequences of actual genes. Critics of behavior genetics expect the opposite, pointing to the repeated failures to replicate associations between genes and behavior as evidence of the shaky theoretical underpinnings of which they have so long complained.

There is an interesting parallel between the search for individual genes that influence behavior and the failed attempt to specify the nonshared environment in terms of measured environmental variables. In each case, investigators began with statistically reliable but causally vague sources of variance, and set out to discover the actual causal processes that produced them. The quest for the nonshared environment, as we have seen, got stuck in the gloomy prospect. Although individual environmental events influence outcomes in the most general sense, they do not do so in a systematic way. One can detect their effects only by accumulating them statistically, using twins or adoptees.

If the underlying causal structure of human development is highly complex, as illustrated in Figure 1, the relatively simple statistical procedures employed by developmental psychologists, geneticists, and environmentalists alike are being badly misapplied. But misapplied statistical procedures still produce what appear to be results. Small relations would still be found between predictors and outcomes, but the underlying complex causal processes would cause the apparent results to be small, and to change unpredictably from one experiment to the next. So individual investigators would obtain "results," which would then fail to replicate and accumulate into a coherent theory because the simple statistical model did not fit the complex developmental process to which it was being applied. Much social science conducted in the shadow of the gloomy prospect has exactly this flavor (e.g., Meehl, 1978).

The gloomy prospect looms larger for the genome project than is generally acknowledged. The question is not whether there are correlations to be found between individual genes and complex behavior—of course there are—but instead whether there are domains of genetic causation in which the gloomy prospect does not prevail, allowing the little bits of correlational evidence to cohere into replicable and cumulative genetic models of development. My own prediction is that such domains will prove rare indeed, and that the likelihood of discovering them will be inversely related to the complexity of the behavior under study.

Finally, it must be remembered that the gloomy prospect is gloomy only from the point of view of the working social scientist. Although frustrated developmental psychologists may be tempted to favor methodologically tractable heuristics over chaotic psychological reality, it is a devil's choice: In the long run, the gloomy prospect always wins, and no one would want to live in a world where it did not. Psychology is at least one good paradigm shift away from an empirical answer to the gloomy prospect, but the philosophical response is becoming clear: The additive effect of genes may constitute what is predictable about human development, but what is predictable about human development is also what is least interesting about it. The gloomy prospect isn't.

Recommended Reading

Gottlieb, G. (1992). (See References)
Lewontin, R.C. (1974). (See References)
Meehl, P.E. (1978). (See References)
Plomin, R., & Daniels, D. (1987). (See References)

Note

1. Address correspondence to Eric Turkheimer, Department of Psychology, 102 Gilmer Hall, P.O. Box 400400, University of Virginia, Charlottesville, VA 22904-4400; e-mail: turkheimer@virginia.edu.

References

Goldsmith, H. (1993). Nature-nurture issues in the behavioral genetic context: Overcoming barriers to communication. In R. Plomin & G. McClearn (Eds.), *Nature, nurture and psychology* (pp. 325–339). Washington, DC: American Psychological Association.

Gottlieb, G. (1991). Experiential canalization of behavioral development: Theory. *Developmental Psychology, 27,* 4–13.

Gottlieb, G. (1992). *Individual development and evolution.* New York: Oxford University Press.

Gottlieb, G. (1995). Some conceptual deficiencies in "developmental" behavior genetics. *Human Development, 38,* 131–141.

Harris, J.R. (1998). *The nurture assumption: Why children turn out the way they do.* New York: Free Press.

Lewontin, R.C. (1974). The analysis of variance and the analysis of causes. *American Journal of Human Genetics, 26,* 400–411.

Meehl, P.E. (1978). Theoretical risks and tabular asterisks: Sir Karl, Sir Ronald, and the slow progress of soft psychology. *Journal of Consulting and Clinical Psychology, 46,* 806–834.

Plomin, R., & Daniels, D. (1987). Why are children in the same family so different from one another? *Behavioral and Brain Sciences, 10,* 1–60.

Rowe, D.C. (1994). *The limits of family influence: Genes, experience, and behavior.* New York: Guilford Press.

Scarr, S. (1992). Developmental theories for the 1990s: Development and individual differences. *Child Development, 63,* 1–19.

Turkheimer, E. (1998). Heritability and biological explanation. *Psychological Review, 105,* 782–791.

Turkheimer, E., Goldsmith, H.H., & Gottesman, I.I. (1995). Commentary. *Human Development, 38,* 142–153.

Turkheimer, E., & Gottesman, I.I. (1991). Is H^2 = 0 a null hypothesis anymore? *Behavioral and Brain Sciences, 14,* 410–411.

Turkheimer, E., & Gottesman, I.I. (1996). Simulating the dynamics of genes and environment in development. *Development and Psychopathology, 8,* 667–677.

Turkheimer, E., & Waldron, M.C. (2000). Nonshared environment: A theoretical, methodological, and quantitative review. *Psychological Bulletin, 126,* 78–108.

This article has been reprinted as it originally appeared in *Current Directions in Psychological Science*. Citation information for this article as originally published appears above.

The Role of Prenatal Maternal Stress in Child Development

Janet A. DiPietro[1]

Johns Hopkins University

Abstract

The notion that a woman's psychological state during pregnancy affects the fetus is a persistent cultural belief in many parts of the world. Recent results indicate that prenatal maternal distress in rodents and nonhuman primates negatively influences long-term learning, motor development, and behavior in their offspring. The applicability of these findings to human pregnancy and child development is considered in this article. Potential mechanisms through which maternal psychological functioning may alter development of the fetal nervous system are being identified by current research, but it is premature to conclude that maternal prenatal stress has negative consequences for child development. Mild stress may be a necessary condition for optimal development.

Keywords

pregnancy; fetus; fetal development; stress

"Ay ay, for this I draw in many a tear,
And stop the rising of blood-sucking sighs,
Lest with my sighs or tears I blast or drown
King Edward's fruit, true heir to the English Crown"

—Queen Elizabeth's response upon learning of her husband's imprisonment in
Shakespeare's *King Henry VI* (Part 3), Act IV, Scene IV

Since antiquity, people have thought that the emotions and experiences of a pregnant woman impinge on her developing fetus. Some of these notions, such as the idea that a severe fright marks a child with a prominent birthmark, no longer persist. However, the premise that maternal psychological distress has deleterious effects on the fetus is the focus of active scientific inquiry today. A resurgence of interest in the prenatal period as a staging period for later diseases, including psychiatric ones, has been fostered by the enormous attention devoted to the hypothesis of fetal programming advanced by D.J. Barker and his colleagues. Fetal programming implies that maternal and fetal factors that affect growth impart an indelible impression on adult organ function, including functioning of the brain and nervous system. That earlier circumstances, including those during the prenatal period, might affect later development is hardly newsworthy to developmentalists. In the 1930s, the Fels Research Institute initiated a longitudinal study of child development that commenced with intensive investigation of the fetal period.

Possible effects of maternal psychological distress during pregnancy range along a continuum from the immediate and disastrous (e.g., miscarriage) to the more subtle and long term (e.g., developmental disorders). Most existing research has focused on the effects of maternal distress on pregnancy itself. For example, there are numerous comprehensive reviews of research indicating that women who express greater distress during pregnancy give birth somewhat earlier to somewhat lighter babies than do women who are less distressed. The focus of this report is on the potential for maternal stress to generate more far-reaching effects on behavioral and cognitive development in childhood.

MECHANISMS AND EVIDENCE FROM ANIMAL STUDIES

There are no direct neural connections between the mother and the fetus. To have impact on the fetus, maternal psychological functioning must be translated into physiological effects. Three mechanisms by which this might occur are considered most frequently: alteration in maternal behaviors (e.g., substance abuse), reduction in blood flow such that the fetus is deprived of oxygen and nutrients, and transport of stress-related neurohormones to the fetus through the placenta. Stress-related neurohormones, such as cortisol, are necessary for normal fetal maturation and the birth process. However, relatively slight variations in these hormones, particularly early in pregnancy, have the potential to generate a cascade of effects that may result in changes to the fetus's own stress response system.

The most compelling evidence of a link between maternal psychological functioning and later development in offspring is found in animal studies. Stress responses in rodents can be reliably induced by a variety of experimental methods. Deliberate exposure of pregnant laboratory animals to stressful events (e.g., restraint) produces effects on offspring. These include deficits in motor development, learning behavior, and the ability to cope effectively in stressful situations. There is a tendency for the effects to be greater in female than in male offspring. Changes in brain structure and function of prenatally stressed animals have also been documented (Welberg & Seckl, 2001). Yet not all documented effects of prenatal stress are negative; mild stress has been observed to benefit, not damage, later learning in rats (Fujioka et al., 2001).

In a series of studies, pregnant rhesus monkeys that were exposed to repeated periods of loud noise were shown to bear offspring with delayed motor development and reduced attention in infancy. A constellation of negative behaviors, including enhanced responsiveness to stress and dysfunctional social behavior with peers, persisted through adolescence (Schneider & Moore, 2000). In general, studies of stress in nonhuman primates find males to be more affected than females. However, although a study comparing offspring of pregnant pigtailed macaques that were repeatedly stressed with offspring of nonstressed mothers did find that the behavior of prenatally stressed males was less mature than the behavior of non-prenatally stressed males, for females the results were reversed. The females born to the stressed mothers displayed more mature behavior than non-prenatally stressed females (Novak & Sackett, 1996). Thus, although most studies have reported detrimental consequences, reports of either no effects or beneficial ones make it clear that much is left to be learned about the specific characteristics of stressors that either accelerate or retard development.

DOES MATERNAL STRESS AFFECT
DEVELOPMENT IN HUMANS?

Several important factors make it difficult to generalize results based on animal studies to humans. First, there are substantial physiological differences inherent to pregnancies in different species. Second, researchers are unable to control the events that transpire after birth in humans. Women who are psychologically stressed before pregnancy are also likely to be stressed after pregnancy, so it is critical that the role of social influences after birth be carefully distinguished from pregnancy effects that are transmitted biologically. Finally, the nature of the prenatal stress studied in animals and humans is very different, and this may pose the greatest barrier to the ability to generalize. In animal research, stressors are external events that are controlled in terms of duration, frequency, and intensity. The closest parallel in human studies is found in the few studies that have taken advantage of specific events, including an earthquake and the World Trade Center disaster, to study the effects on pregnancy in women residing in physical proximity. No such study has examined children's cognitive or behavioral outcomes. However, what is measured in virtually all human studies of "stress" during pregnancy is women's affect, mood, and emotional responses to daily circumstances in their lives. Maternal anxiety and, to a lesser extent, depression are prominent foci of research. Both may reflect emotional responses to stressful circumstances, but they also represent more persistent features of personality. Thus, not only are the physiological consequences and nature of prenatal stress different between animal and human studies, but when human studies detect an association between mothers' prenatal anxiety, for example, and their children's later behavior, it may be the result of shared genes or child-rearing practices related to maternal temperament.

Despite these concerns, there is a small but growing literature indicating that there is a relation between pregnant women's psychological distress and their children's behavioral outcomes. In one study, the ability of 8-month-old infants to pay attention during a developmental assessment was negatively correlated with the amount of anxiety their mothers reported about their pregnancy (Huizink, Robles de Medina, Mulder, Visser, & Buitelaar, 2002). This study is one of the few in which infants' behavior was rated by an independent observer and not a parent. Two separate studies with large numbers of participants found positive associations between maternal distress (primarily anxiety) in the first half of pregnancy and behavioral disorders or negative emotionality at preschool age (Martin, Noyes, Wisenbaker, & Huttunen, 2000; O'Connor, Heron, Golding, Beveridge, & Glover, 2002). Unfortunately, both relied on mothers' reports of their children's problems, so it is impossible to know whether the results simply indicate that anxious mothers perceive their children to be more difficult than nonanxious mothers do. However, new information about potential mechanisms whereby maternal stress might affect fetal development gives plausibility to these results. Maternal anxiety is associated with reduced blood flow to the fetus (Sjostrom, Valentin, Thelin, & Marsal, 1997), and fetal levels of stress hormones reflect those of their mothers (Gitau, Cameron, Fisk, & Glover, 1998).

Remarkably, this handful of published studies represents most of what we know about the effects of maternal distress on child development. There are several additional reports in the literature, but because of problems in methods or analysis, their results are not compelling. As the field matures, methodological, analytical, and interpretational standards will emerge over time.

THE NEXT LEVEL OF INVESTIGATION

The implicit assumption has been that prenatal stress and emotions have consequences for child development after birth because they have more immediate effects on the development of the nervous system before birth. Until recently, the fetal period of development was a black box. Although fetuses remain one of the few categories of research participants who can be neither directly viewed nor heard, opportunities to measure fetal development now exist. As pregnancy advances, the behavioral capabilities of the fetus become similar to those of a newborn infant, although the fetus is limited by the constraints of the uterus. Nonetheless, measurement of fetal motor activity, heart rate, and their relation to each other provides a fairly complete portrait of fetal development. New techniques present an opportunity to examine the manner in which the psychological state of the pregnant woman may affect development prior to birth, and perhaps permanently change the offspring's course of development.

In our first efforts to examine the link between fetal behavior and maternal stress, my colleagues and I relied on commonly used paper-and-pencil questionnaires to measure maternal psychological attributes. In a small study, we found that mothers' perception of experiencing daily hassles in everyday life was inversely related to the degree to which their fetuses' movement and heart rate were in synchrony. Such synchrony is an indicator of developing neural integration (DiPietro, Hodgson, Costigan, Hilton, & Johnson, 1996). In a second study, we found that mothers' emotional intensity, perception of their lives as stressful, and, in particular, feelings that they were more hassled than uplifted by their pregnancy were positively related to the activity level of their fetuses (DiPietro, Hilton, Hawkins, Costigan, & Pressman, 2002). We had previously reported that active fetuses tend to be active 1-year-olds, so fetal associations portend postnatal ones.

Measures of maternal stress and emotions that are based on mothers' self-reports are important only to the extent that they correspond to physiological signals that can be transmitted to the fetus; thus, they provide limited information. We turned to investigating the degree to which maternal physiological arousal, as measured by heart rate and electrical conductance of the skin, a measure of emotionality, is associated with fetal behavior. The results were unexpected in that fetal motor activity, even when it was imperceptible to women, stimulated transient increases in their heart rate and skin conductance.

It became apparent to us that the only way to truly examine the effect of stress on the fetus was to subject women to a standard, noninvasive stressor and measure the fetal response. The stressor we selected was a common cognitive challenge known as the Stroop Color-Word Test. In this test, subjects are asked to read color names that are printed in various colors and so must dissociate the color of the words from their meaning. The test is not aversive but reliably induces physiological arousal. In general, when pregnant women engaged in this task, fetal motor activity was suppressed, although individual responses varied. The degree to which individual women and fetuses responded to the Stroop test was similar from the middle to the end of pregnancy. These results lead us to propose three hypotheses. First, women respond to stress in characteristic ways that fetuses are repeatedly exposed to over the course of pregnancy. This experience serves to sensitize the developing nervous system. Second, there are both short-term and longer-term adaptive responses to stress by the fetus, depending on the intensity and repetitiveness of the stimulation. Finally, the immediacy of the fetal response to the Stroop, as well as to maternal viewing of graphic scenes from a movie on labor and delivery, suggest an additional mechanism whereby maternal stress might affect the fetus. We propose that the fetus responds to changes in the sensory environment of the uterus that occur when maternal heart rate, blood pressure, and other internal functions are abruptly altered. This proposal cannot be readily tested, but hearing is among the first perceptual systems to develop prenatally, and it is well documented that the fetus can perceive sounds that emanate from both within and outside the uterus.

Our final foray into this area of inquiry has been to follow children who participated in our studies as fetuses. Recently, we completed developmental testing on approximately one hundred 2-year-old children. The results, as is often the case in fetal research, surprised us. Higher maternal anxiety midway through pregnancy was strongly associated with better motor and mental development scores on the Bayley Scales of Infant Development, a standard developmental assessment. These associations remained even after controlling statistically for other possible contributing factors, including level of maternal education and both anxiety and stress after giving birth. This finding is in the direction opposite to that which would be predicted on the basis of most, but not all, of the animal research. Yet it is consistent with what is known about the class of neurohormones known as glucocorticoids, which are produced during the stress response and also play a role in the maturation of body organs. Our results are also consistent with findings from a series of studies on physical stress. The newborns of pregnant women who exercised regularly were somewhat smaller than the newborns of women who did not exercise much, but showed better ability to remain alert and track stimuli; the children of the regular exercisers also had higher cognitive ability at age 5 (Clapp, 1996). Exercise and psychological distress do not necessarily have the same physiological consequences to the fetus, but the parallel is intriguing.

CONCLUSIONS

At this time, there is too little scientific evidence to establish that a woman's psychological state during pregnancy affects her child's developmental outcomes. It is premature to extend findings from animal studies to women and children, particularly given the disparity in the way the animal and human studies are designed. The question of whether maternal stress and affect serve to accelerate or inhibit maturation of the fetal nervous system, and postnatal development in turn, remains open. It has been proposed that a certain degree of stress during early childhood is required for optimal organization of the brain, because stress provokes periods of disruption to existing structures (Huether, 1998), and this may be true for the prenatal period as well.

The relation between maternal stress and children's development may ultimately be found to mirror the relation between arousal and performance, which is characterized by an inverted U-shaped curve. This function, often called the Yerkes-Dodson law, posits that both low and high levels of arousal are associated with performance decrements, whereas a moderate level is associated with enhanced performance. This model has been applied to a spectrum of psychological observations, and a parallel with prenatal maternal stress may exist as well. In other words, too much or too little stress may impede development, but a moderate level may be formative or optimal. The current intensive investigation in this research area should provide better understanding of the importance of the prenatal period for postnatal life as investigators direct their efforts toward determining how maternal psychological signals are received by the fetus.

Recommended Reading

Kofman, O. (2002). The role of prenatal stress in the etiology of developmental behavioral disorders. *Neuroscience and Biobehavioral Reviews, 26,* 457–470.
Mulder, E., Robles de Medina, P., Huizink, A., Van den Bergh, B., Buitelaar, J., & Visser, G. (2002). Prenatal maternal stress: Effects on pregnancy and the (unborn) child. *Early Human Development, 70,* 3–14.
Paarlberg, K.M., Vingerhoets, A., Passchier, J., Dekker, G., & van Geijn, H. (1995). Psychosocial factors and pregnancy outcome: A review with emphasis on methodological issues. *Journal of Psychosomatic Research, 39,* 563–595.
Wadhwa, P., Sandman, C., & Garite, T. (2001). The neurobiology of stress in human pregnancy: Implications for prematurity and development of the fetal central nervous system. *Progress in Brain Research, 133,* 131–142.

Acknowledgments—This work has been supported by Grant R01 HD5792 from the National Institute of Child Health and Development.

Note

1. Address correspondence to Janet DiPietro, Department of Population and Family Health Sciences, 624 N. Broadway, Johns Hopkins University, Baltimore, MD 21205; e-mail: jdipietr@jhsph.edu.

References

Clapp, J. (1996). Morphometric and neurodevelopmental outcome at age five years of the offspring of women who continued to exercise regularly throughout pregnancy. *Journal of Pediatrics, 129,* 856–863.
DiPietro, J., Hilton, S., Hawkins, M., Costigan, K., & Pressman, E. (2002). Maternal stress and affect influence fetal neurobehavioral development. *Developmental Psychology, 38,* 659–668.
DiPietro, J.A., Hodgson, D.M., Costigan, K.A., Hilton, S.C., & Johnson, T.R.B. (1996). Development of fetal movement-fetal heart rate coupling from 20 weeks through term. *Early Human Development, 44,* 139–151.
Fujioka, T., Fujioka, A., Tan, N., Chowdhury, G., Mouri, H., Sakata, Y., & Nakamura, S. (2001). Mild prenatal stress enhances learning performance in the non-adopted rat offspring. *Neuroscience, 103,* 301–307.

Gitau, R., Cameron, A., Fisk, N., & Glover, V. (1998). Fetal exposure to maternal cortisol. *Lancet,* 352, 707–708.

Huether, G. (1998). Stress and the adaptive self-organization of neuronal connectivity during early childhood. *International Journal of Neuroscience, 16*, 297–306.

Huizink, A., Robles de Medina, P., Mulder, E., Visser, G., & Buitelaar, J. (2002). Psychological measures of prenatal stress as predictors of infant temperament. *Journal of the American Academy of Child & Adolescent Psychiatry, 41*, 1078–1085.

Martin, R., Noyes, J., Wisenbaker, J., & Huttunen, M. (2000). Prediction of early childhood negative emotionality and inhibition from maternal distress during pregnancy. *Merrill-Palmer Quarterly,* 45, 370–391.

Novak, M., & Sackett, G. (1996). Reflexive and early neonatal development in offspring of pigtailed macaques exposed to prenatal psychosocial stress. *Developmental Psychobiology, 29*, 294.

O'Connor, T., Heron, J., Golding, J., Beveridge, M., & Glover, V. (2002). Maternal antenatal anxiety and children's behavioural/emotional problems at 4 years. *British Journal of Psychiatry, 180*, 502–508.

Schneider, M., & Moore, C. (2000). Effects of prenatal stress on development: A non-human primate model. In C. Nelson (Ed.), *Minnesota Symposium on Child Psychology: Vol. 31. The effects of early adversity on neuro-behavioral development* (pp. 201–244). Mahwah, NJ: Erlbaum.

Sjostrom, K., Valentin, L., Thelin, T., & Marsal, K. (1997). Maternal anxiety in late pregnancy and fetal hemodynamics. *European Journal of Obstetrics and Gynecology, 74*, 149–155.

Welberg, L., & Seckl, J. (2001). Prenatal stress, glucocorticoids and the programming of the brain. *Journal of Neuroendocrinology, 13*, 113–128.

This article has been reprinted as it originally appeared in *Current Directions in Psychological Science*. Citation information for this article as originally published appears above.

Behavior in Adulthood and During Aging Is Affected by Contaminant Exposure in Utero

M. Christopher Newland[1]

Department of Psychology, Auburn University, Auburn, Alabama (M.C.N.)

Erin B. Rasmussen

Department of Psychology, College of Charleston, Charleston, South Carolina (E.B.R.)

Abstract

Environmental contaminants can alter the course of neural development, with consequences that appear in behavior. Such effects extend into adulthood and sometimes accelerate the rate of aging, even when exposure ceases by birth. The neurotoxicant methylmercury provides an interesting case study that reveals much about how disrupted neural development has lifelong consequences. Methylmercury also provides an example of the assessment and management of risks associated with exposure to developmental neurotoxicants.

Keywords

methylmercury; behavioral toxicology; delayed neurotoxicity; development and aging

In April of 1956, two sisters entered the pediatrics department of a hospital in southern Japan. Previously bright, verbal, and active, suddenly they could not walk, their speech was incoherent, and they were delirious. Eventually a number of children from the same neighborhood entered the hospital with nearly identical complaints (Smith & Smith, 1975).

This was the beginning of a major industrial disaster caused by tons of mercury that were being dumped into Minamata Bay. Adults became blind, and children were born with cerebral palsy and mental retardation. By 1993, 2,256 children and adults were diagnosed with Minamata disease in the fishing village that gave methylmercury poisoning its name (Harada, 1995). Methylmercury-contaminated fish were identified as the cause of the disease only after an all-too-familiar practice of blaming the victims for negligence, sinfulness, or drug abuse (Smith & Smith, 1975). (The pattern by which this and other disasters often unfold is captured closely in the fictional allegory *The Plague*, by Camus, 1947/1972.) The events in Minamata led researchers to recognize that developmental disorders can have environmental sources. Now these events are showing that disorders associated with aging may be related to contamination, too. Beginning at about 50 years of age, Minamata residents exposed to methylmercury as adults reported difficulties with such simple activities as buttoning a shirt or toileting themselves without assistance (Kinjo, Higashi, Nakano, Sakamoto, & Sakai, 1993), and this decline in function accelerated with age. Interestingly, death rates in exposed populations were no different from those in nearby villages, so the functional deficits are not necessarily linked to mortality.

In this article, we examine methylmercury neurotoxicity as a case study to illustrate the role that environmental contaminants can play over the course of a life span. We also hope to show how controlled studies can shed light on neural and behavioral mechanisms by which methylmercury has its effects. Such understanding can inform the development of guidelines regarding exposure to neurotoxic substances.

LABORATORY MODELS OF MINAMATA DISEASE

With methylmercury, as with many other chemicals, epidemiological evidence from human populations is correlational and cannot demonstrate causality or identify mechanisms of action. There are simply too many confounding influences. Controlled experimental studies with animals are necessary, especially with neurotoxic substances, because the effects are often irreversible and deliberate human exposure would be reprehensible.

Laboratory investigators have used nonhuman primates and rodents to study methylmercury's toxicity. Investigations with nonhuman primates reproduced the essential features of methylmercury exposure during neural development, resulting in a far better understanding of visual, auditory, and sensorimotor deficits associated with methylmercury and the exposure conditions required to produce them (Rice, 1996). Some primate studies also yielded intriguing evidence that animals that were exposed developmentally and appeared normal as adults showed deficits as they aged, but the sample sizes of these studies were small. Rodent studies had larger sample sizes but usually were less revealing about methylmercury's neurotoxicity. Sometimes no effects could be identified, or they occurred only at very high exposure levels. This discrepancy between primates and rodents sometimes led to suggestions that rats and mice are inappropriate models of human neurotoxicity of methylmercury (and sometimes of other chemicals as well).

We disagree. The difficulties with rodent studies were related to dosing regimens and the behavioral measures employed. Primate studies entailed chronic, low-level exposure regimens and sophisticated behavioral procedures designed to identify subtle effects of exposure. Rodent studies often incorporated acute, high-level exposure that could only result in wildly changing methylmercury concentrations in the brain, so the methylmercury concentration at certain crucial developmental periods could not be ascertained. Sometimes these studies used behavioral measures that are better suited to demonstrating the effects of high exposure levels than to identifying subtle impairments associated with chronic, low-level exposure (Newland & Paletz, 2000).

With appropriate experimental design, the rodent can be an excellent model of human mercury exposure, however. Stable mercury concentrations comparable to those seen in primate studies can be produced in the rodent brain by adjusting methylmercury intake to overcome the exceptionally high levels of mercury-binding hemoglobin in rat blood (because mercury binds readily to sulfur, found in hemoglobin, relatively less mercury is available for transport to the brain in rats than in other mammalian species) and by beginning exposure weeks before mating, to allow for the long time required for methylmercury levels to stabilize. In our studies (Newland & Reile, 1999), female rats consume water containing 0, 0.5, or 6 ppm of mercury (as methylmercury), resulting in intakes averaging about 0, 40, and 500 μg/kg/day, respectively, before mating. The resulting brain concentrations (about 0, 0.5, and 9 ppm) are in a range considered to be low to moderate (Burbacher, Rodier, & Rice, 1990) in mammalian species. These levels are quite stable because of the protracted dosing regimen. Our observations confirm that these are not high exposure levels. It would be impossible to identify rats exposed under our protocol using cage-side observations, even if one were looking specifically for methylmercury-related signs.

PUZZLING ABOUT LEARNING AND MEMORY

Epidemiological studies have correlated methylmercury exposure with mental retardation at high exposure levels (Harada, 1995) and with subtle changes in language and attention tasks at lower levels (Grandjean, Weihe, White, & Debes, 1998). Paradoxically, methylmercury exposure in rats or monkeys has not affected performance on tasks commonly associated with "cognition." Performance is not impaired on discrimination tasks in which one stimulus (an S+) signals the availability of reinforcement and another (an S+) signals that reinforcement is not available. Nor do effects appear after the S+ and S− are reversed and a new discrimination must be acquired. Memory is not impaired either; methylmercury may even have increased delays at which monkeys' performance on a delayed discrimination task began to deteriorate (reviewed in Newland & Paletz, 2000, and Rice, 1996). These tasks emphasize the contextual control of behavior, and they appear to be insensitive to methylmercury. A procedure that emphasizes the selection of behavior by reinforcing events, described shortly, appears to be quite sensitive to methylmercury. A crucial distinction exists here, and it draws from the insight that operant behavior (essentially all voluntary behavior) can be understood by reducing it to a three-term contingency of reinforcement, in which a response-reinforcer relationship is viewed as acting in a stimulus context. First noted more than half a century ago by Skinner, the ability of this dynamic interplay among stimuli, responses, and consequences to account for the formation of impressively complex behavior is among the most widely replicated empirical phenomena in all of psychology.

Experiments can be designed to examine different terms, even if these terms cannot be completely isolated. In a discrimination task, the experimenter changes something about the stimuli that signal which response to perform. Thus, a red light may signal that pressing the left lever produces food, and a green light may signal that pressing the right lever produces food. In a memory task, the stimuli are removed before the opportunity to respond is made available. The response-reinforcer relationship is invariant—one lever press always produces food, for example. Accuracy is often used to measure contextual control over behavior (synonyms include *stimulus control* or *discrimination*).

To emphasize the response-reinforcer relationship, researchers hold the stimulus context constant, but the relative rate of reinforcement available from different response devices changes. In this case, behavior change has little to do with context because that remains constant. Instead, behavior change reflects different response-reinforcer relationships. For example, two levers may both produce food twice a minute for a few sessions, but then one lever produces food four times per minute and the other produces food once per minute. Context still exists (the levers are, after all, different), but its role is deemphasized relative to the role played by the specific response requirements. This thinking has been applied to methylmercury's neurotoxicity as follows (Newland & Paletz, 2000).

Figure 1 illustrates the effect of in utero methylmercury exposure on behavior of squirrel monkeys in a procedure that examines continuous choice under reinforcement contingencies that change occasionally (Newland, Yezhou, Logdberg, & Berlin, 1994). In this experiment, a squirrel monkey faced a panel

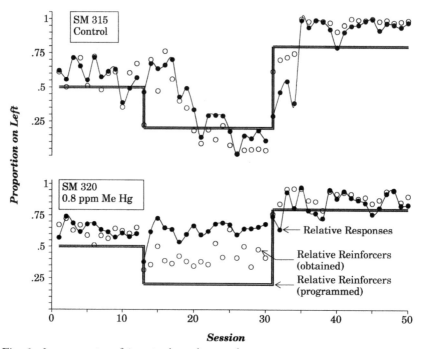

Fig. 1. Lever pressing of 2 squirrel monkeys undergoing transitions in concurrent reinforcement schedules. Initially, one half of the food reinforcers derived from the left lever and one half derived from the right lever. Beginning with the 13th session, only 20% of the reinforcers derived from the left lever, and beginning in the 31st session, 80% of the reinforcers derived from the left lever. Each datum represents a single, 30-min session. The double lines show the proportion of reinforcers programmed to derive from the left lever. Open circles show the proportion of reinforcers obtained from that lever. Closed circles show the proportion of responses made on that lever. Results are shown for a control monkey (top panel) and a monkey exposed in utero to methylmercury (Me Hg; bottom panel). Adapted from "Prolonged Behavioral Effects of in Utero Exposure to Lead or Methyl Mercury: Reduced Sensitivity to Changes in Reinforcement Contingencies During Behavioral Transitions and in Steady State," by M.C. Newland, S. Yezhou, B. Logdberg, & M. Berlin, 1994, *Toxicology and Applied Pharmacology, 126*, p. 8. Copyright 1994 by Academic Press.

containing two levers. In the first phase, pressing the left lever produced food intermittently but unpredictably once a minute. Pressing the right lever produced food under the same schedule of reinforcement. By switching between the two levers, the monkey could receive an average of two reinforcers per minute. (This is called a concurrent schedule of food reinforcement.)

Reinforcement rates changed abruptly at the beginning of the 13th session; the left lever produced food at one quarter the rate of the right lever (one vs. four reinforcers per minute). The behavior of the control monkey, which was not exposed to methylmercury, gradually shifted until the proportion of its responses on the left lever approximated the low proportion of reinforcers delivered by that lever. This steady-state performance in which the relative allocation of behavior approximates the relative availability of reinforcement is called matching and is commonly observed in studies of animals (Davison & McCarthy, 1988) and humans (Kollins, Newland, & Critchfield, 1997).

In contrast, the behavior of the methylmercury-exposed monkey was unperturbed by the new reinforcement rates. This insensitivity also occurred in later transitions, including the one beginning at Session 31 in Figure 1. In behavior therapy interventions (results not shown in the figure), 99% of the reinforcers were programmed to come from one lever, an extreme discrepancy that finally caused exposed monkeys' behavior to change. Three methylmercury-exposed monkeys, and many lead-exposed monkeys, exhibited retarded transitions repeatedly with this procedure; that is, they required many more reinforcers to complete the transition than did unexposed monkeys. These results have been replicated with rodents in as-yet unpublished data.

In this type of study, it is common practice to correlate the relative number of responses on a lever to the relative reinforcement rate obtained from that lever. However, the monkey study just described (Newland et al., 1994) emphasized programmed reinforcement rates instead. An extreme example exemplifies the difference between programmed and obtained reinforcement rates. The experimenter may arrange for (program) one quarter of the reinforcers to derive from the left lever, but if no responses occur on that lever, then 0% of reinforcers are obtained from that lever. Programmed reinforcement rate is a more appropriate variable because (a) the goal is to examine how neurotoxicants alter the way in which structure in behavior reflects structure in the environment and (b) obtained reinforcement proportions are not independent variables, anyway. To see the latter point, note that during the first transition for the methylmercury-exposed monkey (Fig. 1), obtained reinforcement rates lay between programmed rates and response proportions. Obtained reinforcement rates depended on both programmed reinforcement rate and behavior and cannot be considered independent.

METHYLMERCURY EXPOSURE IN UTERO INFLUENCES THE COURSE OF AGING

We now shift from young monkeys to old rats. We followed rats exposed to methylmercury during gestation (as described earlier) throughout life to examine very long-term consequences of such exposure (Newland & Rasmussen, 2000). When the rats were 4 to 6 months of age, we trained them to press a lever nine

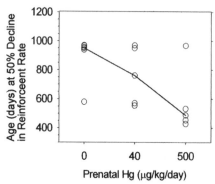

Fig. 2. Decline in reinforcement rates of rats trained to execute response bursts of nine lever presses within 4 s in order to receive food reinforcement. The graph shows the age at which each rat's performance (number of bursts meeting the criterion) declined to 50% of a baseline established when the rat was a young adult. If the rat completed the experiment without experiencing such a decline, a value of 950 days was entered. Results are shown for rats exposed to methylmercury in utero and control rats with no exposure. Adapted from "Aging Unmasks Adverse Effects of Gestational Exposure to Methylmercury in Rats," by M.C. Newland & E.B. Rasmussen, 2000, *Neurotoxicology and Teratology, 22*, p. 825. Copyright 2000 by Elsevier Science, Inc.

times within 4 s. (This is referred to as differential reinforcement of high rate, meaning that high response rates, including those that make up response bursts, are selectively reinforced with food.) We focused on the number of nine-response bursts that met the high-response-rate criterion, as well as on the age at which performance declined to 50% of the levels seen when the rats were young adults.

Aging exerted its own toll on this behavior. Most 2-year-old control rats performed at about 80% of the baseline established when they were young adults, but 1 crossed the 50% threshold (Fig. 2). As the figure illustrates, in utero exposure to methylmercury caused many rats to cross the threshold at a younger age, and the higher the exposure, the younger the age. The exposed animals had not had methylmercury since weaning and probably not since birth because little methylmercury is available in milk (Newland & Reile, 1999). Figure 2 also illustrates the phenomenon known as individual susceptibility, a common finding in behavioral toxicology. In each exposure group, at least 1 rat completed the study without crossing the 50% threshold, and at least 1 rat crossed this threshold; the number showing performance deficits increased with methylmercury dose. Thus, it is not the case that in utero methylmercury exposure shifted the whole population equally. Instead, it appears that some rats are susceptible to showing functional declines as they age, and methylmercury exposure in utero amplified this susceptibility. Incidentally, mortality in these rats was unrelated to exposure, as in Minamata.

DRUG CHALLENGES AND NEUROCHEMICAL MECHANISMS

Can a behavioral mechanism such as reinforcement insensitivity be related to neurotransmitter function? By observing a contaminant's effects in vitro (i.e., on isolated neural tissue), researchers form hypotheses about its neurochemical mechanisms of action. To be meaningful, these hypotheses must be tested with drug challenges, in which a drug with known, specific effects is administered to animals engaging in a behavioral task. Early, and somewhat limited, studies suggested that exposure to methylmercury during development increases sensitivity to d amphetamine, a drug that promotes the activity of dopamine and norepinephrine neurotransmitter systems. We expanded on these studies by including drugs representing several drug classes, selected according to their effects on tissue; by examining a full range of doses; and by using fully adult animals (Rasmussen & Newland, 2001).

We conducted these drug challenges with the same rats described in the previous section; their lever pressing was maintained under the same differential-reinforcement-of-high-rate schedule of reinforcement as in that study. The drug challenges were conducted when the rats were between 6 months and 1 year old. To determine a drug's effect, we injected it before an experimental session and compared the resulting response rates with those seen in control sessions in which either there was no injection or an inert solution was injected. Multiple doses were used. To rule out non-specific effects of the injection process itself, we occasionally injected only the vehicle, the fluid in which the drug was dissolved. Compared with unexposed rats, methylmercury-exposed rats were up to twice as sensitive to d amphetamine; that is, the dose that significantly lowered responding in the methylmercury-exposed rats was one half the dose with the same effect in the unexposed rats. Exposed rats were less sensitive to pentobarbital, which promotes the activity of an inhibitory transmitter called GABA (gamma amino butyric acid). Equally important is the fact that the study demonstrated specificity: Methylmercury-exposed rats showed no differential sensitivity to other drugs tested.

There is substantial evidence that midbrain dopamine, and perhaps norepinephrine, pathways play a role in reinforcement and choice. The methylmercury-exposed rats' sensitivity to amphetamine might indicate that their diminished sensitivity to reinforcing consequences, illustrated in Figure 1, is related to actions of these neurotransmitter systems. In other words, it appears that a behavioral effect of methylmercury exposure, sensitivity to reinforcement, can be linked to a specific neural mechanism, alteration in the dopamine system. Many gaps remain to be filled, including relating d amphetamine's behavioral effects to altered behavioral transitions (illustrated in Fig. 1) before this can be verified.

In a similar vein, pentobarbital's actions might be viewed in light of observations that compounds that promote GABA, like alcohol, pentobarbital, and many tranquilizers, can cause selective amnesia. The diminished sensitivity to pentobarbital associated with methylmercury exposure might be related to reports that methylmercury does not disrupt performance on tasks that tax memory. At present, however, this idea is only speculation.

LINKING ANIMAL AND HUMAN EXPOSURES TO ASSESS RISK

The episode at Minamata showed not only that methylmercury is a hazard, but also that it is found in fish. It is now known that fish is the major source, close to the only source, of human methylmercury exposure worldwide. Therefore, advice about consuming methylmercury will influence the consumption of fish, an excellent source of nutrients important to neural development and cardiovascular health. It is crucial to understand how methylmercury acts, and at what doses, to ensure that advisories are not drawn so cautiously that they reduce fish consumption inappropriately. Laboratory studies are a necessary component of the process of identifying acceptable exposure levels. In our studies, and in some others, the duration, magnitude, and route of exposure were selected after considering the biology underlying methylmercury intake and elimination. However, the studies also model human exposures and therefore can contribute to evaluations of risk. Effects that are dose related, reproducible, and linked to mechanisms of action can be combined with epidemiological studies to arrive at estimates of a *reference dose*, a level of intake that is unlikely to be harmful.

Creativity and skillful application of principles of conditioning in designing behavioral procedures are key to identifying the subtle effects of low-level exposure, and the effects of low doses receive considerable attention in policymaking regarding the even lower exposure levels that people might experience. Even under the best of circumstances, it is necessary to extrapolate to doses lower than those used in laboratories. Studies with economically feasible sample sizes will not detect effects seen in fewer than 10% of subjects, but a 10% prevalence would be a disaster in a human population. The solution to this problem is beyond the scope of this article, but readers might be interested in seeing the creative approaches taken to conducting such extrapolations (Glowa & Mac-Phail, 1995). These approaches exploit the quantitative sophistication of well-designed behavioral experiments.

After reviewing the scientific literature, the U.S. Environmental Protection Agency (EPA) recently set the reference ("safe") dose for methylmercury at 0.1 µg/kg/day, or about one can of tuna per week, for pregnant women. The fetus was the primary concern because it was felt to be the most sensitive to methylmercury's effects. Effects associated with aging might extend concern to the elderly.

The value of 40 µg/kg/day that caused impairments in our rats might seem far removed from the reference dose, but in light of how risk assessment is actually conducted, it may be quite close. Risk assessors acknowledge that there are uncertainties embedded in extrapolating from small, relatively normal, and otherwise healthy rats to a diverse array of people. To accommodate these uncertainties, they simply divide the exposure level used in a laboratory study by one or several powers of 10 to estimate tolerable human exposures. The point of departure for conducting a risk assessment beginning with rats might be 4 and not 40 µg/kg/day, because of the high concentration of hemoglobin in rat blood, but it is not clear how to incorporate this peculiarity of rat blood into risk assessment. Thus, the intake experienced by our animals could be uncomfortably close, by risk-assessment standards, to the level considered unlikely to cause harm in humans.

EPA's reference dose aroused considerable debate because of how it might influence fish consumption. Setting reference doses too low or communicating a message so confusing that it dissuades people from eating fish would be counterproductive. As a state risk assessor told us, "If I tell people to avoid *certain* fish, then they will simply avoid *all* fish and eat burgers and fries instead!"

Fish differ widely in mercury content and in nutrients. For example, sword-fish and shark may contain 10 to 40 times the mercury found in tuna, and ocean salmon may have 10 times less. So only large, long-lived predators (mercury accumulates in the food chain and in long-lived fish) should be avoided. Health agencies recommend avoiding shark, king mackerel, tilefish ("golden bass," "golden snapper"), swordfish, and fish from contaminated waters, but these recommendations are confusing and widely ignored. Swordfish is found on many restaurant menus, and few people know what is contained in processed fish. Perhaps people would be better served if hazards were simply removed from the food supply, so consumers could be assured that the fish they do purchase will not cause harm.

CLOSING COMMENTS

Psychology can make a significant contribution to the environmental health sciences. The experimental analysis of behavior, by applying well-grounded principles of conditioning, already has. Experimental psychology has more than a century's experience in grappling with the difficult problem of studying behavior systematically. This experience has yielded many successes in identifying fundamental behavioral principles and in linking these to nervous system activity. In addition, experimentalists have developed many creative methods for examining behavior in exquisite detail. Clinical psychology, when it draws from science, can contribute to treatment, assessment, and the application of principles. All of this expertise can be used in ways that matter to science and to policy.

Recommended Reading

Clarkson, T.W. (2002). The three modern faces of mercury. *Environmental Health Perspectives, 110*(Suppl. 1), 11–23.

Committee on the Toxicological Effects of Methylmercury, National Research Council. (2000). *Toxicological effects of methylmercury*. Washington, DC: National Academy Press.

Cranmer, J.S. (Ed.). (1996). Neurotoxicity of methylmercury: Indicators and effects of low-level exposure [Special issue]. *Neurotoxicology, 17*(1).

Newland, M.C., & Reile, P.A. (1999). Learning and behavior change as neurotoxic endpoints. In H.A. Tilson & J. Harry (Eds.), *Target organ series: Neurotoxicology* (pp. 311–338). New York: Raven Press.

Weiss, B., Clarkson, T.W., & Simon, W. (2002). Silent latency periods in methylmercury poisoning and in neurodegenerative disease. *Environmental Health Perspectives, 110*(Suppl. 5), 851–854.

Acknowledgments—M.C. Newland wishes to acknowledge support by Grant ES-10865 from the National Institute of Environmental Sciences.

Note

1. Address correspondence to M. Christopher Newland, Experimental Psychology, Auburn University, AL 36849; e-mail: newlamc@auburn.edu.

References

Burbacher, T.M., Rodier, P.M., & Weiss, B. (1990). Methylmercury developmental neurotoxicity: A comparison of effects in humans and animals. *Neurotoxicology and Teratology, 12*, 191–202.

Camus, A. (1972). *The plague* (S. Gilbert, Trans.). New York: Vintage Books. (Original work published 1947)

Davison, M., & McCarthy, D. (1988). *The matching law: A research review*. Hillsdale, NJ: Erlbaum.

Glowa, J.R., & MacPhail, R.C. (1995). Quantitative approaches to risk assessment in neurotoxicology. In L.W. Chang & W. Slikker (Eds.), *Neurotoxicology: Approaches and methods* (pp. 777–787). San Diego, CA: Academic Press.

Grandjean, P., Weihe, P., White, R.F., & Debes, F. (1998). Cognitive performance of children prenatally exposed to "safe" levels of methylmercury. *Environmental Research, 77*, 165–172.

Harada, M. (1995). Minamata disease: Methylmercury poisoning in Japan caused by environmental pollution. *Critical Reviews in Toxicology, 25*, 1–24.

Kinjo, Y., Higashi, H., Nakano, A., Sakamoto, M., & Sakai, R. (1993). Profile of subjective complaints and activities of daily living among current patients with Minamata disease after 3 decades. *Environmental Research, 63*, 241–251.

Kollins, S.H., Newland, M.C., & Critchfield, T.S. (1997). Human sensitivity to reinforcement in operant choice: How much do consequences matter? *Psychonomic Bulletin & Review, 4*, 208–220.

Newland, M.C., & Paletz, E.M. (2000). Animal studies of methylmercury and PCBs: What do they tell us about expected effects in humans? *Neurotoxicology, 21*, 1003–1027.

Newland, M.C., & Rasmussen, E.B. (2000). Aging unmasks adverse effects of gestational exposure to methylmercury in rats. *Neurotoxicology and Teratology, 22*, 819–828.

Newland, M.C., & Reile, P.A. (1999). Blood and brain mercury levels after chronic gestational exposure to methylmercury in rats. *Toxicological Sciences, 50*, 106–116.

Newland, M.C., Yezhou, S., Logdberg, B., & Berlin, M. (1994). Prolonged behavioral effects of in utero exposure to lead or methyl mercury: Reduced sensitivity to changes in reinforcement contingencies during behavioral transitions and in steady state. *Toxicology and Applied Pharmacology, 126*, 6–15.

Rasmussen, E.B., & Newland, M.C. (2001). Developmental exposure to methylmercury alters behavioral sensitivity to *d* amphetamine and pentobarbital in adult rats. *Neurotoxicology and Teratology, 23*, 45–55.

Rice, D.C. (1996). Sensory and cognitive effects of developmental methylmercury exposure in monkeys, and a comparison to effects in rodents. *Neurotoxicology, 17*, 139–154.

Smith, W.E., & Smith, A.M. (1975). *Minamata*. New York: Holt, Rinehart, and Winston.

This article has been reprinted as it originally appeared in *Current Directions in Psychological Science*. Citation information for this article as originally published appears above.

Biological Bases of Maternal Attachment

Dario Maestripieri[1]
Committee on Human Development and Institute for Mind and Biology, The University of Chicago, Chicago, Illinois

Abstract

In recent years, there has been growing interest in investigating the processes affecting caregiving behavior. Recent studies of human and nonhuman primates have suggested that hormones can account, at least in part, for changes in caregiving motivation during pregnancy and the postpartum period and for variability in caregiving motivation and behavior among individuals. Although hormones may not be the primary determinants of caregiving, future research cannot afford to overlook the contribution that biological processes can make to normative and pathological attachment and parenting.

Keywords

attachment; caregiving; hormones; primates

In 1969, Bowlby published the first volume of his trilogy on *Attachment and Loss*. In it, he laid out the basic principles of a new theory aimed at explaining the nature of the social bond between infants and their caregivers, most notably their mothers. After 30 years of research focused on the processes associated with the formation, maintenance, and breaking of infants' bonds with their caregivers, psychologists are now turning their attention to attachment from the caregiver's perspective (George & Solomon, 1999).

Maternal attachment can be viewed as a set of behaviors whose function is to maintain proximity and interaction with the infant. As the early conceptualizations and empirical studies of infant attachment were informed by research with nonhuman primates (hereafter, primates), so the recent research on maternal attachment has been informed by primate studies. For example, both primate and human studies have recently investigated whether motivation for caregiving changes across pregnancy in relation to hormonal changes, whether the first few postpartum days are a sensitive period for this motivation, and whether hormonal variables predict differences in caregiving motivation and behavior among individuals. In this article, I review some recent findings in these three areas of research and discuss similarities and differences between primate and human data.

CHANGES IN CAREGIVING MOTIVATION DURING PREGNANCY

In group-living macaques, caregiving motivation during pregnancy can be measured by the frequency with which females touch, hold, groom, or carry other females' newborn infants. Interactions with young infants are by no means limited to pregnant females. Macaque females of all ages and reproductive stages show some interest in young infants and attempt to interact with them. This suggests that in primates, just as in humans and other mammals, pregnancy hormones (such as estradiol and progesterone) are not necessary for the expression of caregiving motivation. The question addressed by recent primate studies, however, is not whether hormones are necessary for caregiving motivation, but whether the hormonal changes underlying pregnancy enhance caregiving motivation.

A recent study of pigtail macaques reported that the frequency of interaction with infants increased during late pregnancy and peaked the week before birth (Maestripieri & Zehr, 1998). The increase in caregiving motivation during late pregnancy was correlated with an increase in the concentrations of estradiol in the blood and in the estradiol-to-progesterone ratio. This correlational evidence that hormones can affect caregiving motivation was corroborated by experimental manipulations. Rhesus macaque females whose ovaries had been removed increased significantly their frequency of interactions with other females' infants after receiving estradiol in doses similar to those of middle-late pregnancy (Maestripieri & Zehr, 1998). Furthermore, nonpregnant marmoset females treated with estrogen and progesterone in concentrations similar to those of late pregnancy showed a significantly higher motivation to interact with infants than nontreated females (Pryce, Döbeli, & Martin, 1993).

Human pregnancy is characterized by hormonal changes very similar to those occurring in primates and other mammals. Both longitudinal and cross-sectional studies of women in their first pregnancy have shown that, in most cases, women experience increased maternal feelings toward their own fetus at about 20 to 24 weeks of gestation (Corter & Fleming, 1995). Changes in maternal feelings during pregnancy do not appear to be correlated with changes in concentrations of hormones such as estradiol, progesterone, prolactin, or cortisol (Corter & Fleming, 1995). However, it is possible that if changes in maternal attachment during pregnancy were assessed with behavioral and psychophysiological measures (e.g., heart rate responses to infant cries) instead of women's self-reports on their feelings of attachment, an association between changes in caregiving motivation and hormones would become apparent.

IS THERE A POSTPARTUM SENSITIVE PERIOD FOR CAREGIVING MOTIVATION?

Klaus and Kennell (1976) hypothesized that there may be a sensitive period shortly after birth during which it is necessary for mothers to be in close contact with their infants for later child development to be optimal. Many subsequent studies of bonding concluded that the evidence for such a sensitive period was at best equivocal and, consequently, research on bonding was abandoned. Although the concept of mother-infant bonding was extrapolated from animal research, what most human studies attempted to demonstrate (i.e., that slight differences in time spent in contact during the postpartum period would have longlasting consequences for the parent-child relationship) has never been demonstrated in animals either. In fact, a recent reanalysis of the primate data has provided some evidence that the postpartum period may be a sensitive period for caregiving motivation, but not necessarily for infant attachment or development (Maestripieri, 2001).

Naturalistic observations of macaques have shown that a mother whose infant dies shortly after birth may kidnap a newborn from another new mother and adopt it. Occasionally, a new mother with a live infant may adopt another newborn and raise both infants as if they were twins. Interestingly, although infant mortality is by no means limited to the early postpartum period, all cases of newborn adoption have been reported to occur within the first 2 postpartum weeks, suggesting that the potential for adoption is highest during this period.

Experimental studies in which infants have been swapped between mothers also suggest that there is a postpartum sensitive period for caregiving motivation (Maestripieri, 2001). In particular, the evidence suggests that (a) when mother and infant are separated during the sensitive period, the mother is likely to accept her own infant or an alien infant with similar characteristics if reunion occurs before the end of the sensitive period; (b) when mother and infant are separated during the sensitive period, the mother is likely to reject her own infant and any other infant if reunion occurs after the end of the sensitive period; and (c) when mother and infant are separated after the sensitive period and later reunited, the mother is likely to accept her own infant but reject any other infant. These findings are unlikely to be accounted for by learning processes related to recognition of offspring. Rather, they suggest that the physiological changes associated with childbirth and early lactation may be associated with a period of heightened responsiveness to infant stimuli and motivation for caregiving behavior.

Whether humans also have a postpartum sensitive period for caregiving motivation is not clear. Even if such a sensitive period were discovered, its implications for later parenting and child development would remain to be established. It is obvious that human adoption is the product of deliberate choice and that foster parents can provide excellent care. Nevertheless, the fact remains that if hormones and other biological variables have some effects on caregiving motivation, however small these effects might be, psychologists can no longer afford to overlook them.

INDIVIDUAL DIFFERENCES IN CAREGIVING MOTIVATION AND BEHAVIOR

Investigating whether differences in caregiving motivation or behavior among individuals are, at least in part, accounted for by hormonal or other biological variables is probably the greatest challenge for research on maternal attachment. This is because, in both primates and humans, individual differences in motivation and behavior are affected to a great extent by previous experience and the surrounding environment. Therefore, a full understanding of the causes of individual differences in caregiving would require knowledge of the complex interactions among biological, cognitive, and social processes.

Some of the most obvious individual differences in behavior are related to sex. In most mammalian species, there is a clear sex difference in caregiving motivation and behavior, with females being far more involved in caregiving than males. In only a few species of primates do males participate in caregiving, and these cases appear to reflect special reproductive and ecological circumstances.

For example, in New World monkeys such as marmosets and tamarins, females give birth to twins and fathers share the energetic costs of infant carrying with mothers. In rhesus macaques, the sex difference in interest in infants appears in the 1st year of life and persists through adulthood. A rhesus macaque female begins handling newborn infants when she is only a few months old and barely big and strong enough to lift them off the ground. In contrast, males of the same age show little or no interest in interacting with infants. A similar sex difference in interaction with infants has been reported for human children and adolescents in a number of cultures. In humans, such differences may, at least in part, be the product of socialization, and in particular the different expectations that parents in most cultures have for their sons and daughters in terms of childcare roles. In macaques, however, the sex difference in behavior toward infants is unlikely to be the product of socialization because there are no consistent differences in the way mothers, or other group members, interact with males and females during their 1st year of life (Fairbanks, 1996).

An alternative explanation has to do with prenatal hormones. In rhesus macaques, prenatal exposure to male hormones (androgens) is known to affect sex differences in play later in life, so that juvenile females prenatally exposed to excess androgens engage in the rough-and-tumble play that is typical of males (Goy & Phoenix, 1971). Unfortunately, no primate studies to date have investigated the relation between prenatal hormones and caregiving motivation. In a study with humans, however, girls affected by congenital adrenal hyperplasia (a common inherited syndrome in which the adrenal gland overproduces androgens) played less frequently with dolls than unaffected girls, suggesting that prenatal exposure to excess androgens may play a role in the development of sex differences in caregiving motivation (Geary, 1998).

Primate studies investigating differences in caregiving motivation or behavior among adult females have produced conflicting evidence. In a laboratory study of redbellied tamarins, mothers that had poor parenting skills and whose infants did not survive had lower urinary concentrations of estradiol in the last week of pregnancy than mothers that had good parenting skills and whose infants survived (Pryce, Abbott, Hodges, & Martin, 1988). This difference, however, was found only in females without previous caregiving experience, not in experienced mothers. In macaques, not all pregnant females are more interested in infants than nonpregnant females, and individual differences in behavior toward infants are not necessarily related to differences in hormone levels. Rhesus macaque mothers who physically abuse their infants interact more frequently with other females' infants than nonabusive mothers during both pregnancy and lactation. However, the hormonal profiles of abusive and nonabusive mothers are generally similar. Moreover, individual differences in parenting styles during early lactation are largely unrelated to the levels of estradiol and progesterone circulating in the blood of both abusive and nonabusive mothers (Maestripieri & Megna, 2000).

In recent studies of humans, mothers who maintained high levels of estradiol before and after childbirth had higher feelings of attachment to their own infants in the early postpartum days than women whose levels of estradiol were lower (Fleming, Ruble, Krieger, & Wong, 1997). Interestingly, the hormone that was most closely related to maternal behavior in the early postpartum period was not estradiol but the stress hormone cortisol. Higher salivary concentrations of cortisol were associated with more intense caregiving behavior in both firsttime and experienced mothers (Fleming, Steiner, & Corter, 1997). Mothers with higher salivary concentrations of cortisol on the 1st day after childbirth were also more attracted to their own infants' body odor and better able to recognize their infants' odor than mothers with lower cortisol concentrations. Mothers' attraction to infant odors was also affected by previous experience with infants, and experience, rather than cortisol, was the best predictor of individual differences in maternal responsiveness assessed with a questionnaire.

CONCLUSIONS

Taken together, these recent studies of primates and humans suggest that the study of hormonal correlates of individual differences in caregiving, and more generally of biological influences on maternal attachment, is an enterprise that is worth pursuing. Understanding the complex interaction among biological, cognitive, and social variables in the expression of caregiving behavior will not be an easy task. However, we already possess sophisticated theoretical models integrating multiple factors that may affect caregiving motivation and variability in caregiving across the life span and different individuals (e.g., Corter & Fleming, 1995; Pryce, 1995). Such models, along with comparative studies of animal parenting, can stimulate and inform future research on maternal attachment. There are still many important questions that remain to be addressed. Is there an interaction between prenatal hormonal influences and early postnatal experiences in the development of caregiving behavior? Are the influences of biological variables on caregiving mostly limited to firsttime parents, or can these influences still be detected in reproductively experienced individuals? What are the specific similarities and differences between the processes affecting maternal and paternal attachment? Are there any biological correlates of neglectful or abusive parenting? Answering these questions will have important implications for understanding the normative processes underlying maternal attachment, as well as its pathologies.

Recommended Reading

Corter, C., & Fleming, A.S. (1995). (See References)
Maestripieri, D. (1999). The biology of human parenting: Insights from nonhuman primates. *Neuro-science & Biobehavioral Reviews, 23,* 411– 422.

Acknowledgments—This work was supported by National Institute of Mental Health Awards R01-MH57249 and R01-MH62577. I thank Martha McClintock for helpful comments on this manuscript.

Note

1. Address correspondence to Dario Maestripieri, Committee on Human Development, The University of Chicago, 5730 S. Woodlawn Ave., Chicago, IL 60637; e-mail: dario@ccp.uchicago.edu.

References

Bowlby, J. (1969). *Attachment and loss: 1. Attachment*. New York: Basic Books.

Corter, C., & Fleming, A.S. (1995). Psychobiology of maternal behavior in human beings. In M. Bornstein (Ed.), *Handbook of parenting* (pp. 87–116). Hillsdale, NJ: Erlbaum.

Fairbanks, L.A. (1996). Individual differences in maternal styles: Causes and consequences for mothers and offspring. *Advances in the Study of Behavior, 25*, 579–611.

Fleming, A.S., Ruble, D., Krieger, H., & Wong, P.Y. (1997). Hormonal and experiential correlates of maternal responsiveness during pregnancy and the puerperium in human mothers. *Hormones and Behavior, 31*, 145–158.

Fleming, A.S., Steiner, M., & Corter, C. (1997). Cortisol, hedonics, and maternal responsiveness in human mothers. *Hormones and Behavior, 32*, 85–98. Geary, D.C. (1998). *Male, female: The evolution of human sex differences*. Washington, DC: American Psychological Association.

George, C., & Solomon, J. (1999). Attachment and caregiving: The caregiving behavioral system. In J. Cassidy & P.R. Shaver (Eds.), *Handbook of attachment* (pp. 649–670). New York: Guilford Press.

Goy, R.W., & Phoenix, C.H. (1971). The effects of testosterone propionate administered before birth on the development of behaviour in genetic female rhesus monkeys. In C.H. Sawyer & R.A. Gorski (Eds.), *Steroid hormones and brain function* (pp. 193–201). Berkeley: University of California Press.

Klaus, M.H., & Kennell, J.H. (1976). *Maternal-infant bonding*. St. Louis, MO: Mosby.

Maestripieri, D. (2001). Is there mother-infant bonding in primates? *Developmental Review, 21*, 43–120.

Maestripieri, D., & Megna, N.L. (2000). Hormones and behavior in rhesus macaque abusive and nonabusive mothers: 2. Mother-infant interactions. *Physiology and Behavior, 71*, 43–49.

Maestripieri, D., & Zehr, J.L. (1998). Maternal responsiveness increases during pregnancy and after estrogen treatment in macaques. *Hormones and Behavior, 34*, 223–230.

Pryce, C.R. (1995). Determinants of motherhood in human and nonhuman primates: A biosocial model. In C.R. Pryce, R.D. Martin, & D. Skuse (Eds.), *Motherhood in human and nonhuman primates: Biosocial determinants* (pp. 1–15). Basel, Switzerland: Karger.

Pryce, C.R., Abbott, D.H., Hodges, J.H., & Martin, R.D. (1988). Maternal behavior is related to prepartum urinary estradiol levels in red-bellied tamarin monkeys. *Physiology and Behavior, 44*, 717–726.

Pryce, C.R., Döbeli, M., & Martin, R.D. (1993). Effects of sex steroids on maternal motivation in the common marmoset (*Callithrix jacchus*): Development and application of an operant system with maternal reinforcement. *Journal of Comparative Psychology, 107*, 99–115.

Section 1: Critical Thinking Questions

1. What is the point of examining continuing controversies in developmental science? In particular, is it just silly to continue to consider the nature/nuture debate? If not, what can we derive from the discussion, even if it is unrealistic to expect that it will ever, in fact, be the "dead issue" Anastasi declared it to be a half a century ago?

2. Consider the use of animal models to study developmental outcomes in humans. Can you mount both sides of the ethical argument about conducting experimental research with animals that would never be justified with humans (e.g., exposing animals to stress or methylmercury during prenatal development)? What are some of the factors affecting how much it is possible to generalize findings from animal research to humans?

This article has been reprinted as it originally appeared in *Current Directions in Psychological Science*. Citation information for this article as originally published appears above.

Section 2: Infant Processes

Infant research requires methods different from those used with verbal children, and this is one reason for placing the next group of articles in a section defined by age rather than by substantive topic. Infancy researchers also commonly share an interest in the nature/nurture debate, trying to shed light on questions about the biological *origins* of some later achievement. Investigators have often reasoned that if one starts early enough in an infant's life, one can identify biologically-given capacities before experience has had a chance to affect behavior. There is, however, reason to be cautious about such reasoning given that learning occurs surprisingly quickly, within hours of birth (and even *in utero*). Researchers who study infancy also commonly address questions about continuity between earlier and later developmental stages, asking, for example, whether early milestones (walking, first words) predict to later development. Articles in this section address one or more of these issues.

The first, by Bennett Bertenthal, Joseph Campos, and Rosanne Kermoian illustrates the quest to understand how achieving a particular developmental milestone—here independent locomotion—may be related to other major developmental changes. In both correlational and experimental designs, the investigators link self-produced locomotion to the child's fear of heights and the ability to search for hidden objects. Additionally, they describe the evolution of crawling behavior itself, linking physical changes (e.g., arm and leg strength) to behavioral changes (type of locomotion) and discuss implications of their findings for broad developmental processes.

The second article by Chiari Turati asks whether infants are biologically endowed to attend specifically to faces. Such an endowment could jump-start the child on the path toward later skilled face recognition, postulated to have great evolutionary value. Turanti presents empirical evidence that newborns do not have a domain-specific endowment for face preference; rather they have more general perceptual biases leading them to attend to perceptual stimuli of certain kinds. Because faces have those characteristics, they attract attention.

Mark Howe examines one issue of continuity—self-relevant memory. Are older children and adults able to access memories from infancy or perhaps even from the womb? What makes this question so interesting is not simply that they tap memory over a long retention interval. Rather it is that such memories come from a stage of life without language, and perhaps even without other forms of symbolic representation. Howe reviews evidence of prenatal and infant memories, suggesting that the critical ingredient for self-tagged memories is the development of self-awareness.

Roberta Golinkoff and Kathy Hirsh-Pasek address word acquisition. When infants hear a word, how do they know to which of the visible myriad objects it applies? Even if they focus in on the correct object, how do they know if the word refers to the object as a whole or to one of its feature (like shape or color)? They offer an emergentist coalition model (ECM) positing that different processes predominate word acquisition at different times. Specifically, they present data showing that word learning is first based on associative learning linked to objects' perceptual salience, then becomes influenced by social cues, and finally becomes largely controlled by social cues (even overriding objects' perceptual attractiveness).

The final article in this section by Paul Quinn concerns the early emergence of category representation. Quinn begins by explaining the power of grouping individual entities into categories, and the theoretical importance of determining whether categorization emerges before the acquisition of language. Describing data from studies using habituation and preferred looking paradigms, he highlights evidence that infants categorize in a range of domains (e.g., dogs vs. cats; above vs. below), identifies some of the bases for categorization, and suggests some of ways that early categorization may enhance emerging knowledge and language.

An Epigenetic Perspective on the Development of Self-Produced Locomotion and Its Consequences

Bennett I. Bertenthal[1]
Professor of Psychology, University of Virginia

Joseph J. Campos
Professor of Psychology and Director of the Institute of Human Development, University of California, Berkeley

Rosanne Kermoian
Assistant Research Psychologist, University of California, Berkeley

One of the most striking characteristics of early human development is its consistency and stability. Infants show considerable uniformity in the nature and timing of new behaviors. A principal contributor to this early uniformity is the development of species-typical behaviors, such as vocalization, locomotion, and reaching. These behaviors ensure a common set of experiences with far-reaching consequences for development. In this article, we review a specific example of this epigenetic process involving the development of self-produced locomotion.

EXTERNAL VERSUS SELF-PRODUCED FORMS OF EXPERIENCE

The importance of self-produced experiences is often overlooked by researchers, and, indeed, most studies investigating early development focus on the effects of stimulation from the environment. A paradigmatic example is the study of infants' responses to the social stimulation of their caretakers. The infant is viewed as a passive recipient of environmental stimulation, and responses are typically assumed to be contingent on the actions of the caretaker. The alternative view is that infants are active participants in learning about self and environment, and they provide through their own actions at least some of the experiences necessary for further growth and development. In contrast to externally produced forms of stimulation, these new experiences are available to all infants regardless of their rearing environments.

Our own research focuses on how the onset of crawling, the emergence of independent mobility, influences subsequent development. In most infants, crawling emerges between 6 and 9 months of age, and coincides with numerous changes in sensorimotor intelligence, including new ways of coding spatial relations, new concepts about objects, new forms of social communication, a burgeoning of fear, and the further differentiation of other emotions.[2] Is it possible that experiences provided by the emergence of crawling are functionally related to some of these other major developmental changes occurring at the same time? During the past decade, research conducted in our respective labs has shed some light on the answer to this provocative question.

FEAR OF HEIGHTS

During the third quarter of the 1st year, infants show a dramatic increase in the intensity and probability with which they express fear. These changes are so abrupt and so adaptive for survival that it is often assumed that neuromaturational factors are the principal cause of this developmental shift. An especially compelling case is made for fear of heights because it is such a biologically significant behavior. Although we do not dispute a contribution by neuromaturation, our research suggests that the development of fear of heights is considerably more complex, and is based on the interplay between neuromaturation and other factors, especially self-produced locomotor experience.

Wariness of heights is often studied using a "visual cliff." Figure 1 shows a picture of this apparatus, which consists of a large sheet of glass (8 × 4 ft) suspended almost 4 ft above the floor. A narrow board is placed across the middle, dividing the sheet into two sides. On one side (referred to as the shallow side), a textured checkerboard pattern is placed directly under the glass, so that it appears as a rigid and supportable surface. On the other side (referred to as the deep side), the textured checkerboard is placed 4 ft below the glass, so that this side appears as a cliff, or as an apparent drop-off. In most studies, infants are placed on the centerboard and encouraged to cross to the mother, who stands alternately across the deep or shallow sides of the cliff.

Our early observations testing infants on the visual cliff revealed that, contrary to the predictions of other researchers, they did not avoid the deep side (i.e., the apparent drop-off) immediately following the onset of crawling. Instead, it was generally 6 to 8 weeks following the onset of crawling that avoidance was first observed. This observation was subsequently replicated and extended in a series of experiments.[3]

In one study, crawling and pre-crawling infants were tested on the visual cliff at the same age (7.3 months). Infants were held 3 ft above the glass surface

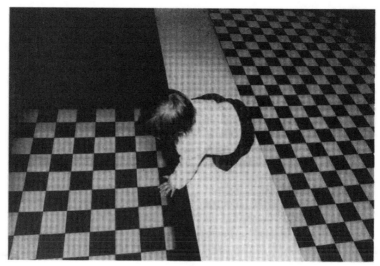

Fig. 1. Photograph of infant crawling on the visual cliff.

46

of the cliff by an experimenter, and slowly lowered onto the surface. During this descent, their heart rate was measured and compared with their heart rate during a baseline period. In general, heart rate decelerates in states of orienting and attentiveness, and accelerates in states of defensiveness or fearfulness.[4] Pre-crawling infants showed no significant cardiac changes as they were lowered onto either side of the visual cliff (see Fig. 2). By contrast, crawling infants showed significant cardiac acceleration when lowered onto the deep side, and no cardiac change when lowered onto the shallow side.

Although these results suggested that crawling experience affected fear of heights, they were by no means definitive. Logically, crawling experience could covary with any number of other developmental variables that might contribute to the development of fear of heights. The challenge of subsequent research was to show that the relation between crawling experience and visual-cliff performance was causal and not merely correlative. To do so entailed a series of converging experiments.

The most convincing experiment was one in which locomotor experience was manipulated in a quasi-experimental manner. A group of precrawling infants were given 40 hr of locomotor experience in their homes by their caregivers, who placed them in infant walkers for some period of time each day. These walkers enable infants to locomote by supporting them in a small seat that is attached to a frame on wheels. Infants with walker experience were tested with the descent paradigm on the visual cliff. An age-matched control group of precrawling infants without walker experience was also tested on the visual cliff. The results provided

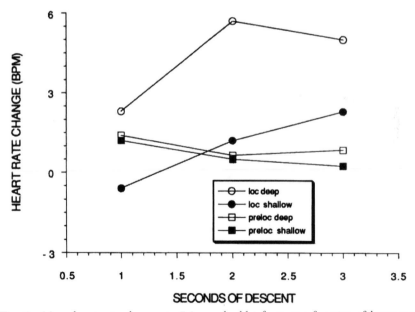

Fig. 2. Mean heart rate changes in 7.3-month-old infants as a function of locomotor experience. Data are plotted to show second-by-second heart rate changes during descent onto deep and shallow sides of the visual cliff. Heart rate change is calculated using beats per minute (BPM). Loc = crawling infants; preloc = precrawling infants.

firm support for the conclusion that experiences with self-produced locomotion contribute to the development of fear of heights. Specifically, the group of pre-crawling infants with walker experience showed heart rate acceleration when lowered onto the deep side of the visual cliff; the age-matched control group showed only a slight deceleratory shift.

Another study confirmed that the relation between locomotor experience and fear of heights was not task-specific. In this experiment, wariness of heights was tested by encouraging infants to locomote across the deep and shallow sides

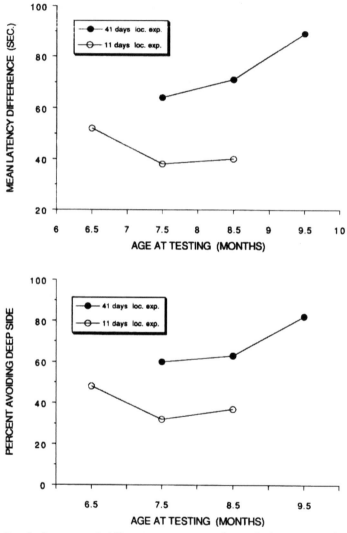

Fig. 3. Results from a visual-cliff experiment testing infants who began to crawl at 6, 7, or 8 months of age. The top panel shows the mean latency differences between moving onto the deep and shallow sides of the visual cliff as a function of both locomotor experience (loc. exp.) and age at testing. The bottom panel shows the percentage of infants not cross-ing the deep side of the cliff as a function of locomotor experience and age at testing.

of the cliff. To assess independently the effects of age of onset of crawling and crawling experience, infants who began to crawl at 6, 7, or 8 months of age were tested after 11 or 41 days of locomotor experience. The probability of an infant crossing the cliff, as well as the latency (or elapsed time) to begin crossing, were significantly related to crawling experience, but not to the age of onset of crawling (see Fig. 3).

Taken together, these results offer compelling evidence that crawling experience contributes significantly to the development of fear of heights. The explanation for this relation is still not completely understood, but we do know that falling experiences alone are not sufficient to account for this developmental shift on the visual cliff. A more plausible interpretation for this shift is that active control of locomotion, unlike passive locomotion, demands continuous updating of one's orientation relative to the spatial layout. This information is provided through multimodal sources, such as visual and vestibular coding of angular acceleration. With locomotor experience, changes in angular acceleration detected by the visual system are mapped onto analogous changes detected by the vestibular system. Fear or avoidance ensues when the expected mapping between visual and vestibular information is violated. This violation occurs when infants are placed on the deep side of the visual cliff, because angular acceleration on the retina is scaled to the distance of the nearest visible texture, whereas no such scaling occurs for the vestibular system.[5] As a consequence, visual and vestibular specification of self-motion become discrepant, and produce an aversive, vertiginous response by infants, not unlike what happens to adults when looking down from a very high skyscraper.[6]

SPATIAL SEARCH

The search for hidden objects is another skill that is linked to crawling experience. It is fairly well established that young infants are rarely successful in searching for a hidden object following a displacement of themselves or the object. Perhaps the best known example of this deficit is the A-not-B error shown by infants on Piaget's object-permanence test. In this test, infants continue to search in a previously successful location even after they observe the toy hidden somewhere else. This situation changes around 8 to 9 months of age, when infants begin to show correct search for a displaced object. The temporal correspondence between this developmental shift in search behavior and the onset of crawling led a number of investigators to suggest a causal connection between crawling experience and the development of new search skills.

Two recent experiments support this predicted relation. The first study tested hands-and-knees-crawling infants, precrawling infants, and precrawling infants with walker experience (mean age = 8.5 months) on a series of hiding tasks corresponding to Piaget's object-permanence scale.[7] Hands-and-knees-crawling and walker-assisted precrawling infants passed more items on this scale than did precrawling infants. Infants with the most crawling experience (9 weeks) passed tasks that involved searching for objects hidden in a new, spatially discriminable location, whereas precrawling infants were not able to pass even a task involving a single hiding location if a second (unused) hiding location was present.

The second study involved a different task, but the results were similar.[8] Hands-and-knees-crawling, belly-crawling, and precrawling infants (mean age = 7.5 months) were tested on trials in which a toy was hidden in one of two differently colored containers placed in front of the infant. After the hiding was completed, either the infant or the table was rotated 180° so that the correct left-versus-right location of the hidden toy was reversed. The results revealed that crawling experience was systematically related to search performance when the infant was moved, but not when the table was rotated (see Table 1). When the infant was rotated, hands-and-knees-crawling infants searched the correct container more often than predicted by chance, precrawling infants searched the incorrect container more often than predicted by chance, and belly-crawling infants showed a mixed response.

How does crawling experience contribute to infants' searches for hidden objects? Prior to the onset of crawling, infants remain in one location for extended periods of time. They are thus fairly successful in coding the location of an object with a body-centered frame of reference. Following the onset of crawling, infants are moving much more often, and it becomes inefficient for them to code the location of an object using a body-centered frame of reference. During the initial stages of this transition, infants are likely to show much greater variability in performance, which is exactly what we observed with belly-crawling infants. From our perspective, it is the greater variability in performance that occurs during this time that drives the system to a new level of organization. The newly emergent search strategy no longer relies on a body-centered frame of reference, but instead uses landmarks or some other strategy, such as visual tracking, for continually updating the location of an object.

It is noteworthy that search performance was related to locomotor experience only in the infant-rotation condition. This condition, compared with the table-rotation condition, more closely approximates the experience of infants following the onset of crawling. Infants learn from this experience that they must update their spatial code for the location of an object following a self-displacement. Apparently, the new search response that emerges with crawling experience does not generalize immediately to other conditions in which this response would also improve performance.

Table 1. *Number of infants showing correct and incorrect search for hidden toy on first trail*

	Search	
Infant group	Correct	Incorrect
Infant-displacement condition		
Precrawling	5	15
Belly crawling	3	7
Hands-and-knees crawling	13	5
Table-displacement condition		
Precrawling	11	9
Belly crawling	3	7
Hands-and-knees crawling	10	8

THE ORGANIZATION OF CRAWLING BEHAVIOR

A complementary theme highlighted by the preceding research is that all forms of locomotor experience are not equivalent, and that the transition from belly crawling to hands-and-knees crawling is especially important. This developmental transition shares much in common with the other shifts reviewed. Indeed, the development of hands-and-knees crawling offers one of the clearest examples of how the selection of new behaviors by infants represents an emergent process based on the confluence of multiple organismic and environmental factors.

In a recently completed study, we assessed longitudinally the development of crawling in six infants.[9] Kinematic analyses of interlimb coordination revealed that the most stable pattern of movement corresponds to a diagonal coupling of the limbs, in which diagonally opposite limbs, such as the right arm and left leg, move simultaneously, and 180° out of phase with the other pair of limbs. The development of this diagonal pattern is an emergent process fueled by the initial experience of moving on hands and knees. Limb movements corresponding to a diagonal pattern are rarely observed prior to the time when the infant develops sufficient strength to support the torso off the ground. By contrast, a diagonal pattern is observed a little more than 50% of the time just 1 to 2 weeks after the torso is supported off the ground (see Fig. 4).

Our interpretation for this finding is that hands-and-knees crawling requires that the torso remain supported and balanced during forward progression; these requirements are irrelevant during the preceding stage of belly crawling and creeping. Once infants develop sufficient strength in their arms and legs to support the torso, they begin to explore the various interlimb patterns available for movement, such as moving only one limb at a time or moving both limbs on the same side of the body at the same time. Following a relatively brief opportunity to explore the various interlimb patterns available to them, infants converge on the same diagonal pattern because it provides greater efficiency and stability than any of the alternatives.

Two points should be emphasized about this developmental shift. First, the transition to hands-and-knees crawling begins with a period during which success in producing forward prone progression is quite variable. This experience informs the infant that the previous interlimb organization is no longer adequate for the

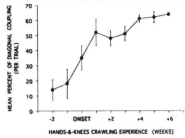

Fig. 4. Mean percentage of time that limbs are diagonally coupled during crawling. Data are plotted from 2 weeks prior (−2) to the onset of hands-and-knees crawling through 6 weeks following (+6) the onset of hands-and-knees crawling.

new task. Gradually, the infant converges on a new form of interlimb patterning representing the most dynamically stable organization given the task at hand. Second, these developmental changes are neither prescriptive nor obligatory, but rather represent the natural outcome of a system governed by trying to achieve the most dynamically efficient solution. It is noteworthy that this sequence of increased variability followed by greater stability and greater generalizability is a common theme that cuts across many different developmental theories.[10]

GENERALIZATIONS ABOUT DEVELOPMENT

At a specific level, the findings from this research program provide compelling evidence that locomotor experience is functionally related to the development of a number of new behavioral forms. At a more general level, these findings lend support to three important generalizations about the developmental process.

First and foremost, our research program shows that some of the most significant early experiences are those produced by the infant's own actions. This finding represents a radical departure from the traditional perspective of viewing these actions as merely products and not processes of development. Moreover, it confirms our contention that some of the relevant factors contributing to the uniformity of early behavioral development are indeed experiential. An important goal for future research is to assess the generalizability of our finding to determine whether other forms of self-generated experiences, such as those produced by sitting or reaching, also contribute to the developmental process.

Second, our findings underscore the limitations invoked by assuming a linear model of development. Such a model makes the simplistic assumption that performance continues to improve at a constant rate as experience increases. Logically, this prediction is problematic because most behaviors reach an asymptotic level of performance and then show no further improvement. Moreover, the results from many studies are not consistent with the expectation that change occurs at a constant rate. For instance, the development of a diagonal gait pattern following the onset of hands-and-knees crawling corresponds to an abrupt nonlinear change rather than a monotonically increasing function. Our experience is that the application of linear models, such as linear regression, to the study of the effects of experience sometimes produces misleading or incorrect results.[11]

Finally, this research underscores the importance of conceptualizing development from a systems perspective. Developmental change is rarely attributable to a single cause. For example, self-produced locomotor experience contributes to search for hidden objects, but so do improved trunk control, ability to sequence actions, and increased visual attentiveness.[7] It is essential that investigators conceptualize early development as responsive to multiple factors that interrelate and subsume organism-environment coactions. From this perspective, behavioral development is multidetermined, relational, and emergent.

Acknowledgments—The research described in this review was supported by National Institutes of Health Grants HD16195 and HD23144, and also by a grant from the John U. and Catherine T. MacArthur Foundation. We thank Jean-nine Pinto for her helpful comments.

Notes

1. Address correspondence to Bennett I. Bertenthal, Department of Psychology, Gilmer Hall, University of Virginia, Charlottesville, VA 22903-2477.

2. A comprehensive review of these developmental changes is presented in B.I. Bertenthal. J.I. Campos, and K.C Barrett, Self-produced locomotion: An organizer of emotional, cognitive, and social development in infancy, in *Continuities and Discontinuities in Development*, R.N. Emde and R.I. Harmon, Eds. (Plenum, New York, 1984).

3. J.J. Campos, B.I. Bertenthal, and R. Kermoian. Early experience and emotional development: The emergence of wariness of heights, *Psychological Science*, 3, 61–64 (1992).

4. J.J. Campos, Heart rate: A sensitive tool for the study of emotional development, in *Developmental Psychobiology: The Significance or Infancy*, L.Y. Lipsitt, Ed. (Erlbaum, Hillsdale. Ni, 1976); L.A. Sroufe and E. Waters, Heart rate as a convergent measure in clinical and developmental research, *Merrill-Palmer Quarterly*, 23, 3–27 (1977).

5. T. Brandt, W. Bles, F. Arnold, and T.S. Kapteyn, Height vertigo and human posture, *Advances in Oto-Rhino-Otolaryngology*, 89, 88–92 (1979).

6. For more details, see B.I. Bertenthal and J.J. Campos, A systems approach to the organizing effects of self-produced locomotion during infancy, in *Advances in infancy Research*, Vol. 6, C. Rovee-Collier and L. Lipsitt. Eds. (Ablex, Norwood, NI, 1990).

7. R. Kermoian and J.J. Campos, Locomotor experience: A facilitator of spatial cognitive development, *Child Development*, 59, 908–917 (1988).

8. D.L. Bai and B.I. Bertenthal, Locomotor status and the development of spatial search skills, *Child Development*, 63, 215–226 (1992).

9. R.L. Freedland and B.I. Bertenthal, Developmental changes in interlimb coordination: Transition to hands-and-knees crawling, *Psychological science*, 5, 26–32 (1994).

10. G. Edelman, *Neural Darwinism* (Basic Books, New York. 1987); E. Thelen, Evolving and dissolving synergies in the development of leg coordination, in *Perspectives on the Coordination of Movement*, S. Wallace, Ed. (Elsevier, Amsterdam, 1989).

11. B.I. Bertenthal and J.J. Campos, A reexamination of fear and its determinants on the visual cliff, *Psychophysiology*, 21, 413–417 (1984).

This article has been reprinted as it originally appeared in *Current Directions in Psychological Science*. Citation information for this article as originally published appears above.

Why Faces Are Not Special to Newborns: An Alternative Account of the Face Preference

Chiara Turati[1]

Università degli Studi di Padova, Padova, Italy

Abstract

Newborns' visual preference for faces might be regarded as a proof of the existence of a specific innate bias toward this class of stimuli. However, recent research has shown that this putatively face-specific phenomenon might be explained as the result of the combined effect of nonspecific perceptual constraints that stem from the general properties of visual processing shortly after birth. General, nonspecific biases may tune the system toward certain aspects of the external environment, allowing, through experience, the emergence of increasingly specialized processes devoted to faces.

Keywords

face preference; newborns; cognitive specialization; perceptual constraints

In daily life, a glance at a face may provide an observer with an impressive amount of different types of information that are of great help in social and cognitive interactions with the surrounding environment. Within milliseconds, the observer can accurately and effortlessly determine the person's age, sex, and mood, whether the person is familiar or not, what his or her identity is, the direction of his or her gaze, and so on. How do these remarkable face-processing capacities emerge? Some authors suggest that, because of the relevance of faces in human life, natural selection led to the evolution of innate face-specific devices that are available prior to any postnatal experience and enable the individual to interact successfully with the world. In contrast, other authors hold that the extensive and prolonged experience that almost everyone commonly has with faces gradually renders people exceptional experts in recognizing individual faces.

An important contribution toward resolving this long-standing issue may come from the study of an intriguing phenomenon observed a few hours after birth, when visual experience with faces is still minimal. When presented with facelike and nonfacelike patterns, newborns spontaneously look longer at and orient more frequently toward the configuration that represents a face (Fig. 1). Early reports of newborns' preference for faces (Fantz, 1963) were subsequently supported by studies that, with a few exceptions, demonstrated this phenomenon with both static and moving stimuli, and both schematic and veridical images of faces (Johnson & Morton, 1991; Macchi Cassia, Turati, & Simion, in press; Valenza, Simion, Macchi Cassia, & Umiltà, 1996). What induces newborns to look longer at a face? Is there an innate face-specific mechanism devoted to this purpose? Or, on the contrary, does newborns' face preference stem from the general properties of perceptual processing?

Fig. 1. The schematic configurations (facelike stimulus on the left, nonfacelike stimulus on the right) used in studies on newborns' face preference (Johnson & Morton, 1991; Valenza, Simion, Macchi Cassia, & Umiltà, 1996).

HISTORICAL BACKGROUND AND THEORETICAL FRAMEWORK

Real faces possess a series of nonspecific perceptual characteristics, such as the complexity of the face configuration and the high contrast of its inner features, that by themselves would strongly attract newborns' attention. However, until recently, the general modes of processing of nonface visual stimuli did not seem sufficient to fully explain the preference that infants devote to faces. The most influential model of newborns' visual preferences (the linear system model; Banks & Ginsburg, 1985) succeeded in explaining preferences for a variety of visual configurations but failed to entirely account for newborns' preference for facelike patterns (Kleiner, 1993; Valenza et al., 1996). This state of the art strongly supported the possibility that innately specified mechanisms dedicated to faces are present at birth.

According to a model proposed independently by Johnson and Morton (1991) and de Schonen and Mathivet (1989), newborns' tendency to prefer faces is mediated by primitive subcortical[2] circuits whose only purpose is to orient newborns' gaze toward faces. By ensuring that infants have visual experience with this class of stimuli, these subcortical structures favor the gradual emergence of specialized cortical circuits that subserve face processing in adults. This position combines the idea that evolution adaptively provided human newborns with a device specifically tuned to faces with the view that visual experience plays a prominent role in the normal development of adults' highly sophisticated face-processing abilities. In fact, the model excludes the existence of a face-specific cortical system that is active from birth and proposes that this system gradually develops as a result of extensive visual experience with faces. Nevertheless, at the same time, the model posits that such experience is guaranteed by virtue of an innate face-specific, content-determined subcortical bias.

The model proposed by Johnson and Morton (1991) and de Schonen and Mathivet (1989) is rooted in a cognitive neuroscience perspective that considers domain-specific cognitive structures as emerging gradually from the interaction between tiny innate constraints and the structure of the input provided by the species-typical environment (Elman et al., 1996). In accord with this approach, the model says that brain specialization and domain specificity are the product of gradual developmental processes, rather than already present at birth. However, although the cognitive neuroscience perspective highlights the absence of domain-specific processes and structures in early cognitive development, the model posits, in the case of faces, a specific representational bias at a lower neural level, that is, in subcortical rather than cortical tissue. Cognitive neuroscience models of the development of other domain-specific cognitive abilities, such as language, do not need to posit such specific representational biases.

Recent developmental models of linguistic competence deny the presence of an innate, prespecified system for language. Rather, it appears that the auditory system is designed to maximally amplify and detect those changes in the auditory input particularly relevant for the development of linguistic processing at a certain age (Werker & Vouloumanos, 2001). In this manner, nonspecific constraints of the perceptual system, interacting with the systematic variations present in the surrounding environment, allow increasing neurocognitive specialization of linguistic processes. General experience expectant sensory and learning mechanisms are considered sufficient to explain the development and attunement of this domain-specific cognitive competence.

Recent studies suggest that the development of face-processing skill follows a similar trajectory. That is, the face-processing system narrows with development, being progressively tuned to human faces. For example, it has been shown that 9-month-olds and adults are able to discriminate between human faces but not monkey faces, whereas 6-month-olds recognize facial identity when tested with both human faces and monkey faces (Pascalis, de Haan, & Nelson, 2002). This loss of ability with age parallels the well-known course of speech perception. During the first year of life, infants preserve the capacity to discriminate phonetic variations from their native language, but lose the ability to discriminate phonetic differences in unfamiliar languages. In other words, young infants are able to distinguish fine phonetic differences not used in their native language, but with development, their discrimination abilities progressively focus exclusively on the phonetic differences of their native language. These findings suggest that the progressive tuning of the perceptual and cognitive systems to specific types of information may be a general trend in the development of early cognition.

AN ALTERNATIVE PROPOSAL ON NEWBORNS' PREFERENCE FOR FACES

In light of these considerations, the research group I collaborate with in Padua, Italy, undertook a series of studies with the goal of investigating the perceptual biases that cause the human face to be a frequent focus of newborns' visual attention. Our goal was to ascertain whether such biases are domain-specific or general, and to determine how they guide and shape the emerging face-learning abilities. We maintained that the presence at birth of general, nonspecific constraints on visual processing might be sufficient to trigger the emergence of the functional specialization for faces observed later in development. Specifically, the domain-specific face system may arise from innate domain-general predispositions that tune the system toward certain aspects of the external environment, allowing, through experience, the development of increasingly specialized processes.

Newborns' Preference for Domain-General Structural Properties

In our research program, we began to look for domain-general structural properties that faces might share with nonface geometric stimuli. The rationale was that if we were able to demonstrate that such nonspecific structural properties are preferred when they appear in nonface stimuli, it would be reasonable to presume that the same perceptual properties also play a role in newborns' preference for faces. In particular, our attention was focused on two different perceptual properties that are typical of faces. The first, termed *up-down asymmetry*, refers to the presence of more patterning in the upper than in the lower part of the configuration (Simion, Valenza, Macchi Cassia, Turati, & Umiltà, 2002). The second, termed *congruency*, refers to the existence of a congruent spatial relation between the spatial disposition of the inner features and the shape of the outer contour, with the greater number of inner elements located in the widest portion of the configuration (Macchi Cassia, Valenza, Pividori, & Simion, 2002). Both these properties characterized the facelike patterns used in almost all the experiments in which newborns' face preference was demonstrated (Fig. 1), but may also be found in non-facelike stimuli.

In our first study, newborns were presented with three pairs of stimuli, each composed of a top-heavy configuration (i.e., more elements in the upper part than in the lower part) and a bottom-heavy configuration (i.e., more elements in the lower part than in the upper part; see Fig. 2). In all comparisons, newborns oriented more frequently to and looked longer at the stimuli with a higher density of elements in the upper part. These results suggested that up-down asymmetry is one of the structural properties that governs newborns' visual preferences in simple nonface, geometric configurations (Simion et al., 2002). In line with the model developed by Acerra, Burnod, and de Schonen (2002), results of a recent study indicate that congruency is also able to induce a visual preference at birth. When congruent and noncongruent nonface configurations were presented to infants, they reliably preferred the congruent pattern (Macchi Cassia et al., 2002).

These outcomes strongly suggest that newborns' putatively specific preference for faces might be explained as the result of the cumulative effect of nonspecific perceptual biases present shortly after birth, because preferences for at least two general structural properties contained in the typical facelike patterns are evident in the case of configurations that do not look anything like faces but share these same perceptual properties. However, it might be the case that newborns' face preference is in fact driven by the specific structure of faces, and that other, general perceptual constraints determine visual preferences in the case of nonface objects. In other words, the fact that preferences in nonface visual stimuli may be due to nonspecific structural properties that these stimuli share with faces does not totally exclude the possibility that qualitatively different processes are responsible for newborns' preferences in the case of faces.

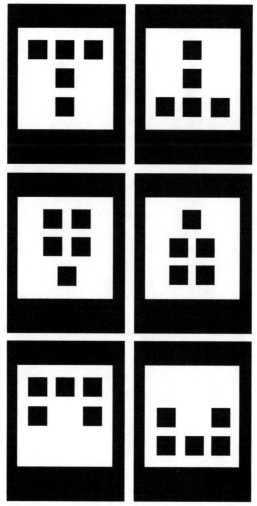

Fig. 2. Nonfacelike stimuli used to study infants' preference for up-down asymmetry (Simion, Valenza, Macchi Cassia, Turati, & Umiltà, 2002).

Specific Versus Nonspecific Factors Inducing Newborns' Preference for Faces

In order to disentangle this issue, we carried out a series of experiments using a set of nonface stimuli with the same number of inner elements and the same head-shaped contour usually displayed in facelike configurations (Fig. 3; Turati, Simion, Milani, & Umiltà, 2002). We were thus able to determine the role of up-down asymmetry in inducing newborns' preference for faces by directly comparing infants' reactions to a facelike configuration and a top-heavy nonface pattern (Fig. 3, top panel). In this comparison, newborns did not show any visual preference. In a second comparison, a pattern with the inner elements positioned in a facelike arrangement but lower than in a face was contrasted with a top-heavy pattern in which the elements were in the upper portion but did not form a face

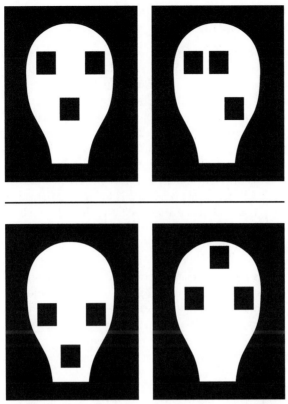

Fig. 3. Stimuli used to study the role of specific versus nonspecific factors in newborn's face preference (Turati, Simion, Milani, & Umiltà, 2002). In one comparison, a facelike pattern was paired with a nonfacelike stimulus with the same number of elements in the upper portion (top panel). In a second comparison, a nonfacelike configuration with the elements placed in the upper portion of the pattern was contrasted with a configuration that had inner elements positioned in a facelike arrangement, but placed in the lower portion of the pattern (bottom panel).

configuration (Fig. 3, bottom panel). Newborns preferred the top-heavy pattern, even though it did not represent a face. This pattern of results has been replicated recently with images of real faces (Macchi Cassia et al., in press).

The results of these experiments indicate that the specific facelike spatial arrangement of the elements within the pattern did not affect newborns' visual behavior, which was instead governed by the up-down asymmetry in the inner features. These results firmly support the idea that nonspecific preferred structural properties may account for newborns' preferential visual response to face stimuli. Thus, in order to explain the first steps in the development of specialization for face processing, it does not seem necessary to assume the existence of a specific innate cortical or subcortical bias toward faces. The earliest basis of face specialization appears to lie in the general functioning of the visual system, which constrains newborns to attend to certain broad classes of visual stimuli that include faces.

HOW DOES NEWBORNS' FACE PREFERENCE AFFECT FACE-LEARNING ABILITIES?

An important and scarcely investigated issue related to the phenomenon of newborns' face preference concerns its impact on face-learning abilities at birth and in the first months of life. On the one hand, innate predispositions toward faces might enhance and potentiate learning, facilitating face recognition and discrimination. On the other hand, the face preference might restrain and limit the type of information that newborns process within faces. Specifically, the presence of the preferred structure that schematically defines a face might constrain newborns to process the overall face pattern holistically, without attending to the distinctive features that distinguish individual faces. Note that this latter possibility is tenable also if newborns' face preference is induced by nonspecific structural properties. It is possible that the nonspecific preferred structural information that biases newborns' visual attention toward facelike patterns interferes with the discrimination and recognition of the inner elements within the overall configuration.

To address this issue, we tested newborns' ability to detect salient changes and extract perceptual commonalities related to the inner elements of facelike configurations (Turati & Simion, 2002). The results showed that newborns were able to discriminate one facelike pattern from another by relying on the shape of their inner features. This indicates that newborns' face-learning abilities are not different from their abilities to learn nonface configurations. Once again, newborns' face-processing capacity seems to be governed by general, rather than specific, rules that apply indifferently to face or nonface stimuli. Thus, newborns' face preference does not directly affect their face-learning processing right at birth. Nevertheless, newborns' preference for faces might give rise to a cascade of events, acting as a bias that provides infants with the opportunity to learn more and more about faces in the first months of life. This extensive experience with faces may allow the gradual development of increasingly specialized face processing.

Recommended Reading

Johnson, M.H. (1993). Constraints on cortical plasticity. In M.H. Johnson (Ed.), *Brain development and cognition: A reader* (pp. 703–721). Cambridge, MA: Blackwell.

Kanwisher, N. (2000). Domain specificity in face perception. *Nature Neuro-science, 3*, 759–763.

Pascalis, O., & Slater, A. (2003). *The development of face processing in infancy and early childhood: Current perspectives.* Huntington, NY: Nova Science Publishers.

Tarr, M.J., & Gauthier, I. (2000). FFA: A flexible fusiform area for subordinate level visual processing automatized by expertise. *Nature Neuroscience, 8*, 764–769.

Acknowledgments—This research was supported by the Ministero dell'Università e della Ricerca Scientifica e Tecnologica (Grant No. 2001112485_004). I am deeply indebted to F. Simion, E. Valenza, and V. Macchi Cassia for their precious guidance within this field of research and their indispensable contribution in all phases of the studies discussed here.

Notes

1. Address correspondence to Chiara Turati, Dipartimento di Psicologia dello Sviluppo e della Socializzazione, Università degli Studi di Padova, via Venezia, 8 - 35131 Padova, Italy; e-mail: chiara.turati@unipd.it.

2. Brain structures (circuits) situated beneath the outer layer of the brain, the cerebral cortex, are referred to as subcortical. Circuits in the cerebral cortex are referred to as cortical.

References

Acerra, F., Burnod, I., & de Schonen, S. (2002). Modelling aspects of face processing in early infancy. *Developmental Science, 5,* 98–117.

Banks, M., & Ginsburg, A.P. (1985). Infant visual preferences: A review and new theoretical treatment. In H.W. Reese (Ed.), *Advances in child development and behavior* (Vol. 19, pp. 207–246). New York: Academic Press.

de Schonen, S., & Mathivet, E. (1989). First come, first served: A scenario about the development of hemispheric specialization in face recognition during infancy. *European Bulletin of Cognitive Psychology, 9,* 3–44.

Elman, J.L., Bates, E.A., Johnson, M.H., Karmiloff-Smith, A., Parisi, D., & Plunkett, K. (1996). *Rethinking innateness: A connectionist perspective on development.* Cambridge, MA: MIT Press.

Fantz, R.L. (1963). Pattern vision in newborn infants. *Science, 140,* 296–297.

Johnson, M.H., & Morton, J. (1991). *Biology and cognitive development: The case of face recognition.* Oxford, England: Basil Blackwell.

Kleiner, K.A. (1993). Specific versus non-specific face recognition device? In B. de Boysson-Bardies, S. de Schonen, P. Jusczyk, P. McNeilage, & J. Morton (Eds.), *Developmental neurocognition: Speech and face processing in the first year of life* (pp. 103–108). New York: Academic Press.

Macchi Cassia, V., Turati, C., & Simion, F. (in press). Can a non-specific bias toward top-heavy patterns explain newborns' face preference? Psychological Science.

Macchi Cassia, V., Valenza, E., Pividori, D., & Simion, F. (2002, April). *Facedness vs non-specific structural properties: What is crucial in determining face preference at birth.* Poster presented at the International Conference on Infant Studies, Toronto, Ontario, Canada.

Pascalis, O., de Haan, M., & Nelson, C.A. (2002). Is face processing species-specific during the first year of life? *Science, 296,* 1321–1323.

Simion, F., Valenza, E., Macchi Cassia, V., Turati, C., & Umiltà, C. (2002). Newborns' preference for up-down asymmetrical configurations. *Developmental Science, 5,* 427–434.

Turati, C., & Simion, F. (2002). Newborns' recognition of changing and unchanging aspects of schematic faces. *Journal of Experimental Child Psychology, 83,* 239–261.

Turati, C., Simion, F., Milani, I., & Umiltà, C. (2002). Newborns preference for faces: What is crucial? *Developmental Psychology, 38,* 875–882.

Valenza, E., Simion, F., Macchi Cassia, V., & Umiltà, C. (1996). Face preference at birth. *Journal of Experimental Psychology: Human Perception and Performance, 22,* 892–903.

Werker, J.F., & Vouloumanos, A. (2001). Speech and language processing in infancy: A neurocognitive approach. In C.A. Nelson & M. Luciana (Eds.), *Handbook of developmental cognitive neuroscience* (pp. 269–280). Cambridge MA: MIT Press.

This article has been reprinted as it originally appeared in *Current Directions in Psychological Science*. Citation information for this article as originally published appears above.

Memories From the Cradle

Mark L. Howe[1]

Department of Psychology, Lakehead University,
Thunder Bay, Ontario, Canada

Abstract

How far back can we, as adults, remember details of our life experiences? Current popular and scientific beliefs are contradictory, with the latter stipulating that personal memories do not begin until the late preschool years (age 4–5 years) and the former claiming that we not only remember being born, but can also remember *in utero* experiences. In this review, these beliefs are examined in a scientific context and evaluated in terms of empirical data about the development of early memory. The theory proposed here is that memories for personal experiences are not possible until the advent of the cognitive self, around the age of 18 to 24 months. This age is much earlier than that proposed as the age of the earliest memories in other scientific accounts and much later than that proposed in popular beliefs about early memory. New data from a cross-sectional and longitudinal study of early memory development and the emergence of the self clearly show the origins of personal memory coincide with the emergence of the early self.

Keywords

autobiographical memory; early memory; self and memory

The debate concerning whether memories from our earliest days persist dates back to the early philosophers and, in psychology, to the beginnings of the 20th century (e.g., Freud, 1916–1917/1963; Rank, 1924/1994; Thorndike, 1905). Today, our courtrooms provide a new venue for this debate, particularly as it concerns memories of traumatic childhood experiences. The residue of very early experiences is said to affect our later behavior regardless of whether we consciously recollect these memories. Indeed, such memories, including those of intrauterine life and of being born, are said to shape a child's future psychological health. Like repressed memories of sexual abuse before them, memories of birth and intrauterine life are said to lie hidden in the recesses of the unconscious, but to sometimes spontaneously or intentionally become conscious (e.g., Chamberlain, 1998; Janov, 2000).

Despite the growing number of reports of memories of life in the womb and the birth experience, there is no scientific evidence to substantiate these claims. Indeed, scientists have suggested that our personal histories do not enter memory until a much later age (e.g., 4 or 5 years), and that the emergence of personal memories is associated with the development of sophisticated language-based representational skills. Here, too, the evidence is found wanting: Although language may be an important concomitant of memory more generally, it is not a key to the beginning of autobiographical memory (i.e., the ability to recollect specific events that happened to oneself; see Howe, 2000).

THE DEVELOPMENTAL SCIENCE OF EARLY MEMORY

So, when does memory for personally experienced events begin? In order to answer this question, we need to know (a) when it is possible to encode, store, and retrieve information from experience (after all, if it is not possible to encrypt information at the time events occur, how could it be possible to retrieve that information later?) and (b) when it is possible to know these events are ones that happened to "me." In what follows, I summarize what developmental science has to say about these two issues.

Early Memory

There is evidence of habituation (a decrement in responding following repeated presentation of the same stimulus), classical conditioning, and "exposure" learning *in utero*. In this latter case, the fetus is exposed to a stimulus (e.g., a sound, the mother's voice) and later, following birth, exhibits a preference for that same stimulus. Although this research on the shaping of stimulus preferences *in utero* is interesting, it is not clear that such "memories" constitute what is normally referred to as autobiographical memory. Indeed, it is not clear that memory for personal experiences exists early in infancy, despite evidence that both implicit and explicit recollective capacities[2] are present and operational in very young infants (Rovee-Collier, Hayne, & Colombo, 2001). Infants exhibit memory for acts they have seen even once, as indicated by their ability to imitate them (see Howe, 2000). As well, very young infants (e.g., 3-month-olds) show memory for a variety of complex associations and visual sequences, and such memories sometimes last for 3 months or more (see Howe, 2000; Rovee-Collier et al., 2001). Indeed, with certain experimental procedures (e.g., elicited imitation), some infants have exhibited memory lasting for a period of 9 months or more.

Thus, studies have demonstrated remarkable memorial accomplishments in fetuses and young infants, whose memory skills have traditionally been considered severely impoverished. However, these studies do not demonstrate the longevity of these early learned events in memory, nor do they establish that these memories are of the same caliber as those that we normally refer to as autobiographical. For example, there is little or no evidence that 6-month-olds can retain event sequences for periods longer than 9 to 12 months. Those few studies that have been conducted in this area show that very long-term retention of early experiences is the exception rather than the rule. Moreover, when infants and toddlers do exhibit long-term retention over protracted periods of time, what is retained is quite fragmentary, poorly integrated, and frequently recalled incorrectly and inconsistently (see Howe, 2000). Thus, despite popular claims about the prodigious nature of early memory for birth and prebirth experiences, what evidence exists indicates that quite the opposite is true. Although it could be argued that these "memories" need not be consciously recollected in order for them to influence our current behaviors and psychological profile (although they are said to become conscious with the right effort), this would seem to be a moot point given that memories even in the first year of life are not very stable in the first place.

Autobiographical Memory and the Self

So, when does autobiographical memory begin? The earliest scientifically documented childhood memories recalled by adults happened to them when they were around 2 years of age (see Howe, 2000). That we cannot recall events that happened to us prior to that age is bothersome given that researchers now know that memory is functioning prior to the onset of autobiographical memory. Indeed, as any review of the scientific literature makes clear, it is not the child's ability to remember events per se that suddenly changes, making possible the first autobiographical memories. What changes are two interrelated components: the integrity or quality of memory traces and the durability of memory traces. Both of these changes occur because of developments in another domain, namely, the advent of the cognitive self.

Memories for personal experiences behave much like memory in general. One tenet of memory is that it benefits in both quality and durability from organization. For example, children's ability to categorize information (e.g., dogs and cats as animals) helps them remember information about exemplars from that category. Similarly, it is not until one has a self to whom events occur that there can be autobiographical memory. Prior to the articulation and recognition of an independent self, there is no referent around which personally experienced events can be organized, and memories for such events may be no better organized than memories for other experiences in domains in which there is no referent or organizational structure available.

Coincidentally, the advent of an independent, recognizable self occurs around the age of 18 to 24 months. Although conjecture about the nature and function of the self has a long tradition, and the nature and course of its early development is still the focus of intense research, there is agreement concerning two key facts: (a) At birth, infants are most likely not aware of their separateness from the environment, and they acquire this awareness following a gradual process of individuation that starts at birth. (b) There are at least two fundamental aspects of the self, the "I," which is a subjective sense of the self, and a "me," which is an objective sense of the self that includes the unique and recognizable features and characteristics that constitute the self concept (see Howe, 2000). It is this cognitive self that is critical to autobiographical memory because it is this sense of the self that contains the features necessary for encoding events as personal in memory.

The cognitive self has been measured using mirror self-recognition tasks in which, for example, infants show full self-recognition by touching their own nose rather than pointing to the mirror following the surreptitious application of a spot of rouge to their nose. It is at this point in their development that children also start to show signs of self-consciousness (e.g., shy smiling, gaze aversion, self-touching) when confronted with their images. Collectively, these behaviors provide a consistent picture of infants who recognize themselves as independent beings with unique features, an achievement that most people agree is a developmental milestone indicating the ability to represent oneself as an object of knowledge and imagination.

Because it is at this age when the cognitive self has recognizable features that can serve to organize memories of personally experienced events, it is now when autobiographical memory begins. Although a number of other factors contribute to the stability of autobiographical memory (e.g., changes in attention, strategy use, knowledge), as they do to all memories, it is this emergence of the independent self that is pivotal to the onset of autobiographical remembering. It is at this point that (a) there is a self to which events happen that can be encoded along with the features of the events themselves, and (b) events take on personal significance, something that is key to the longevity of autobiographical memories no matter when they are formed. As is the case with other categories, it is because the self is a viable cognitive entity with recognizable features that the encoding of such features into functional memory traces becomes possible. Although the advent of this cognitive self means that its features are *potentially encodable*, there is no guarantee that they will be encoded. Whether they will be encoded is determined probabilistically and is contingent on the same variables controlling the encoding of any other feature (e.g., salience, attention, centrality to the event). Such fluctuations in what is encoded can also explain individual differences in the age of the earliest autobiographical memories (see Howe, 2000). Thus, having a viable cognitive self sets the lower limit of when autobiographical memories can be formed, but does not mandate that such memories will be formed.

Interestingly, the changes that conspire to bring about this cognitive self are maturationally driven rather than socially and experientially driven. That is, although age differences exist in the timing of this acquisition, neither the child's sex nor social experiences (e.g., socioeconomic status, birth order, number of siblings) are related to the onset of self-recognition. Moreover, maltreated infants whose aberrant caretaking environments result in delays or deviations in their emotional development as it relates to the self are not delayed in mirror self-recognition. By contrast, infants who have delayed maturation (e.g., Down syndrome, familial mental retardation, autism) do show delays in visual self-recognition, and their eventual success at self-recognition is contingent on reaching a mental age comparable to that of nondelayed infants who succeed at the task. Finally, there is mounting evidence for a link between the establishment of the self and constitutional factors such as stress reactivity (a higher reactivity to stressors is correlated with earlier self-recognition) and temperament (more difficult temperament is associated with earlier self-recognition).

Although they may not control the timing of self-recognition, social and experiential factors do contribute to children's mirror-image reactions. For example, normally developing children frequently react positively toward their mirror images, whereas children from adverse environments show more neutral or even negative reactions to their images. This raises the interesting possibility that social and experiential factors contribute to the featural content of early autobiographical memories. Regardless, the achievement of this "critical mass" of awareness of, and knowledge about, the self serves to provide a new organizer and regulator of experience and the foundation of autobiographical memory.

Evidence

What evidence is there to support this claim? To begin, as already noted, the earliest scientifically reliable autobiographical recollections by adults are from around the age of 18 to 24 months (see Howe, 2000). This is the same time that the cognitive self appears. Of course, simply because two events co-occur does not mean that one causes the other. A stronger case for the importance of the self to the onset of autobiographical memory comes from experimental evidence that the attainment of a recognizable, cognitive self is linked in some way to changes in event memory.

To date, there have been only two studies that have directly examined the link between the self and early autobiographical memory while controlling for extraneous variables. In the first (Harley & Reese, 1999), a series of regression analyses controlled for vocabulary growth, parental conversational style (high vs. low in elaboration), and nonverbal (deferred imitation) memory abilities. The results showed that mirror self-recognition was directly related to the presence of memories for specific events in young children (19 months old at the beginning of the study and 32 months old at the termination of the study). The second study (Howe, Courage, & Edison, in press) also found that mirror self-recognition was directly related to memory for personal events. This study incorporated both cross-sectional and longitudinal measures of language development, mirror self-recognition, and memory for specific events; the participants were 15, 16, 17, 18, 19, 20, 21, 22, and 23 months old in the cross-sectional portion of the study, and a separate sample of 15-month-olds was recruited for the longitudinal portion of the study and tested every 2 weeks until they were 23 months old. Children who were self-recognizers had better event memory than those who were not self-recognizers regardless of language ability and length of the retention interval (up to 12 months). In the group whose abilities were tracked longitudinally, no child was successful on the event memory task prior to achieving self-recognition. Overall, these results provide strong support for the claim that self-recognition is the organizational mechanism that ushers in the personalization of event memory.

CONCLUSIONS AND FUTURE DIRECTIONS

Although a strong logical, theoretical, and empirical case has been made concerning the origins of personal memory at the age of 18 to 24 months, a number of questions remain. First, what is the role of language in this transition? Are experiences that are encoded prior to the use of language easy to translate into words once children become verbally facile? Second, does the ability to verbally recall preverbal events vary as a function of the distinctiveness of the experience in memory, whether it is traumatic, and whether it has continued personal significance? Current evidence indicates that memory for traumatic experiences and memory for other distinctive events behave similarly (Howe, 2000). Third, are there changes in storage that militate against retention of early experiences? For example, does the acquisition of knowledge transform what is already in storage? Do changes in knowledge, particularly about the self, alter the personal significance of experiences, transforming them from ones that were once personally significant to events that are simply an interesting curiosity and are now more likely to be forgotten? Finally, do we need to have conscious access to past memories for them to exert their influence on us? Given what we know about implicit memory, the answer is no. But questions concerning implicit memory may be moot because implicit memories (a) are not autobiographical in nature and (b) can be made explicit with a little introspection.

Although a number of questions remain, it is clear that memories for experiences prior to the age of 24 months are not likely to survive intact into adulthood. Certainly, such recollections would be vague, fragmentary, and disorganized relative to what we normally think of as autobiographical memory. Herein lies the potential problem with trying to extract so-called hidden memories from early in life—first, there is no scientific evidence that they exist and, second, trying to recollect memories that do not exist invariably results in false memories, ones that portray an earlier event in a manner consistent with our current needs and desires. For now, it is safe to say that we do not remember being born or our *in utero* experiences. We do, however, have excellent imaginations, ones that can not only create "memories" but also affect the memories we do carry with us from childhood. Which ones are real and which ones are false is not always easy to tell apart; but memories thought to originate before the age of 2 are very likely *not* to be true.

Recommended Reading

Howe, M.L. (2000). (See References)
Rovee-Collier, C., Hayne, H., & Colombo, M. (2001). (See References)

Acknowledgments—The author's work is supported by grants from the Natural Sciences and Engineering Research Council of Canada.

Notes

1. Address correspondence to Mark L. Howe, Department of Psychology, Lakehead University, 955 Oliver Rd., Thunder Bay, Ontario, Canada P7B 5E1; e-mail: mark.howe@lakeheadu.ca.

2. Explicit memory involves a conscious attempt to recollect specific experiences or prior learning episodes. In tests of explicit memory, individuals are specifically instructed to remember information. Implicit memory does not require a conscious attempt to remember specific information. Rather, memory is inferred from changes in performance on tasks that do not demand recall or recognition of the prior learned event itself.

References

Chamberlain, D.B. (1998). *The mind of your newborn baby.* Berkeley, CA: North Atlantic Books.
Freud, S. (1963). Introductory lectures on psychoanalysis. In J. Strachey (Ed.), *The standard edition of the complete psychological works of Sigmund Freud* (Vols. 15–16, pp. 243–496). London: Hogarth Press. (Original work published 1916–1917)
Harley, K., & Reese, E. (1999). Origins of autobiographical memory. *Developmental Psychology, 35,* 1338–1348.
Howe, M.L. (2000). *The fate of early memories: Developmental science and the retention of childhood experiences.* Washington, DC: American Psychological Association.

Howe, M.L., Courage, M.L., & Edison, S.C. (in press). When autobiographical memory begins. In S. Algarabel, A. Pitarque, T. Bajo, S.E. Gathercole, & M.A. Conway (Eds.), *Theories of memory: Vol. 3*. New York: Psychology Press.

Janov, A. (2000). *The biology of love*. Amherst, NY: Prometheus Books.

Rank, O. (1994). *The trauma of birth*. New York: Dover Publications. (Original work published 1924)

Rovee-Collier, C., Hayne, H., & Colombo, M. (2001). *The development of implicit and explicit memory*. Philadelphia: John Benjamins.

Thorndike, E.L. (1905). *The elements of psychology*. New York: Seiler.

Baby Wordsmith: From Associationist to Social Sophisticate

Roberta Michnick Golinkoff[1]
University of Delaware
Kathy Hirsh-Pasek
Temple University

Abstract

How do infants acquire their first words? Word reference, or how words map onto objects and events, lies at the core of this question. The emergentist coalition model (ECM) represents a new wave of hybrid developmental theories suggesting that the process of vocabulary development changes from one based in perceptual salience and association to one embedded in social understanding. Beginning at 10 months, babies learn words associatively, ignoring the speaker's social cues and using perceptual salience to guide them. By 12 months, babies attend to social cues, but fail to recruit them for word learning. By 18 and 24 months, babies recruit speakers' social cues to learn the names of particular objects speakers label, regardless of those objects' perceptual attraction. Controversies about how to account for the changing character of word acquisition, along with the roots of children's increasing reliance on speakers' social intent, are discussed.

Keywords

word learning; language development

There is power in language. It can start wars or ruin marriages. Readers of these words barely remember a time when they did not have language. But every word you know had to be learned. Imagine bending over your car engine with your mechanic and being told, "Your zorch is shot." You follow your mechanic's eyes and body orientation to the part he is examining. That rusty metal protrusion must be the zorch. How do we learn the mapping between words and the objects and events they represent?

THE WORD-LEARNING PROBLEM

Establishing a Word's Referent: Perceptual, Social, and Linguistic Cues

Infants are motivated to learn names for the same reason that adults are: Knowing what to call something allows one to share the contents of one's mind with another person (Bloom & Tinker, 2001), even when the object is not present. Indeed, a great deal is known about the course of word learning. At 10 months, babies have an average comprehension vocabulary of 50 words, saying virtually nothing. By 30 months, average production vocabulary soars to 550 words (see Table 1; Fenson, Dale, Reznick, Bates, Thal, & Pethick, 1994), and children speak in full sentences.

Table 1. *Median number of words (and ranges) in the comprehension and production vocabularies of children at different ages, according to parental report from the MacArthur Communicative Development Inventory (CDI)*

Age (months)	Comprehension*		Production	
	Median	Range	Median	Range
10	42	11–154	2	0–10
12	74	31–205	6	2–30
18	–	–	75	14–220
24	–	–	308	56–520
30	–	–	555	360–630

Note. From ages 18 to 30 months the CDI does not include comprehension vocabulary. This table is adapted from figures in Fenson, Dale, Reznick, Bates,Thal, & Pethick (1994).

Describing vocabulary growth, however, is only a first step toward unpacking the mechanisms behind word learning. How do words get "hooked" to objects and events? How do we (or children) learn that zorch refers to that whole rusty protrusion rather than to the object's color or size? Any object presents an array of possible referents, a problem Quine (1960) called the indeterminacy of reference. A number of diverse theories have arisen to explain how children solve this problem.

One theory is that children approach the word-learning problem with a set of constraints or principles biasing them to entertain certain hypotheses about word reference over others. For example, children seem to attach names to whole objects rather than to parts (Markman, 1989; Golinkoff, Mervis, & Hirsh-Pasek, 1994).

A second theory dismisses Quine's conundrum, claiming that children map words onto the most salient objects or actions in the environment. Early word learning is but word–object associations (learned links) between noticeable (moving, brightly-colored) objects and concurrent sound sequences (words).

Finally, a third solution suggested by the family of social-pragmatic theories proposes that infants are attuned to the social cues speakers offer when labeling objects. Eighteen-month-olds, for example, only learn novel words when it is clear that objects are being labeled for their benefit (Baldwin, Markman, Bill, Desjardins, Irwin, & Tidball, 1996). If a speaker is on the telephone, toddlers resist learning a novel name for an object in front of them, even if the name is uttered with great excitement. This "failure" is adaptive: Fully 50% of parents' talk is not about the child's focus of attention (Baldwin et al., 1996). To learn words, children must note more than just the temporal contiguity between a verbal label and an object they are attending to.

Although the description of these theories is a bit of a caricature, each family of theories emphasizes only a part of the word-learning process and appeals to one causal mechanism as paramount. There have been a number of calls for hybrid theories that recognize the complexity of word acquisition and integrate diverse inputs (e.g., Waxman & Lidz, 2006). The emergentist coalition model (ECM; Hollich et al., 2000) offers one example that has yielded fruit.

Tracing the Changing Process of Word Learning

The ECM recasts the issue of word learning by asking which components of which theories govern word learning at different phases of development; rather than providing an overall snapshot, it tracks changing strategies over time. Progress has been made in testing this more complex account (e.g., Hollich et al., 2000); in fact, the ECM is currently the only hybrid model that has been empirically evaluated. Here we present evidence illustrating how complex models of word learning can be put to the test. By examining infants' shifting use of associative and social strategies across time, we offer a glimpse of evidence for a piece of the ECM.

Three Fundamental Tenets of the ECM

The model has three basic tenets. First, children are sensitive to multiple cues in word learning: perceptual, social, and linguistic (see Fig. 1). Second, word-learning cues change their relative importance over time. Although a range of cues in the coalition is always available, not all cues are equally utilized in the service of word learning. Children beginning to learn words rely on a perceptual subset of the available cues in the coalition. Only later do they recruit social cues like other people's eye gaze and handling of objects to learn words.

Third, the principles of word learning are emergent, changing over time. Infants may start with an immature principle of reference, such that a word will be mapped to the most salient object from the infant's point of view. Later, children sensitive to speaker intent map a word onto an object from the speaker's point of view.

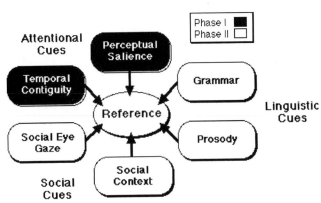

Fig. 1. The coalition of cues available for establishing word reference and utilized differently across developmental time. Children shift from Phase I, a reliance on attentional cues such as how compelling an object is (perceptual salience) and the coincident appearance of an object and a label (temporal contiguity), to Phase II, a greater dependency on social and linguistic cues like eye gaze and grammar. By 12 months, dependence on Phase I cues has begun to wane and shift to the social cues in Phase II.

CHANGING PROCESSES IN WORD LEARNING:
THE EVIDENCE

To investigate transformations in the word-learning process, a method was needed that could measure comprehension and that could succeed with children between 10 and 24 months. Comprehension provides a sensitive index of word-learning competence not restricted by factors that may limit language production, such as articulatory control or motivation to talk. Further, the method must permit the putative cues involved in word learning to be placed in competition so that infants' relative reliance on these cues can be gauged. Hollich et al. (2000) created just such a method using infant visual fixation on target objects as the dependent variable. Babies saw two objects, one interesting (more salient) and one boring (colorless and motionless). Standing between the objects, which were placed on a table out of the infant's reach, a speaker verbally labeled either the interesting or boring object and used social cues like eye gaze and sometimes handling to indicate which object was being labeled. The method ensured that children were learning words and not just examining interesting objects. After word training and a test to see if children learned the name of the target object, another new, deliberately ambiguous label was introduced that the child had not previously heard. This "new label" trial tested whether children would continue to stare at the named, target object even in the presence of another name or would look away or look at the alternative object upon hearing a new name. In a final "recovery trial," infants were asked to look again at the original object.

These different kinds of test trials in combination constitute a powerful test of word learning. If children are operating at the associative level, failing to use social cues, they should simply attach the label to the object they find most interesting. Alternatively, children sensitive to social cues should learn the name for the object that the speaker labels, even if it is boring.

Hollich et al. (2000) found that, by 24 months, children convincingly used social information, learning the names for both the interesting and boring objects. Nineteen-month-olds were still attracted to perceptual cues even though they could use social information to learn the label for the boring object.

Twelve-month-olds showed an entirely different pattern. Social information was necessary, but not sufficient, to ensure word learning. They only learned the novel word when social and perceptual cues were "in alignment," or when children heard the speaker label the interesting object. They failed to learn a word when the speaker labeled the boring object. Had 12-month-olds been pure associationists, they should have mismapped the word, thinking that the novel word labeled the interesting object regardless of speaker cues. The fact that they did not do this suggests they detected the speaker's social cues.

Is there ever a time in word acquisition when children mismap labels, relying totally on the use of perceptual salience? Pruden, Hirsh-Pasek, Golinkoff, and Hennon (in press) found that, unlike their older peers, 10-month-olds were pure associationists, mapping a novel word onto the object that they found the most interesting, regardless of which object the speaker labeled. Ten-month-olds acted as if social cues to reference did not exist.

These data suggest that the processes infants use for word learning change over time. Beginning as associationists, children move to attending to social cues, and then to recruiting the speaker's social cues to decide which object is being named.

WHAT CAUSES DEVELOPMENTAL CHANGE?

The discovery that word-learning processes change across the first 2 years of life raises additional questions. How does the perceptually driven 10-month-old become the socially aware 19-month-old? One interesting possibility is that around the end of the first year, infants come to recognize people as intentional beings who have goals, act autonomously, and act rationally (e.g., Gergely & Csibra, 2003). Once infants understand other beings as having minds and intentions distinct from their own, they can recognize the relevance of those intentions for word learning. Noting speaker intent allows infants to tap into the lexicons of accomplished word learners so that they might add to their store of vocabulary items.

There is, however, another account of the shift to the use of social cues. As Perner and Ruffman (2005) argued, what appears to be sensitivity to social intent may be the ability to form an association between speaker gaze and speaker talk. With word-learning experience, children may note that people generally look at things they talk about. This may lead children to begin to use social cues like eye gaze for word mapping even before they understand the social intent behind the use of those cues. Even this more restrictive social sensitivity would confer advantages to learners. Once children restrict word-to-world mappings to those objects that adults look at, they have narrowed the range of word referents. Of course, this restricted range still leaves many alternative referents for a novel label (e.g., the shape, color, or size of the object). Here, principles or constraints such as "pay attention to shape" (Smith, 2000) or "label the whole object" (Markman, 1989) may also help children narrow their referent choices.

A less restrictive social account that assumes children have access to speaker intent allows for more rapid word learning. Once children can make inferences about what the speaker intends to label, they can learn words incidentally, from conversation. Thus, the use of social information under either account enhances word learning. Whether the use of social information is seen as accessing a speaker's intent or as a more restricted association of words with social cues, one can begin to explain why early word learning (at least production) is so slow (1 to 2 words per week) relative to the fast-paced learning that occurs around 19 months of age, when children use social information.

Is it ever possible to distinguish between the use of associative cues versus social intent? Finding definitive evidence to disconfirm reductionist views and affirm accounts that impute more sophisticated capabilities to children is not a simple problem. One preliminary way is to pit associative and social cues against each other, as is done in the ECM framework (Hollich et al., 2000). Another is to examine corollary findings suggesting children's sensitivity to social intent. That research is abundant. By 18 months, for example, children complete a task on which an adult has feigned failure. Successful completion depends on inferring adult intention (Meltzoff, 1995). Finally, studies involving autistic children allow us to separate the effect of attention to social cues from that of interpreting the intention behind them. Since autistic children appear not to have the ability to detect social intent, they learn words associatively (Hennon, 2002; Priessler & Carey, 2005). Perhaps autistic children's vocabularies fail to grow at a rapid rate for this reason.

Tests of hybrid models of word learning speak to much larger issues within developmental psychology. Word learning is deceptively simple, calling upon a range of processes that seem to take on different values for the learner over time. The ECM provides a window onto cognitive complexity and onto the various routes by which word learning can occur. In this way, the ECM parallels current trends in the exploration of social development that take multiple levels of influence into account. In the study of cognitive development, this is rare. Understanding the various pathways to word learning has implications for crafting interventions that are targeted to the processes children actually use at different ages to learn words.

Considering word learning from this vantage point might also inform the controversy about how and when children develop an understanding of other minds (e.g., Perner & Ruffman, 2005). That is, children must come to appreciate that others have thoughts, feelings, and perceptions different from their own. In communication, this translates into the very motivation for learning language: Wanting to share what one knows with someone who does not yet know it (Bloom & Tinker, 2001). Concurrently, children should pay special attention to social cues used in the context of language, for these cues provide a conduit to what is on the mind of another person. In this sense, the study of word learning offers yet another inroad into the study of how children conceptualize other minds.

Since Plato's time, scholars have discussed how words map onto the world. We have witnessed unparalleled progress in understanding both the course of word learning and the mechanisms fueling that development. The birth of words is a psychological watershed in language acquisition. The research reviewed here suggests that competing theories are best united under a hybrid view that incorporates changing mechanisms of development. Our next task is to understand how children who begin as associationists become social sophisticates.

Recommended Reading

Golinkoff, R.M., Hirsh-Pasek, K., Bloom, L., Smith, L., Woodward, A., Akhtar, N. Tomasello, M., & Hollich, G. (Eds.) (2000). *Becoming a word learner: A debate on lexical acquisition.* New York: Oxford University Press.
Hollich, G.J., Hirsh-Pasek, K., Golinkoff, R.M., Brand, R.J., Brown, E., Chung, H.L., Hennon, E., & Rocroi, C. (2000). (See References)
Waxman, S.R., & Lidz, J. (2006). (See References)

Acknowledgments—This research was supported by Grants SBR9601306 and SBR9615391 to both authors from the National Science Foundation.

Note

1. Address correspondence to Roberta M. Golinkoff, School of Education, University of Delaware, Newark, DE 19716; e-mail: roberta@udel.edu.

References

Baldwin, D.A., Markman, E.M., Bill, B., Desjardins, N., Irwin, J.M., & Tidball, G. (1996). Infants' reliance on a social criterion for establishing word–object relations. *Child Development, 67,* 3135–3153.

Bloom, L., & Tinker, E. (2001). The intentionality model and language acquisition: Engagement, effort, and the essential tension. *Monographs of the Society for Research in Child Development, 66*(Serial No. 267).

Fenson, L., Dale, P., Reznick, S., Bates, E., Thal, D., & Pethick, S. (1994). Variability in early communicative development. *Monographs of the Society for Research in Child Development, 59*(Serial No. 242).

Gergely, G., & Csibra, G. (2003). Teleological reasoning in infancy: The naïve theory of rational action. *Trends in Cognitive Sciences, 7,* 287–292.

Golinkoff, R.M., Mervis, C.V., & Hirsh-Pasek, K. (1994). Early object labels: The case for a developmental lexical principles framework. *Journal of Child Language, 21,* 125–155.

Hennon, E.A. (2002). *How children with autistic disorder use attentional and intentional social information for word learning.* Unpublished doctoral dissertation, Temple University.

Hollich, G.J., Hirsh-Pasek, K., Golinkoff, R.M., Brand, R.J., Brown, E., Chung, H.L., Hennon, E., & Rocroi, C. (2000). Breaking the language barrier: An emergentist coalition model for the origins of word learning. *Monographs of the Society for Research in Child Development, 65*(3, Serial No. 262).

Markman, E.M. (1989). *Categorization and naming in children: Problems of induction.* Cambridge, MA: The MIT Press.

Meltzoff, A.N. (1995). Understanding the intentions of others: Reenactment of intended acts by 18-month-old children. *Developmental Psychology, 31,* 838–850.

Perner, J., & Ruffman, T. (2005). Infants' insight into the mind: How deep? *Science, 308,* 214–216.

Preissler, M.A., & Carey, S. (2005). The role of inferences about referential intent in word learning: Evidence from autism. *Cognition, 97,* 813–823.

Pruden, S.M., Hirsh-Pasek, K., Golinkoff, R.M., & Hennon, E.A. (in press). The birth of words: Ten-month-olds learn words through perceptual salience. *Child Development.*

Quine, W.V.Q. (1960). *Word and object.* Cambridge, England: Cambridge University Press.

Smith, L. (2000). Learning how to learn words: An associative crane. In R.M. Golinkoff, K. Hirsh-Pasek, L. Bloom, L.B. Smith, A.L. Woodard, N. Akhtar, M. Tomasello, & G. Hollich (Eds.), *Becoming a word learner: A debate on lexical acquisition* (pp. 51–80). New York: Oxford University Press.

Waxman, S.R. & Lidz, J. (2006). Early word learning. In D. Kuhn & R. Siegler (Eds.), *Handbook of child psychology* (6th ed., Vol. 2). New York: Wiley.

Category Representation in Young Infants

Paul C. Quinn[1]

Department of Psychology, Washington & Jefferson College, Washington, Pennsylvania

Abstract

Results obtained from a novelty-preference procedure indicate that young infants possess abilities to organize objects into perceptual categories that have conceptual significance for adults. This work suggests that the initial construction of category representations is not dependent on language, formal instruction, or specialized processes, and that category development may proceed through a process of enrichment.

Keywords

infant perception; categorization; knowledge acquisition

Imagine a mental life in which each represented entity (i.e., object, relation, event) was unrelated to every other stored entity, and an environmental experience in which each novel entity encountered was unrelated to all internally represented entities. Intellectual functioning and adaptive responding would be difficult, if even possible, under such conditions because both rely on the ability to relate familiar experiences to each other and to novel experiences. Cognitive scientists believe that our mental life as humans is coherent because of organizing structures called *category representations*—mental representations for similar or like entities. Category representations are believed to underlie our ability to categorize, that is, to respond equivalently to discriminably different entities from a common class.

A way to think about category representations is to envision file folders. We use file folders to organize information into meaningful groupings, and we may have mental files, or category representations, to hold information about various object classes. In this way, we enable intellectual functioning to be mediated by a cognitive system in which objects are related through a set of interconnected category representations.

HISTORICAL CONTEXT

Because of the recognition that categorization has to begin at some point during development, there has been interest in when and how category representations are initiated. A lingering tradition has been to consider the acquisition of category representations to be a late achievement (i.e., of childhood or even early adolescence) that is dependent on the emergence of naming and language, the receipt of formal instruction, and the possession of logical reasoning skills (e.g., Bruner, Olver, & Greenfield, 1966).

Ideas about the development of category representations during childhood began to change as ideas about adult concepts began to evolve, particularly through the work of Rosch (1978). Embracing the family-resemblance view of concepts originally formulated in the philosophy literature, Rosch argued that object categories can be individuated by bundles of correlated attributes. For example, birds have feathers, beaks, two legs, and an ability to chirp, whereas dogs have fur, snouts, four legs, and an ability to bark. If Rosch's view is correct, then an organism that can detect such correlations and compile them into separate representations is capable of categorization. It follows that some of the abilities involved in grouping objects into distinct categories may be present before the emergence of language, instruction, and logic. Consequently, it becomes important to examine the categorization abilities of prelinguistic infants, as it may be from these abilities that the complex concepts of adults develop.

CATEGORIZATION IN INFANTS

To study early categorization, researchers have used a procedure that capitalizes on the established finding that young infants prefer novel stimuli. Infants are presented with a number of different photographic exemplars, all of which are from the same category, during a series of familiarization trials. Subsequently, during a preference test, the infants are presented with two novel stimuli, one from the familiar category and the other from a novel category. Generalization of familiarization to the novel instance from the familiar category and a preference for the novel instance from the novel category (measured in looking time) are taken as evidence that the infants have on some basis grouped together, or categorized, the instances from the familiar category and recognized that the novel instance from the novel category does not belong to this grouping (or category representation). This conclusion is also contingent on the results of control experiments showing that the preference for the novel category is not simply the result of a preexisting preference or a failure to discriminate among the instances of the familiar category.

Investigations conducted with this familiarization/novelty-preference procedure have revealed that young infants are capable of representing a variety of complex object categories at different levels of inclusiveness. For example, 3- to 4-month-olds can represent instances of animals and furniture at both general (e.g., mammal, furniture) and more specific (e.g., cat, dog, chair, table) levels (reviewed in Quinn, in press-b). Researchers have now moved beyond demonstration studies, and begun to investigate a number of interrelated questions regarding *how* infants form category representations.

ISSUES

Information Used to Form Category Representations

One question concerns the basis for category formation by infants participating in the familiarization/novelty-preference procedure. Given the young age of the infants, and the fact that the stimuli are static photographs, the infants are undoubtedly using perceptual attributes that can be found on the surfaces of the exemplars. One strategy that has been used to identify the cue (or cues) that infants use to form a particular category representation is to demonstrate that infants form the category representation when the cue is present, but not when the cue is absent. Such a strategy has been used to determine how, for example, infants form distinct category representations for cats versus dogs (Quinn & Eimas, 1996). Because the two species have considerable perceptual overlap—both possess facial features, a body torso, four legs, fur, and a tail—the diagnostic information is not obvious.

It is possible that subtle differences, not noticeable upon cursory inspection, in one attribute, the pattern of correlation across a number of attributes, or the overall Gestalt might be used to form the category representations. Interestingly, in one study, infants formed the category representations when the exemplars presented during familiarization and test trials displayed only information from the head region (minus the body region), but did not form the category representations when the exemplars displayed only information from the body region (minus the head region). In another study, infants were familiarized with whole cats or dogs, and the test stimuli were hybrids: a novel cat head on a novel dog body versus a novel dog head on a novel cat body (Spencer, Quinn, Johnson, & Karmiloff-Smith, 1997). Black-and-white examples of the test stimuli are presented in Figure 1. The infants' performance indicated that their category representations were based on the head region (and not the body region). These studies suggest that information from the head region provides infants with a sufficient (and possibly necessary) basis to form individuated category representations for cats and dogs.

Although the experiments were successful in demonstrating that head information is used by infants to form category representations for cats versus dogs, some limitations should be acknowledged. Given the silent, static nature of the stimuli, we do not know the extent to which infants might rely on head information when categorizing instances of cats and dogs encountered in the natural environment. Real cats and dogs display different movement patterns and make different communicative sounds, and it is possible that such movement and sound information might also be diagnostic of category membership.

Another limitation is that we do not know the extent to which the head information would be relied on by infants who are presented with different category contrasts. When cats or dogs are contrasted with birds, horses, or humans, for example, other cues, such as the number of legs, the shape of the body, or the typical posture, may become important in the formation of exclusive category representations for cats and dogs.

Fig. 1. Black-and-white examples of the cat-dog hybrid stimuli used in Spencer, Quinn, Johnson, and Karmiloff-Smith (1997). Copyright by John Wiley & Sons. Reprinted with permission.

These examples suggest that category representations may be anchored by multiple static and dynamic attributes, any one or subset of which may be used by infants in a particular context. The task of determining those attributes and identifying the conditions in which they are diagnostic of category membership has begun, and will likely continue for some time, given the cognitive complexity created by the large number of categories, each of which must be differentiated from a large number of contrast categories.

Category Formation Versus Category Possession

Another issue regarding the category representations of infants is whether they are formed online, during the course of each experiment, or whether the experiments simply tap into category representations that were constructed on the basis of previous experience. One variable to consider in deciding this issue is the experimental task. Data from the familiarization/novelty-preference procedure have been interpreted in terms of category formation. That is, infants are presumed to construct a category representation as more and more exemplars from the familiar category are presented (see Mareschal, French, & Quinn, 2000, for an explicit computational model of the on-line category-formation process). Another variable to consider is age. With increasing age, infants have more real-world experience, and are thus more likely to tap their own knowledge base when performing in laboratory experiments.

Even with task and age as guidelines, it is difficult to determine the precise mix of perceptual process and knowledge access responsible for the category representations mediating performance in a particular experiment. Consider, for example, the performance of young infants presented with a mammal-furniture contrast in a familiarization/novelty-preference experiment. Given that the infants are not likely to have observed (at least directly) mammals such as elephants or hippopotamuses or the particular furniture exemplars presented in the task, one might be tempted to say that the participating infants rely largely, if not exclusively, on perceptual processing, and that they form the category representations during the course of the familiarization trials. However, parents are known to read to infants from picture books that may depict exemplars of animals, and infants are likely to have at least some visual experience with generic furniture items such as chairs and tables. Moreover, even young infants may be able to recognize that unfamiliar mammals are more like familiar animals (e.g., humans) than furniture items (Quinn & Eimas, 1998). Thus, even in an experiment that is designed as a study of category formation, young infants may recruit information from a preexisting knowledge base that in part determines their preference behavior.

Order of Emergence

Category representations may exist at different levels of inclusiveness and form hierarchically organized systems of knowledge representation. Human adults can, for example, represent "mammal" or "animal" at a global or superordinate level, "cat" at an intermediate or basic level, and "Siamese cat" at a specific or subordinate level. The conventional wisdom was that the basic level was the first to be acquired by children, and that development consisted of grouping together basic-level representations to form the superordinate level, and differentiating the basic level to form the subordinate level. However, experimental evidence supporting the basic-before-superordinate view has been called into question, and a number of recent studies of infants from a variety of age groups, as well as simple computer simulations, have provided evidence that global category representations are formed earlier and more readily than basic-level representations (reviewed in Quinn, in press-b). The greater efficiency of global category representation may be due to the attributes that characterize a global category being more discriminable and more frequently encountered (e.g., legs vs. wheels in the case of animals vs. vehicles) than the properties that distinguish each basic-level category from the same global structure (e.g., specific values of the same features—leg length, wheel diameter). Increasing frequency of experience with objects in a domain should result in a greater likelihood that those objects will be represented at the basic and eventually subordinate levels. The results of these latest studies thus support a differentiation-driven view of early category development.

Category Representations Are Not Just for Objects

Can young infants also form category representations that are defined by the positional relations of objects? Recent studies suggest that infants between 3 and 10 months of age can form category representations for spatial relations such as above versus below, left versus right, and between (Quinn, in press-a). These studies have also provided evidence for two developmental changes. First, category representations of spatial relations may initially be limited to the objects depicting the relations. The idea is that the early representations are in terms of specific objects, so that "a above b" and "c above d" have nonoverlapping representations. Later representations become more abstract so that various objects can be presented in the same relation and the equivalence of the relation is maintained despite this variation (Quinn, Cummins, Kase, Martin, & Weissman, 1996). Second, category representations for different spatial relations may emerge at different points during development. In particular, infants may initially encode the location of a target relative to a single landmark (e.g., "the bowl is above the table"), and later encode the location of a target in relation to multiple landmarks that define a local spatial framework (e.g., "the bowl is between the fork and spoon"; Quinn, Norris, Pasko, Schmader, & Mash, 1999). The ability to form category representations for spatial relations early in development should make it possible for infants to experience objects in organized spatial arrangements, rather than as spatially disconnected entities located in unrelated positions.

IMPLICATIONS

Infants' early, but nevertheless correct, parsing of the world implies that some of the conceptual representations of children and adults are informational enrichments of the perceptual category representations formed by young infants (Quinn & Eimas, 1997). For example, in the domain of objects, infants may develop a category representation for "animal" by encountering various animals over time and joining together into a common representation perceived attributes such as an elongated body shape, skeletal appendages, facial attributes bounded by a head shape, movement patterns, and communicative sounds. The observable static and dynamic attributes that can be detected from the surfaces and trajectories of exemplars via perception can subsequently be supplemented by a name and by less apparent information regarding biological structures and functions, acquired by means of tutors and language, such as "has a heart" and "can reproduce" (Millikan, 1998; Waxman & Markow, 1995). Language can thus serve as an additional input system that delivers information that further defines representations already established through vision (and other sensory modalities), with the result that conceptual representations such as "animal" or "animate" become possible.

This view does not deny that innate core knowledge or specialized abstraction processes may also serve as supports in the process of further knowledge acquisition by older infants, children, and adults (Carey, 2000; Mandler, 2000). However, the work reported here suggests that (a) young infants correctly parse much of the world about them and (b) these parsings underlie the process of further knowledge acquisition. The representation of category information by young infants appears to form the primitive base from which adult conceptions are developed.

Current questions center on the factors that govern the early parsing abilities of infants and how the initial parsings can lead to complex knowledge categories. Future research will continue to focus on the nature of the attributes that infants use to represent category information, the mix of on-line learning versus access of previously acquired knowledge used in generating category representations, and the order of emergence of category representations at different levels of exclusiveness.

Recommended Reading

Madole, K.L., & Oakes, L.M. (1999). Making sense of infant categorization: Stable processes and changing representations. *Developmental Review, 19,* 263–296.

Pauen, S. (2000). Early differentiation within the animate domain: Are humans something special? *Journal of Experimental Child Psychology, 75,* 134–151.

Quinn, P.C., & Johnson, M.H. (1997). The emergence of perceptual category representations in young infants: A connectionist analysis. *Journal of Experimental Child Psychology, 66,* 236–263.

Rakison, D., & Butterworth, G. (1998). Infants' use of object parts in early categorization. *Developmental Psychology, 34,* 49–62.

Younger, B.A., & Fearing, D.D. (2000). A global-to-basic trend in early categorization: Evidence from a dual-category habituation task. *Infancy, 1,* 47–58.

Acknowledgments—Preparation of this article was supported by National Science Foundation Research Grant BCS-0096300. The author thanks Peter Eimas for comments on the initial draft.

Note

1. Address correspondence to Paul C. Quinn, Department of Psychology, Washington & Jefferson College, Washington, PA 15301; e-mail: pquinn@washjeff.edu.

References

Bruner, J.S., Olver, R.R., & Greenfield, P.M. (1966). *Studies in cognitive growth.* New York: Wiley.

Carey, S. (2000). The origin of concepts. *Journal of Cognition and Development, 1,* 37–41.

Mandler, J.M. (2000). Perceptual and conceptual processes. *Journal of Cognition and Development, 1*, 3–36.

Mareschal, D., French, R.M., & Quinn, P.C. (2000). A connectionist account of asymmetric category learning in early infancy. *Developmental Psychology, 36*, 635–645.

Millikan, R.G. (1998). A common structure for concepts of individuals, stuffs, and real kinds: More mama, more milk, and more mouse. *Behavioral and Brain Sciences, 21*, 55–100.

Quinn, P.C. (in press-a). Concepts are not just for objects: Categorization of spatial relation information by young infants. In D.H. Rakison & L.M. Oakes (Eds.), *Early category and concept development: Making sense of the blooming, buzzing confusion*. Oxford, England: Oxford University Press.

Quinn, P.C. (in press-b). Early categorization: A new synthesis. In U. Goswami (Ed.), *Blackwell handbook of childhood cognitive development*. Oxford, England: Blackwell.

Quinn, P.C., Cummins, M., Kase, J., Martin, E., & Weissman, S. (1996). Development of categorical representations for above and below spatial relations in 3- to 7-month-old infants. *Developmental Psychology, 32*, 942–950.

Quinn, P.C., & Eimas, P.D. (1996). Perceptual cues that permit categorical differentiation of animal species by infants. *Journal of Experimental Child Psychology, 63*, 189–211.

Quinn, P.C., & Eimas, P.D. (1997). A reexamination of the perceptual-to-conceptual shift in mental representations. *Review of General Psychology, 1*, 271–287.

Quinn, P.C., & Eimas, P.D. (1998). Evidence for a global categorical representation for humans by young infants. *Journal of Experimental Child Psychology, 69*, 151–174.

Quinn, P.C., Norris, C.M., Pasko, R.N., Schmader, T.M., & Mash, C. (1999). Formation of a categorical representation for the spatial relation between by 6- to 7-month-old infants. *Visual Cognition, 6*, 569–585.

Rosch, E. (1978). Principles of categorization. In E. Rosch & B.B. Lloyd (Eds.), *Cognition and categorization* (pp. 27–48). Hillsdale, NJ: Erlbaum.

Spencer, J., Quinn, P.C., Johnson, M.H., & Karmiloff-Smith, A. (1997). Heads you win, tails you lose: Evidence for young infants categorizing mammals by head and facial attributes. *Early Development and Parenting, 6*, 113–126.

Waxman, S.R., & Markow, D.B. (1995). Words as invitations to form categories: Evidence from 12- to 13-month-old infants. *Cognitive Psychology, 29*, 257–302.

Section 2: Critical Thinking Questions

1. Just as some would argue that it is impossible to separate nature and nurture, some would also argue that it is impossible to separate cognition from affect or emotion. From the articles in this section, identify one or more illustrations of ways in which cognitive and social (interpersonal) constructs intersect. Can you find one or more phenomena discussed in these articles for which you believe it would be useful to look for this interplay?

2. Nature/nurture is not the only persistent contrast that has been a mainstay of discussion in developmental psychology. Another has been continuity/discontinuity: Does development occurs in a continuous manner with gradual, quantitative change or does it occur abruptly, with qualitative change? Consider one or more of the achievements covered in these articles (e.g., acquisition of self-locomotion, word acquisition, self-relevant memory). Should the phenomenon be characterized as undergoing gradual or sudden changes? Is the answer determined by theory or data? What difference would it make whether you view a developmental change as continuous or discontinuous?

This article has been reprinted as it originally appeared in *Current Directions in Psychological Science*. Citation information for this article as originally published appears above.

Section 3: Cognitive Development

The previous section on infant development addressed several topics that are also core topics in cognitive development—attention, memory, language, and categorization. The current section expands on that work by covering some additional core topics (e.g., symbolic development, theory of mind), exploring cognitive development as it continues throughout the life span, and examining neurological underpinnings of cognitive change.

In the first article, Dima Amso and B.J. Casey combine research showing age-linked changes in cognitive behaviors with imaging data (magnetic resonance imaging, or MRI; functional MRI, or fMRI; and diffusion tensor imaging, or DTI) to draw conclusions about biological mechanisms that underlie behavioral changes. They conclude that the order in which brain regions mature parallels the order in which cognitive developmental milestones emerge. They also provide converging evidence for the neurological processes identified in correlational studies by reporting imaging data recorded while participants learn new skills.

The second article, by Paul Harris, Marc de Rosnay, and Francisco Pons, explores children's progressive understanding of theory of mind (TOM) which includes understanding (a) that others have mental states (e.g., knowledge, feelings, beliefs), (b) that others' mental states may or may not match the child's mental state or reality, and (c) that others' mental states affect their actions and utterances. The authors report correlational and experimental research linking TOM development to language and conversation (e.g., faster acquisition in children whose mothers talk more about mental states) and then discuss and evaluate possible reasons for the link between language and TOM.

Judy DeLoache focuses on the very young child's developing "representational insight," that is, understanding that one thing can stand for another. Children are tested by showing them a small object being hidden in a model room and asking them to find an analogous larger object in a larger room. At 30, but not at 24 months of age, children can use the information from the model to guide their search. Variations on the task show that 24-month-olds have difficulty understanding "dual representation," that is, that one thing can simultaneously have an existence in its own right and stand for something else. This research reveals the development of the foundation for understanding the symbols that play a central role in cognitive development throughout the years that follow.

The article by Rochel Gelman also addresses the early emergence of an important core of cognition—the cardinal counting principle—which refers to understanding that when one counts a collection, the final count tag (word) gives the total number of objects. Based on young children's difficulty reporting the total number of objects in traditional counting tasks, earlier theorists (most notably Piaget) had concluded that children do not understand this concept until 4 or 5. However, findings from a new task in which children were asked to count to check prior arithmetic predictions led Gelman to conclude that children have conceptual understanding of cardinal number as young as 2-1/2 or 3 years.

The final article in this section, by Timothy Salthouse, concerns age-related cognitive change in later portions of the life span. Salthouse reports data from a variety of studies with adults ranging in age from roughly 20 to 90 years. Performance on tests of reasoning, memory, and line-pattern judgments show a linear decline with age across the entire age span tested. Performance on a vocabulary task also declines in a linear relation with age, but these declines do not begin until about 50. The linear pattern of decline argues against explaining cognitive declines as a function of specific life events (e.g., retirement). Salthouse discusses adults' strategies for coping successfully with age-linked declines, and identifies key questions that need to be resolved as the field attempts to explain the declines.

Beyond What Develops When: Neuroimaging May Inform How Cognition Changes With Development

Dima Amso[1] and B.J. Casey

Sackler Institute for Developmental Psychobiology, Weill Medical College of Cornell University

Abstract

There is no single methodology that can fully explain the nature of human development and learning. Yet, headway is being made on how cognitive milestones are achieved during development with the use of magnetic resonance imaging (MRI) technology. With this methodology, it is possible to assess changes in brain structure, function, and connectivity. Recent findings suggest that both progressive and regressive processes—as opposed to simple linear patterns of change—underlie changes in cognitive abilities. Functional MRI studies suggest that both biological maturation and learning correspond to a fine-tuning of neural systems with enhanced recruitment of task-relevant regions. This fine-tuning of cortical systems corresponds with their enhanced connectivity with cortical and subcortical circuitry. In sum, imaging has helped to move the field of cognitive development beyond questions of what develops and when, to how these changes may occur.

Keywords

neuroimaging; cognitive development; learning

Developmental cognitive psychology is the study of how individuals' cognitive abilities change over time and of the emergent processes that support those changes. Behavioral measures used to assess cognitive development typically vary by the age of the population of interest. For example, investigations in infancy are often dependent on looking-time measures, while studies in children use verbal-report or manual-response (button-press, joystick) measures. In either case, the measure obtained is an indirect estimate of some underlying process or body of knowledge. Broadly speaking, such measures have been most successful at addressing what develops and when.

Although traditional research methods have been informative in understanding cognitive change over time, recent advances in brain-imaging methods promise to be useful at addressing the biological mechanisms underlying those changes. The methods that will be emphasized in this article are all forms of magnetic resonance imaging (MRI) that provide information about structure, function, and brain connectivity.

One could argue that neuroimaging provides no unique information to the study of cognitive development. That is, identifying a structure with which a function is associated (i.e., brain mapping) is interesting, but it provides no more information about cognitive development than can be obtained from simple behavioral measures. When, between populations, performance differs along some dimension of interest, behavioral data can be informative about developmental processes. However, infants and children may arrive at the same behavioral outcomes adults do by using very different neural pathways and associated cognitive strategies. In such cases, having only behavioral information may be misleading, resulting in the formulation of models and theories that devalue the contribution of other factors to development.

Understanding the development of pathways underlying cognition and the experiences that alter those pathways is imperative to the study of cognitive development. As noted by Karmiloff-Smith (1994), "the mind does not begin with pre specified modules; rather, development involves a gradual process of modularization" (p. 693). Perhaps the single greatest contribution that neuroimaging can make to the study of cognitive development involves unmasking the biological mechanisms that support developmental behavioral change. Before the advent of sophisticated imaging techniques, assumptions about relationships between the brain and behavior had no empirical grounding. We suggest that imaging techniques provide a unique opportunity to assess biological and behavioral changes simultaneously, allowing for quantitative evidence of brain–behavior associations. We provide evidence from developmental studies of cognitive control during learning to illustrate these contributions. Learning to predict environmental information is a key element of cognitive development. Knowing what to expect and in which context to expect it is critical to planning and maintaining appropriate thoughts and actions. Although learning to predict certain events in the world (e.g., anticipatory eye movements in response to regularly presented stimuli) may be intact early in development, the ability to adjust behavior when these predictions are violated develops more gradually as the underlying neural circuitry is organized (Casey, Amso, & Davidson, in press).

IMAGING METHODOLOGIES: WHAT THEY DO AND DO NOT REVEAL ABOUT DEVELOPMENT

MRI technologies have introduced a new set of tools for capturing features of brain development in living, developing humans. This method permits repeated scanning of the same individual over time, thus providing precise measurements of neuroanatomical changes during learning and development. MRI became especially important to cognitive and developmental scientists when its functional capabilities were discovered and developed. Whereas MRI is used to produce structural images of the brain, the functional component of MRI (fMRI) provides an index of brain activity by measuring changes in localized blood-oxygen levels in the living brain (e.g., Kwong et al., 1992). The assumption that these localized increases in blood oxygenation reflect increases in neuronal activity has found empirical grounding in combined fMRI and electrophysiology studies of nonhuman primates (Logothetis, Pauls, Augath, Trinath, & Oeltermann, 2001).

While fMRI provides a measure of brain function and can help identify regional changes with development, diffusion tensor imaging (DTI) provides an index of brain connectivity. DTI measures change in the microstructure of white matter (tissue containing nerve fibers with fatty insulating material called myelin), based on the properties of water diffusion (e.g., Pierpaoli, Jezzard, Basser,

Barnett, & Di Chiro, 1996). Diffusion of water in white-matter tracts is constrained by myelin and the orientation and regularity of fibers. Water diffuses more readily in parallel to a tract than perpendicular to it—a phenomenon called anisotropic diffusion—and thus can provide information about directionality of connectivity. MRI can be sensitized to water diffusion to quantify myelination and white-matter microstructure in the living brain in order to provide information about changes in connectivity with development (Klingberg, Vaidya, Gabrieli, Moseley, & Hedehus, 1999; Liston et al., in press). This technique can be informative as to how regional connectivity relates to the development of behavior and changes in cortical activity underlying that behavior.

Conventional imaging methods have advanced the field of developmental neuroscience by providing evidence of changes in structural architecture and functional organization in the living brain as it develops. However, magnetic resonance (MR) methods (e.g., MRI, fMRI, DTI) only provide indirect measures of brain structure, function, and connectivity. Differences in the volume of a structure or amount of activity, as measured by MR methods, lack the resolution to definitively characterize the mechanisms of change. Evidence from histology, the microscopic study of tissue, suggests that brain development is a dynamic process of regressive and progressive processes. As such, developmental changes observed using MR techniques may reflect a combination of these processes.

HOW DOES THE STRUCTURAL AND FUNCTIONAL ORGANIZATION OF THE HUMAN BRAIN CHANGE WITH COGNITIVE DEVELOPMENT?

Several imaging studies have mapped the neuroanatomical course of human brain development. Longitudinal MRI studies (Gogtay et al., 2004; Sowell et al., 2004) have shown that cortical maturation parallels developmental cognitive milestones. Regions supporting primary functions, such as motor and sensory systems, mature earliest (see Fig. 1). Next come temporal and parietal association cortices involved in basic language skills and spatial attention. Evidence suggests that higher-order association areas, such as the prefrontal and lateral temporal cortices, which integrate primary sensorimotor processes and modulate basic attention and language processes, mature last (see Fig. 1; Gogtay et al., 2004; Sowell et al., 2004). This progression has been determined via MRI-based studies showing that loss of cortical gray-matter (which contains mostly cell bodies) volume occurs earliest in the primary sensorimotor areas and latest in the dorsolateral prefrontal cortex (e.g., Gogtay et al., 2004; Sowell et al., 2004). The prevalent hypothesis that changes in gray-matter volume detected by MR reflect synapse formation and elimination cannot be supported by imaging studies because of the limited resolution of this methodology.

Cross-sectional studies of normative brain maturation during childhood and adolescence have shown similar patterns, leading to the conclusion that gray-matter loss during this period reflects a sculpting process of the immature brain (e.g., Caviness, Kennedy, Richelme, Rademacher, & Filipek, 1996). While gray-matter volume has an inverted-U-shaped pattern of development, increases in white-matter volume and density with age are roughly linear (Gogtay et al., 2004). These

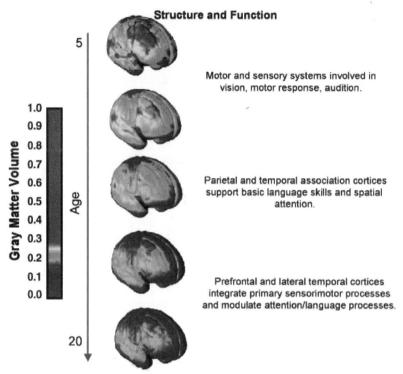

Structure and Function

Motor and sensory systems involved in vision, motor response, audition.

Parietal and temporal association cortices support basic language skills and spatial attention.

Prefrontal and lateral temporal cortices integrate primary sensorimotor processes and modulate attention/language processes.

Fig. 1. The sequence of gray-matter maturation (indicated by loss) with age. Areas in blue correspond to the specific cortices undergoing gray-matter loss. These structures and their functional significance are described to the right. Adapted from Gogtay et al., 2004.

changes presumably reflect ongoing myelination of axons, which enhances neuronal conduction and may play a role in the speed of cognitive processing.

How do these changes in brain structure relate to cognitive development? With development, a child's capacity to filter competing information and suppress inappropriate actions, termed cognitive control, improves dramatically; thus susceptibility to interfering and competing actions diminishes with maturity (Casey, Amso, & Davidson, in press). Durston, Thomas, Worden, Yang, and Casey (2002) used a go/no-go task in combination with fMRI to examine the neural basis of cognitive control and its development. In a go/no-go task, subjects are presented with stimuli to which they are instructed either to respond (go trials) or withhold a response (no-go trials). In an attempt to isolate cognitive and neural processes underlying susceptibility to interference, they parametrically manipulated the number of responses a subject made before having to withhold a response. The ability to accurately withhold a response decreased as the number of preceding responses increased. Simultaneously, the imaging data showed that inhibiting a response to a less-frequent nontarget was associated with increased activity in the ventral prefrontal cortex and the striatum, one of the nuclei that make up the basal ganglia, located below the cerebral cortex. Activity in the ventral prefrontal cortex correlated with performance across age, with children making more errors overall and maximally recruiting the ventral prefrontal cortex, even when a single response preceded them withholding a response.

These findings suggest that susceptibility to interference from competing sources is paralleled by maturational differences in recruitment of underlying frontostriatal circuitry, especially in the prefrontal cortex. Collectively, imaging studies of cognitive control show that children recruit larger, more diffuse prefrontal regions when performing these cognitive tasks than adults do. Activity within brain regions that correlates with task performance becomes more focal or fine-tuned with age, whereas brain regions not correlated with such task performance diminish in activity with age, as shown by cross-sectional (Brown, Lugar, Coalson, Miezin, Petersen, & Schlaggar, 2005) and longitudinal studies (Durston et al., 2006; see Fig. 2).

There are only a few examples of the use of DTI to study cognitive development. One such study (Liston et al., in press) used activation maps from the Durston et al. (2002) developmental-fMRI study discussed earlier to identify

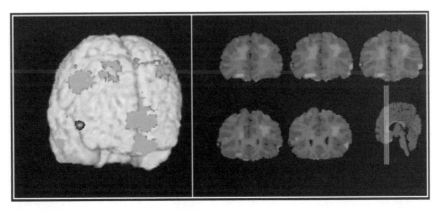

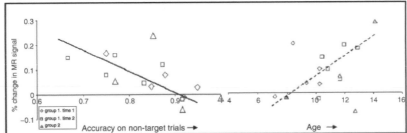

Fig. 2. Regressive and progressive changes with development. Red areas indicate increases in activity in regions associated with cognitive control with age. Blue areas are those that do not correlate with cognitive-control task performance and show attenuated activity with age. The graphs show correlations between activity of key brain areas (ventral prefrontal cortex) during performance of a go/no-go task with behavioral performance and age. These data reflect the increased impulsivity observed as children move into the early stages of adolescence and that later diminishes in adulthood. Adapted from "A Shift From Diffuse to Focal Cortical Activity With Development," by S. Durston, M.C. Davidson, N. Tottenham, A. Galvan, J. Spicer, J.A. Fossella, & B.J. Casey, 2006, *Developmental Science*, 9, p. 5. Copyright 2006 by Blackwell Publishers. Adapted with permission.

fiber tracts that play a role in control over behavior. Specifically, they examined the degree of connectivity between the prefrontal cortex and the striatum, two brain regions in which activity has been shown to correlate with task performance. Levels of connectivity in the frontostriatal and a comparison fiber tract (the corticospinal fiber tract) both correlated with age, but only frontostriatal connectivity correlated with performance on the cognitive-control task (go/no-go paradigm). These findings suggest that the development of prefrontal connectivity and function contributes to a developing capacity for cognitive control.

The results from this select review of studies indicate that changes in prefrontal cortical volume, function, and connectivity as measured by MRI, fMRI, and DTI correspond with a developing capacity for cognitive control. The MRI data showed protracted development of lateral prefrontal cortical thickness. The fMRI data showed fine-tuning of prefrontal activity with development as the pattern of activity shifted from a diffuse to more focal pattern. The DTI results suggest that enhanced prefrontal connectivity may contribute to changes in cognitive abilities with development.

HOW DOES THE STRUCTURAL AND FUNCTIONAL ORGANIZATION OF THE HUMAN BRAIN CHANGE WITH LEARNING?

As development is an interactive process between biological maturation and experience, it is important to examine neural changes with learning. One of the first studies to examine learning with fMRI showed cortical changes as subjects learned sequential finger movements (Karni, Meyer, Jezzard, Adams, Turner, & Ungerleider, 1995). Activity in the primary motor cortex during motor-sequence learning was apparent within a single imaging session and increased over weeks of training. Specifically, activity in task-relevant regions became increasingly enhanced with training, whereas task-irrelevant regions become less active over time. This pattern, in adults, mimics the observed changes in cross-sectional (Brown et al., 2005) and longitudinal (Durston et al., 2006) developmental data described previously.

The previously described studies (Durston et al., 2002; Liston et al., in press) examined the neural mechanisms supporting changes in how behavior is altered when learned expectations are violated (i.e., inhibiting a response to a less frequent non-target). Recently, Amso, Davidson, Johnson, Glover, and Casey (2005) used fMRI to examine neural mechanisms underlying simple learning in adults. A common measure of learning from developmental psychology is preference for novelty as measured by looking times. In novelty-preference paradigms, a stimulus becomes familiar or learned through repeated exposures. Adjusting behavior when these learned or expected events are violated is an essential element of cognitive control (Casey et al., in press), aspects of which are present early in life. Understanding the neural bases for these preferences may constrain developmental theories for how these abilities emerge. In this study, subjects were presented with cue and target stimuli in alternation. The frequency manipulation was designed so that frequent and novel target stimuli were preceded by and had an equal probability of co-occurrence or association with the same cue. The association manipulation was such that the target stimulus was identical in the novel and frequent-association condition. Here the manipulation rested solely on the probability of its co-occurrence with the preceding cue stimulus.

The behavioral results from this study showed longer response times to novel target stimuli—i.e., stimuli with a lower frequency of occurrence across the experiment—as well as learning-related behavioral changes (shorter response times) for both frequently occurring and frequently associated stimuli. The imaging results showed increased activity in the striatum to novel targets and increased left hippocampal activity to novel associations. The hippocampus was preferentially active to the infrequent association, suggesting its involvement in learning of new associations or linking a cue with a novel target (see Fig. 3). These behavioral and imaging findings are interesting in light of the developmental work using novelty preferences and lookingtime measures to show learning in infants. The findings suggest that novelty preference is not based in a single system, but is rather a manifestation of various learning mechanisms that are interacting with the environment. When learned associations are violated is when cognitive control is needed to adjust behavior appropriately, and the previously described studies suggest that this ability is what changes most with development.

WHAT HAS BEEN LEARNED AND FUTURE DIRECTIONS

How has imaging informed the understanding of cognitive development? First, the imaging studies of development and learning suggest that both progressive and regressive processes, as opposed to simple linear patterns of change, underlie changes in cognitive abilities and that these changes may differ regionally across the brain. In development, cortical-thickness changes occur last in higher cortical regions of the lateral prefrontal and temporal cortex and occur in an inverted U-shaped progression, with an increase and subsequent decrease. Second, development and learning correspond to a fine-tuning of neural systems with enhanced recruitment of task-relevant regions and suppression of less task-relevant regions. Finally, these changes correspond with enhanced connectivity of cortical circuitry as measured by DTI. Each of these imaging methods has begun to provide insight on how changes in cognitive processing occur with development. Neuroimaging and other sophisticated techniques such as computational modeling (Munakata & McClelland, 2003) permit the mechanisms supporting the behaviors under investigation to be more precisely characterized. This approach allows for formulation of testable theories and models of development that are consistent with neurobiology.

Recommended Reading

Casey, B.J., Tottenham, N., Liston, C., & Durston, S. (2005). Imaging the developing brain: What have we learned about cognitive development? *Trends in Cognitive Sciences, 9,* 104–109.

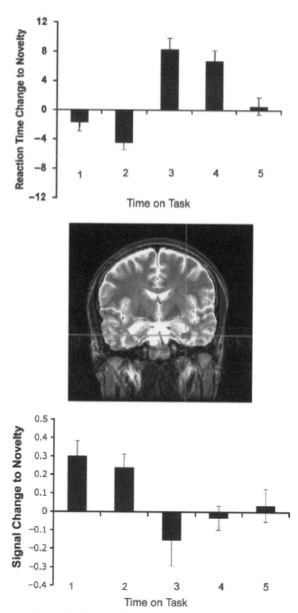

Fig. 3. Infrequent (novel) relative to frequent association comparison. Top graph illustrates changes in reaction time to the novel relative to the frequent association. A greater response to the novel relative to the frequent association indicates learning; results show that learning is not evident at sampled time points early in the task, but becomes increasingly evident later, as participants are more exposed to the task structure. Image (center) shows hippocampal activity to novelty. Bottom graph shows pattern of activation (as measured by signal change) in the hippocampus to novel relative to frequent association as a function of time on task. Adapted from Amso, Davidson, Johnson, Glover, & Casey (2005).

Gogtay, N., Giedd, J.N., Lusk, L., Hayashi, K.M., Greenstein, D., Vaituzis, A.C., Nugent, T.F., Herman, D.H., Clasen, L.S., Toga, A.W., Rapoport, J.L., & Thompson, P.M. (2004). (See References)

Liston, C., Watts, R., Tottenham, N., Davidson, M., Niogi, M., Ulug, A., & Casey, B.J. (in press). (See References)

Acknowledgments—This work was supported in part by R01 MH63255, R01 DA018879, R21 DA15882, and P50 MH062196 awarded to B.J. Casey.

Note

1. Address correspondence to Dima Amso, Sackler Institute for Developmental Psychobiology, Weill Medical College of Cornell University, 1300 York Avenue, Box 140, New York, NY 10021; e-mail: dia2004@med.cornell.edu.

References

Amso, D., Davidson, M.C., Johnson, S.P., Glover, G., & Casey, B.J. (2005). Contributions of the hippocampus and the striatum to simple association and frequency-based learning. *Neuroimage, 27,* 291–298.

Brown, T.T., Lugar, H.M., Coalson, R.S., Miezin, F.M., Petersen, S.E., & Schlaggar, B.L. (2005). Developmental changes in human cerebral functional organization for word generation. *Cerebral Cortex, 15,* 275–280.

Casey, B.J., Amso, D., & Davidson, M.C. (in press). Learning about learning and development with neuroimaging. In M. Johnson & Y. Munakata (Eds). *Attention and performance XXI: Processes of change in brain and cognitive development.* Cambridge, MA: MIT Press.

Caviness, V.S., Kennedy, D.N., Richelme, C., Rademacher, J., & Filipek, P.A. (1996). The human brain age 7–11 years: A volumetric analysis based on magnetic resonance images. *Cerebral Cortex, 6,* 726–736.

Durston, S., Thomas, K.M., Worden, M.S., Yang, Y., & Casey, B.J. (2002). An fMRI study of the effect of preceding context on inhibition. *Neuroimage, 16,* 449–453.

Durston, S., Davidson, M.C., Tottenham, N., Galvan, A., Spicer, J., Fossella, J.A., & Casey, B.J. (2006). A shift from diffuse to focal cortical activity with development. *Developmental Science, 9,* 1–8.

Gogtay, N., Giedd, J.N., Lusk, L., Hayashi, K.M., Greenstein, D., Vaituzis, A.C., Nugent, T.F., Herman, D.H., Clasen, L.S., Toga, A.W., Rapoport, J.L., & Thompson, P.M. (2004). Dynamic mapping of human cortical development during childhood through early adulthood. *Proceedings of the National Academy of Sciences, USA, 101,* 8174–8179.

Karmiloff-Smith, A. (1994). Precis of: *Beyond modularity: A developmental perspective on cognitive science. Behavioral and Brain Sciences, 17,* 693–745.

Karni, A., Meyer, G., Jezzard, P.A., Adams, M.M., Turner, R., Ungerleider, L.G. (1995). Functional MRI evidence for adult motor cortex plasticity during motor skill learning. *Nature, 377,* 155–158.

Klingberg, T., Vaidya, C.J., Gabrieli, J.D., Moseley, M.E., & Hedehus, M. (1999). Myelination and organization of the frontal white matter in children: A diffusion tensor MRI study. *Neuroreport, 10,* 2817–2821.

Kwong, K.K., Belliveau, J.W., Chesler, D.A., Goldberg, I.E., Weisskoff, R.M., Poncelet, B.P., Kennedy, D.N., Hoppel, B.E., Cohen, M.S., & Turner, R. (1992). Dynamic magnetic resonance imaging of human brain activity during primary sensory stimulation. *Proceedings of the National Academy of Sciences, USA, 89,* 5675–5679.

Liston, C., Watts, R., Tottenham, N., Davidson, M., Niogi, M., Ulug, A., & Casey, B.J. (in press). Frontostriatal microstructure predicts individual differences in cognitive control. *Cerebral Cortex.*

Logothetis, N., Pauls, J. Augath, M., Trinath, T. & Oeltermann, A. (2001). Neurophysiological imvestigation of the basis of the fMRI signal. *Nature, 412,* 150–157.

Munakata, Y., & McClelland, J.L. (2003). Connectionist models of development. *Developmental Science, 6*, 413–429.

Pierpaoli, C., Jezzard, P., Basser, P.J., Barnett, A., & Di Chiro, G. (1996). Diffusion tensor MR imaging of the human brain. *Radiology, 201*, 637–648.

Sowell, E.R., Thompson, P.M., Leonard, C.M., Welcome, S.E., Kan, E., & Toga A.W. (2004). Longitudinal mapping of cortical thickness and brain growth in normal children. *Journal of Neuroscience, 24*, 8223–8231.

This article has been reprinted as it originally appeared in *Current Directions in Psychological Science*. Citation information for this article as originally published appears above.

Language and Children's Understanding of Mental States

Paul L. Harris[1]
Harvard University

Marc de Rosnay
Cambridge University

Francisco Pons
University of Aalborg, Denmark

Abstract

Children progress through various landmarks in their understanding of mind and emotion. They eventually understand that people's actions, utterances, and emotions are determined by their beliefs. Although these insights emerge in all normal children, individual children vary in their rates of progress. Four lines of research indicate that language and conversation play a role in individual development: (a) Children with advanced language skills are better at mental-state understanding than those without advanced language skills, (b) deaf children born into nonsigning families lag in mental-state understanding, and (c) exposure to maternal conversation rich in references to mental states promotes mental-state understanding, as do (d) experimental language-based interventions. Debate centers on the mechanism by which language and conversation help children's understanding of mental states. Three competing interpretations are evaluated here: lexical enrichment (the child gains from acquiring a rich mental-state vocabulary), syntactic enrichment (the child gains from acquiring syntactic tools for embedding one thought in another), and pragmatic enrichment (the child gains from conversations in which varying perspectives on a given topic are articulated). Pragmatic enrichment emerges as the most promising candidate.

Keywords

mind; emotion; language; conversation

In the past 20 years, a large body of research has shown that normal children progress through a series of landmarks in their understanding of mental states. At around 4 years of age, children understand that people's actions and utterances are guided by their beliefs, whether those beliefs are true or false. At around 5 to 6 years of age, they come to realize that people's emotions are also influenced by their beliefs (Pons, Harris, & de Rosnay, 2003). This gradual acquisition of what is now routinely known as a *theory of mind* can be illustrated with the classic fairy tale of Little Red Riding Hood. When 3-year-olds are told that the wolf is waiting for Little Red Riding Hood, they typically fail to realize that she mistakenly expects to be greeted by her grandmother as she knocks at the cottage door. By contrast, 4- and 5-year-olds understand Little Red Riding Hood's false belief. Yet many 4-year-olds and some 5-year-olds say that when she knocks, she must be afraid of the wolf—the very wolf that she does not know about! By the age of 6 years, however, most children fully grasp Little Red Riding Hood's naïveté. They understand not

Fig. 1. A test of children's understanding of the relationship between belief and emotion. Children are shown the picture at the top (a) and told that the rabbit is eating a carrot. A fox is hidden under a flap depicting a bush. Children are then invited to lift the bush, to see the fox hidden behind it (b), and then to replace the bush "so that the rabbit can't see the fox." Next, the children are asked whether the rabbit knows there is a fox hiding behind the bush and how the rabbit feels—happy, just alright, angry, or scared—by selecting one of the four face choices (c). Four- and five-year-olds often acknowledge that the rabbit does not know that the fox is hiding behind the bush, but still claim that the rabbit is scared (Pons, Lawson, Harris, & de Rosnay, 2003).

only that she fails to realize that a wolf is waiting to eat her, but also that she feels no fear. An illustrative test of children's understanding of the relationship between belief and emotion is shown in Figure 1.

Children's acquisition of a theory of mind emerges in orderly steps (Wellman & Liu, 2004; Pons et al., 2003), but individual children vary markedly in their rate of progress. In this article, we review four lines of evidence indicating that language and conversation play a key role in helping children develop an understanding of mental states. We then ask about the causal mechanism involved.

CHILDREN'S LANGUAGE SKILL AND MENTAL-STATE UNDERSTANDING

Among normal children and children with autism, accuracy in the attribution of beliefs and emotions has been correlated with language skill (Happé, 1995; Pons, Lawson, Harris, & de Rosnay, 2003). It could be argued that this correlation shows that a theory of mind facilitates language acquisition. However, longitudinal research has offered little support for such an interpretation. Astington and Jenkins (1999) found that pre-schoolers' theory-of-mind performance was not a predictor of subsequent gains in language. Rather, the reverse was true: Language ability was a good predictor of improvement in theory-of-mind performance. Children with superior language skills—particularly in the domain of syntax—made greater progress over the next 7 months than other children did in their conceptualization of mental states.

Restricted Access to Language: The Case of Deafness

Does a child's access to language, as well as a child's own language skill, affect his or her theory of mind? When children are born deaf, they are often delayed in their access to language, including sign language. Late signers are particularly common among deaf children born to hearing parents because the parents themselves rarely master sign language. Late signers—like children with autism—are markedly delayed in their understanding of mental states. By contrast, deaf children who learn to sign in a home with native signers are comparable to normal children in their performance on theory-of-mind tasks (Peterson & Siegal, 2000).

Even when efforts are made to bypass problems that late signers might have in grasping the language of such tasks—for example, by substituting a nonverbal (Figueras-Costa & Harris, 2001) or pictorial (Woolfe, Want, & Siegal, 2002) test of mental-state understanding—late signers still have marked difficulties. By implication, late-signing children are genuinely delayed in their conceptualization of mental states; it is not simply that they have difficulty in conveying their understanding when the test is given in sign language.

Maternal Conversation and Mental-State Understanding

Two recent studies show that, even when children have normal access to language, mothers vary in their language style and this style appears to affect children's mental-state understanding. Ruffman, Slade, and Crowe (2002) studied mother–child pairs on three occasions when the children ranged from 3 to 4 years of age. On each occasion, they recorded a conversation between mother and child about a picture book and measured the child's theory-of-mind performance and linguistic ability. Mothers' use or nonuse of mental-state language—terms such as *think, know, want,* and *hope*—at earlier time points predicted children's later theory-of-mind performance. Moreover, the reverse pattern did not hold.

The experimental design used in this study allowed the role of maternal conversation to be clarified in important ways. First, it was specifically mental-state references that predicted children's theory-of-mind performance; other aspects of maternal discourse, such as descriptive comments (e.g., "She's riding a bicycle") or causal comments (e.g., "They have no clothes on because they're in the water"), had no impact on children's theory-of-mind performance over and above the effect of mental-state utterances. Second, children's earlier language abilities also predicted their later theory-of-mind performance independently of their mothers' mental-state discourse.

The study by Ruffman et al. (2002) focused on false-belief tasks mastered somewhere between 3 and 4 years of age. We investigated whether mothers' mental-state discourse is linked to children's performance on a more demanding task typically mastered at around 5 or 6 years of age. Recall the story of Little Red Riding Hood: Only around the age of 5 or 6 years do many children realize that Little Red Riding Hood feels no fear of the wolf when she knocks at the door of grandmother's cottage. In a study of children ranging from 4½ to 6 years (de Rosnay, Pons, Harris, & Morrell, 2004), we found that mothers' use of mentalistic terms when describing their children (i.e., references to their children's psychological attributes as opposed to their behavior or physical attributes) and their children's own verbal ability were positively associated not only with correct false-belief attributions, but also with correct emotion attributions in tasks utilizing stories akin to that of Little Red Riding Hood. Moreover, mothers' mentalistic descriptions predicted children's correct emotion attributions even when the sample was restricted to children who had mastered the simpler false-belief task. So, even after children have mastered the false-belief task, there is still scope for maternal discourse to help the child make further progress in understanding mental states.

Four important conclusions emerge from these studies. First, mothers who talk about psychological themes promote their children's mental-state understanding. Second, it is unlikely that psychologically precocious children prompt more mental-state language in their mothers; rather, the direction of causation is from mother to child. Third, mere talkativeness on the part of a mother does not promote mental-state understanding—it is the mother's psychological language that is critical. Fourth, mothers' psychological orientation has sustained influence: This influence is evident among 3-year-olds and 6-year-olds alike. The effect of maternal language is not restricted to false-belief understanding. It also applies to the later understanding of belief-based emotions.

Language-Based Interventions

So far, we have summarized correlational findings demonstrating a link between language and mental-state understanding. However, experimental language interventions also produce gains in mental-state understanding. In one study, Lohmann and Tomasello (2003) pretested a large group of 3-year-olds. Those who failed a standard test of false belief received various types of intervention and were then retested using other false-belief tasks. The most effective intervention for improving children's understanding of false belief combined two factors: (a) the presentation of a series of objects, some of which had a misleading appearance (e.g., an object that looked initially like a flower but turned out to be a pen); and (b) verbal comments on what people would say, think, and know about the perceptible properties and actual identity of these objects. Hale and Tager-Flusberg (2003) also found that language-based interventions were effective in improving children's false-belief understanding. In one intervention, children discussed story protagonists who held false beliefs. In a second intervention, they discussed story protagonists who made false claims. In each case, the children were given corrective verbal feedback if they misstated what the protagonists thought or said. Both interventions proved very effective in promoting 3-year-olds' grasp of false belief.

These intervention studies confirm that conversation about people's thoughts or statements has a powerful effect on children's understanding of belief. One additional finding underscores the critical role of conversation. When Lohmann and Tomasello (2003) presented children with various misleading objects but offered minimal verbal comment—other than a request to look at the objects— the impact on children's mental-state understanding was negligible.

HOW DOES LANGUAGE HELP?

Given the converging evidence just described, the claim that language makes a difference for children's developing theory of mind is convincing. Not only do children's own language abilities predict their rate of progress in understanding the mind, but their access to conversation, especially conversation rich in mentalistic words and concepts, is an equally potent and independent predictor.

Despite this solid evidence for the role of language, there is disagreement over how exactly it helps. Consider the type of comments that a mother might make as she and her preschool child look at a picture book—"I think it's a cat" or "I don't know whether it's a dog" (Ruffman et al., 2002, p. 740). It could be argued that such comments help the child develop an understanding of mental states because the words *think* and *know* draw the child's attention to mental processes. But there are other possible explanations. For example, such comments are also syntactically distinctive: They embed a proposition (". . . it's a cat" or ". . . whether it's a dog") in another clause containing a mental verb ("I think . . ." or "I don't know . . ."). Mastery of the way propositions can be embedded in other clauses might help children to conceptualize mental states that take particular states of affairs as their target. Mental-state understanding often calls for an appreciation of the way in which a mental state such as a thought, a belief, or a hope is targeted at a particular state of affairs. But also, such comments play a role in the pragmatics of conversation. More specifically, they set out a claim (e.g., ". . . it's a cat") and they convey the particular perspective of the speaker toward that claim. Accordingly, such comments might underline the way people can vary in the mental stance or perspective they adopt toward a given claim. In short, mentalistic comments contain distinctive words (e.g., *think* and *know*), grammatical constructions (e.g., embedded propositions), and pragmatic features (e.g., the enunciation of individual perspectives). Which factor is critical? It is too early to draw firm conclusions, but the evidence increasingly points to the importance of pragmatic features.

First, two recent studies with children speaking languages other than English suggest that the syntax of embedded propositions is not the reason why language skill correlates with theory-of-mind understanding. In German, *want* sentences such as "Mother wants George to go to bed" must be rendered with a that proposition —"Mutter will, dass George ins Bett geht" (literally, "Mother wants *that* George into the bed goes"). Perner, Sprung, Zauner, and Haider (2003) studied whether early exposure to, and understanding of, the *want*–that structure is associated with good performance on standard theory-of-mind tasks, but they found no evidence supporting such a relationship. Similarly, a study of Cantonese-speaking children failed to uncover any link between mastery of verbs that can serve to embed another proposition and theory-of-mind under-standing, once general language competence had been taken into account (Cheung et al., 2004).

Second, our findings (de Rosnay et al., 2004) make both the lexical and the syntactic explanations problematic. Maternal usage of terms like *think* and *know* together with their embedded propositions might plausibly help children to understand false beliefs because when they attribute a false belief to someone children will need to use the same linguistic constructions. For example, to describe Little Red Riding Hood's mistaken belief, it is appropiate to say: "She thinks that it's her grandmother" or "She doesn't know that it's a wolf." However, the attribution of emotion, including belief-based emotion, does not call for the use of mental-state terms with embedded propositions. It simply calls for appro-priate use of particular emotion terms. "Little Red Riding Hood felt happy as she knocked at the cottage." Yet we found that mothers' mental discourse not only helped children understand false beliefs, but also helped them move on to under-stand belief-based emotions. An emphasis on pragmatics can readily explain this twofold impact: Mothers disposed to talk about varying individual beliefs regard-ing a given situation will probably also articulate the feelings that flow from those individual beliefs.

CONCLUSIONS

People often observe other people's facial expressions and bodily postures for clues to their mental life. Indeed, a great deal of research on the early develop-ment of a theory of mind has focused on infants' skill at interpreting these non-verbal clues. However, in contrast to any other species, human beings are also able to talk to each other about their mental lives. They can talk about their feel-ings, compare their beliefs, and share their plans and intentions.

The research reviewed here shows that such conversations play a key role in helping children to make sense of mental states. We are on the brink of designing longitudinal and intervention studies that will help us determine just how con-versation helps children in this endeavor. So far, research on children's mental-state understanding has mainly focused on the milestone of understanding false beliefs. We have shown here, however, that maternal discourse is also linked with how well children attribute belief-based emotions to other people, and specifically that this link holds true even among children who have already mastered false beliefs.

In the future, it will be important to study various other milestones in children's mental-state understanding. For example, only around age 5 or 6 do children understand that the emotions people actually feel may not correspond to the emotions that they express. Also, it is not until middle childhood that children fully understand self-conscious emotions such as guilt—or understand that it is possible to feel conflicting emotions about the same situation. In the future, researchers can focus on these developmental advances to better understand the influence of parents' conversation on children's mental-state understanding. If it is found that the same type of parental conversation style (e.g., coherent psychological discourse) has a pervasive influence across different aspects of mental-state understanding, then it will become less likely that specific lexical or semantic features of discourse are the crucial factor. Instead, as we have noted, it will be more plausible to assume that some parents elucidate a variety of mental states in conversation with their children. That elucidation is not tied to particular lexical terms or syntactic constructions. Instead, it reflects a wide-ranging sensitivity to individual perspectives and nurtures that same sensitivity in children.

Researchers may also consider the implications of mental-state understanding for children's behavior and social relationships. An increasing body of evidence indicates that good performance on theory-of-mind tasks is correlated with the ability to form relationships with peers (Pons, Harris, & Doudin, 2002). A plausible—but as yet untested—interpretation is that children's mental-state understanding helps them both to initiate and to maintain friendships. This hypothesis can be tested by assessing the impact of a discourse-based intervention not just on children's mental-state understanding, but also on their relationships with peers.

Finally, researchers may look forward to an important bridge between developmental and clinical psychology. The mother who is alert to her child's mental states, who accurately puts thoughts and feelings into words, and who nurtures her child's sensitivity to different mental perspectives may have an effect on her child that is not unlike that of a clinician or therapist who fosters a reflective stance in his or her patients.

Recommended Reading

Astington, J.A., & Baird, J. (Eds.). (2005). *Why language matters for theory of mind*. New York: Oxford University Press.

de Rosnay, M., Pons, F., Harris, P.L., & Morrell, J. (2004). (See References)

Harris, P.L. (1996). Desires, beliefs and language. In P. Carruthers & P.K. Smith (Eds.), *Theories of theories of mind* (pp. 200–220). Cambridge, England: Cambridge University Press.

Harris, P.L. (2000). Understanding emotion. In M. Lewis & J. Haviland-Jones (Eds.), *Handbook of emotions* (2nd ed., pp. 281–292). New York: Guildford Press.

Peterson, C.C., & Siegal, M. (2000). (See References)

Note

1. Address correspondence to P.L. Harris, 503A Larsen Hall, HGSE, Harvard University, Appian Way, Cambridge, MA 02138; e-mail: paul_harris@gse.harvard.edu.

References

Astington, J.W., & Jenkins, J.M. (1999). A longitudinal study of the relation between language and theory-of-mind development. *Developmental Psychology, 35,* 1311–1320.

Cheung, H., Hsuan-Chih, C., Creed, N., Ng, L., Wang, S.P., & Mo, L. (2004). Relative roles of general and complementation language in theory-of-mind development: Evidence from Cantonese and English. *Child Development, 75,* 1155–1170.

de Rosnay, M., Pons, F., Harris, P.L., & Morrell, J. (2004). A lag between understanding false belief and emotion attribution in young children: Relationships with linguistic ability and mothers' mental state language. *British Journal of Developmental Psychology, 22,* 197–218.

Figueras-Costa, B., & Harris, P.L. (2001). Theory of mind in deaf children: A non-verbal test of false belief understanding. *Journal of Deaf Studies and Deaf Education, 6,* 92–102.

Hale, C.M., & Tager-Flusberg, H. (2003). The influence of language on theory of mind: A training study. *Developmental Science, 6,* 346–359.

Happé, F.G.E. (1995). The role of age and verbal ability in the theory of mind task performance of subjects with autism. *Child Development, 66,* 843–855.

Lohmann, H., & Tomasello, M. (2003). The role of language in the development of false belief understanding: A training study. *Child Development, 74,* 1130–1144.

Perner, J., Sprung, M., Zauner, P., & Haider, H. (2003). *Want that* is understood well before *say that, think that,* and false belief: A test of de Villiers's linguistic determinism on German-speaking children. *Child Development, 74,* 179–188.

Peterson, C.C., & Siegal, M. (2000). Insights into theory of mind from deafness and autism. *Mind and Language, 15,* 123–145.

Pons, F., Harris, P.L., & Doudin, P.-A. (2002). Teaching emotion understanding. *European Journal of Psychology of Education, 17,* 293–304.

Pons, F., Harris, P.L., & de Rosnay, M. (2003). Emotion comprehension between 3 and 11 years: Developmental periods and hierarchical organization. *European Journal of Developmental Psychology, 2,* 127–152.

Pons, F., Lawson, J., Harris, P.L., & de Rosnay, M. (2003). Individual differences in children's emotion understanding: Effects of age and language. *Scandinavian Journal of Psychology, 44,* 347–353.

Ruffman, T., Slade, L., & Crowe, E. (2002). The relation between children's and mothers' mental state language and theory-of-mind understanding. *Child Development, 73,* 734–751.

Wellman, H.M., & Liu, D. (2004). Scaling of theory of mind tasks. *Child Development, 75,* 523–541.

Woolfe, T., Want, S.C., & Siegal, M. (2002). Signposts to development: Theory-of-mind in deaf children. *Child Development, 73,* 768–778.

This article has been reprinted as it originally appeared in *Current Directions in Psychological Science*. Citation information for this article as originally published appears above.

Early Understanding and Use of Symbols: The Model Model

Judy S. DeLoache[1]

Professor of Psychology, University of Illinois,
Urbana-Champaign

The hallmark of human cognition is symbolization: There is nothing that so clearly distinguishes us from other creatures as our creative and flexible use of symbols. Cultural creations such as writing systems, number systems, maps, and models—to name a few—have enabled human knowledge and reasoning to transcend time and space.

My working definition of an external, artifactual symbol is that it is any entity that someone intends to stand for something other than itself. Note that this definition is agnostic about the nature of symbols; virtually anything can be a symbol, so long as some person intends that it be responded to not as itself, but in terms of what it represents. Adults are so experienced and skilled with symbols and symbolic reasoning that they simply assume that many of the novel entities they encounter will have symbolic import. They appreciate that such entities should be responded to as representations of something other than themselves—and readily do so. My research reveals that children only gradually adopt this assumption. Despite the centrality of symbolization in human cognition and communication, young children are very conservative when it comes to detecting and reasoning about symbol–referent relations.

SYMBOLIC DEVELOPMENT

Becoming a proficient symbolizer is a universal developmental task; full participation in any culture requires mastery of a variety of culturally relevant symbols and symbol systems, in addition to language and symbolic gestures. Children make substantial progress in this task in the first years of life. In Western societies, older infants and toddlers start to learn about pictures and pictorial conventions. Most preschool children are taught the alphabet and numbers, many begin to read, and some even start to do simple arithmetic. Many young children also encounter a variety of less common symbols, such as maps, models, musical notation, and computer icons.

Symbolic development plays a prominent role in many theories of child development, and there is a substantial body of empirical work focusing on the development of particular symbol systems, especially drawing, reading, and mathematical competence.[2] My research addresses the general issue of how very young children first gain insight into novel symbol–referent relations and how they begin to use symbols as a source of information and a basis for reasoning.

In our research, my colleagues and I present young children with a particular symbolic representation—most often a scale model, picture, or map—that provides information needed to solve a problem. Use of the symbol requires (a) some awareness of the relation between symbol and referent, (b) mapping the corresponding elements from one to the other, and (c) drawing an inference about one based on knowledge of the other. The majority of our research has involved scale models. Because young children rarely, if ever, encounter real models in which the symbol maps onto a specific referent, we can use scale models to examine how children first gain insight into and exploit a novel type of symbol–referent relation.

In our standard task, the model stands for a room (either a full-sized real room or a tentlike, portable room). The model is very realistic, and there is a high degree of physical similarity between the objects—items of furniture—within the model and the room. The model is in the same spatial orientation as the room, but it is located outside the room, so the child can see only one space at a time. The model–room relation is explicitly and elaborately described and demonstrated for the 2- to 3-year-old children. In the task, children watch as a miniature toy is hidden behind or under a miniature item of furniture in the model, and they are told that a larger version of the toy is hidden with the corresponding piece of furniture in the room. ("Watch! I'm hiding Little Snoopy here. I'm going to hide Big Snoopy in the same place in his big room.") If the children appreciate the relation between the two spaces, then their knowledge of the location of the miniature toy in the model can be used to figure out where to search for the larger toy in the room, and vice versa. (It does not matter whether subjects see the hiding event in the model or the room. For convenience, I refer to the situation in which the hiding event occurs in the model.)

In numerous studies, 36-month-old children have typically succeeded in this task (>75% errorless retrievals), but 30-month-olds have usually performed very poorly (<20% correct).[3–6] Failure in the task is not due to memory or motivational factors: Virtually all children can retrieve the toy they actually observe being hidden in the model. Nevertheless, the younger children fail to relate their knowledge of the model to the room. These children understand that there is a toy hidden in the room, and they readily search for it. What they do not realize is that they have any way of knowing—other than by guessing—where it is.

A MODEL OF SYMBOL UNDERSTANDING AND USE

Research conducted with this and related tasks has led to the development of a heuristic, conceptual model of young children's understanding and use of symbols (see Fig. 1). (To avoid confusion, henceforth, I use the term Model, with a capital *M*, to refer to the conceptual model.) Although this Model is intended to apply to symbol use more broadly, in this review, I use our work with scale models to illustrate the Model's features. The Model incorporates several factors we have discovered to be important in young children's symbol use (left side of Fig. 1), including characteristics of the symbol itself (salience), the symbol–referent relationship (iconicity), the symbol user (experience), and the social context (instruction). As is apparent from the figure, these factors interact in complex ways to determine performance.

The end point of the Model is the behavior of using a symbol as a source of information (right side of Fig. 1), which always requires mapping between symbol

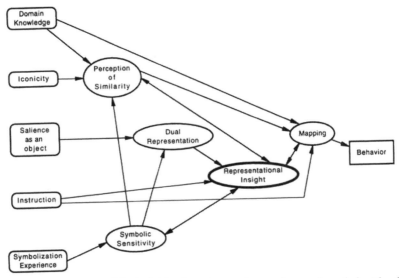

Fig. 1. A heuristic model of children's understanding and use of symbols. The five rounded rectangles on the left represent factors demonstrated or hypothesized to affect the behavior of interest (symbol use), represented by the rectangle on the far right. The ellipses represent intervening variables assumed to mediate between the manipulated factors and children's behavior. Because we have not yet investigated the role of domain knowledge, it is not discussed in this article.

and referent. Numerals must be mapped onto the appropriate quantities; the individual elements on a road map must be mapped onto the corresponding roads and cities in the real world. In the model task, the individual objects—items of furniture—within the model must be mapped onto the corresponding objects in the room. The relation between the hidden toy and its hiding place must also be mapped from one space to the other.

Representational insight, the basic realization of the existence of a symbol–referent relation, is the pivotal element in the Model. The level of awareness of this relation varies from explicit metacognitive knowledge that a given symbol represents some particular referent, such as an adult might have, to an implicit and inexpressible sense of relatedness, such as a young child might have. My research has repeatedly shown both that representational insight can be surprisingly difficult for young children to achieve and that developmental progress can be very rapid.

It is obvious that the social context of symbol use is important. Much symbolic development involves direct instruction by other, more knowledgeable people. Children are explicitly taught the alphabet and numbers and how to read and do math. In the model task also, direct instructions play an important role: Three-year-olds succeed in the standard task in which the relation between the model and room is explicitly described and demonstrated for them, but they perform very poorly when less complete instructions are given.[7] Children have to be told about the model–room relation to achieve representational insight.

Another variable that plays an important role in young children's symbol use has to do with the symbol–referent relation. Iconicity refers to physical similarity between symbol and referent. Many symbol–referent relations are purely arbitrary and conventional, with no physical resemblance at all—for example, numerals, letters, and musical notation. Some are partially iconic: Maps preserve spatial relations, but have few other iconic features. Other symbols are highly iconic: A color photograph, for example, closely resembles its referent. Except for size, the scale model used in my research looks very much like the room it represents.

Iconicity generally facilitates symbol use: The more a symbol resembles its referent, the easier it is to perceive the similarity between the two. Perception of similarity facilitates both the achievement of representational insight and mapping. In the model task, similarity has been shown to be very important, both in terms of surface similarity of the individual objects within the two spaces and in terms of the overall resemblance between the model and the room. For example, 3-year-olds are highly successful if the furniture in the two spaces is highly similar, but they perform poorly if there is a low level of similarity. When object similarity is high and, in addition, model and room are similar in overall size, even 2½-year-olds succeed in the model task.[4]

Note that the Model specifies two-way influences between representational insight and perception of similarity. A child who realizes that a symbol and referent are related will presumably search for similarity between the elements within them, thus leading to improved mapping. For example, in the model task, a child who realizes that the model and room are related will actively look for similarities between the individual items within the spaces.

DUAL REPRESENTATION

Another important factor is the salience of the physical properties of the symbol. All symbols of the sort under consideration have both a concrete and an abstract nature. A consequence is that understanding and using them requires what I have termed dual representation—simultaneously representing both the concrete and the abstract nature of a symbol.[3] To the extent that one's attention is drawn to the physical properties of a symbol, it will be more difficult to appreciate its symbolic status. As Langer[8] said, a peach would be a poor symbol because "we are too much interested in peaches themselves."

To succeed in our task, the child must mentally represent the model both as a real, concrete object (or set of objects) and, at the same time, as an abstract symbol for something other than itself. The high salience of the model and young children's keen interest in it prevent them from representing it both ways. They pay attention to the model itself, encoding and remembering the location of the hiding event in it, but that memory representation remains separate from their mental representation of the room. Hence, they fail to use their knowledge about the model to draw an inference about the room.

The dual representation hypothesis has received strong support from the confirmation of a series of counterintuitive but theoretically motivated predictions. First, I reasoned that because a picture is much less salient and interesting as an object than a model is, substituting a picture for the model should make our task easier (even though two-dimensional stimuli are generally less informative and effective than three-dimensional ones).[3] As predicted, 2½-year-old children succeeded when pictures, but not a model, were used to convey the location of a hidden toy.

Second, we attempted to decrease the physical salience of the model by placing it behind a window, thus preventing the children from touching it or interacting directly with it. We reasoned that denying children access to the model would decrease its salience as an object, hence making it easier for them to achieve dual representation. The predicted improvement in the performance of a group of 2½-year-olds occurred. In a third study in this series, we attempted instead to increase the salience of the model by letting children play with it for several minutes before testing them in the standard task. The idea was that playing with and manipulating the model would make it more salient as an object and hence would make dual representation more difficult to achieve. The predicted poor performance by a group of 3-year-olds occurred.[9]

We recently conducted an even more stringent test of dual representation by attempting to eliminate the need for it.[10] In this study, we endeavored to convince a group of 2½-year-old children that a "shrinking machine" could shrink a troll doll and a room. Our reasoning was that if children believe the machine has shrunk the room (into the scale model of that room), then there is no representational relation between model and room. Instead, there is an identity relation: The model *is* the room. Hence, the task of retrieving the hidden toy is simply a memory problem. Therefore, we predicted that 2½-year-olds, who typically fail the standard model task, would succeed in the nonsymbolic shrinking-room task.

In the orientation, the child was introduced to "Terry the Troll" (a troll doll with vivid fuschia hair) and was shown "Terry's room" (a tent-like, portable room that had been used in many previous model studies). Then the shrinking machine (an oscilloscope with flashing green lights) was introduced, and its remarkable powers were demonstrated. The troll was placed in front of the machine, which was "switched on," and the child and experimenter waited in the adjoining area, listening to computer-generated "sounds the shrinking machine makes while it's working." The child then returned to discover a miniature troll in place of the original one. Figure 2 shows the troll before and after the "shrinking event." The child was then shown that the machine could also make the troll "get big again." A similar demonstration showed the power of the machine to shrink and enlarge Terry's room. The sight of the model in place of the room was very dramatic.

The child then watched as the experimenter hid the larger doll somewhere in the portable room. After waiting while the machine shrank the room, the child was asked to find the hidden toy. The miniature troll was, of course, hidden in the model in the place corresponding to where the child had seen the larger troll being hidden in the room. Thus, just as in the model task, the child had to use his or her knowledge of where the toy was hidden in one space to know where to search in the other. However, in this task, the child thought the room and model were the same thing. (Both the experimenters and the parents were convinced that all but one child firmly believed the shrinking-room scenario. Remember, most of these children also believe in the tooth fairy.)

Fig. 2. The incredible shrinking troll. The panel on the left shows the troll positioned in front of the shrinking machine; the panel on the right shows the troll after the shrinking event.

As predicted, performance was significantly better in this nonsymbolic task than in a control task involving the usual symbolic relation between the model and the room. This superior performance occurred even though the shrinking-room scenario was more complicated and the delay between the hiding event and the child's retrieval was much longer than in the standard model task. This study thus provides very strong support for the dual representation hypothesis.

DEVELOPMENTAL PROGRESS

A key element in the Model is the individual's symbolization experience, which includes both general experience with a variety of symbols and specific experience with any particular type of symbol. Such experiences lead to the development of symbolic sensitivity, a general expectation or readiness to look for and detect the presence of symbolic relations between entities. Experience responding to a given entity as a representation of something other than itself increases an individual's readiness to respond to other entities in an abstract rather than concrete mode.[11] Symbolic experience, and hence symbolic sensitivity, increases naturally with age.

Evidence for the role of symbolic sensitivity comes from a series of standard transfer-of-training studies. Children who are first tested in a relatively easy task (i.e., one in which they detect the symbol–referent relation and perform well) subsequently perform better in a more difficult task (i.e., one their age group normally fails). Thus, 2½-year-olds who did well using a picture to guide their search for a hidden toy subsequently succeeded using a model as a source of information. Children of the same age also showed significant transfer from a relatively easy model task to the standard task. Three-year-old children who first participated in the task with high similarity between model and room were subsequently successful with low similarity between the two spaces, although 3-year-olds typically fail the latter task.[6]

Symbolic sensitivity is the primary mechanism for developmental change in the Model. As a function of experience using symbols, children increasingly expect and look for relations between entities. As children become more sensitive to the possibility of symbolic relations, they become capable of detecting them with less support. Thus, high levels of iconicity are less important for older children than for younger children, less explicit instructions suffice, and so forth. Dual representation is more readily achieved: Anticipating a symbolic relation, children focus less on the concrete characteristics of a symbol and more on its abstract, representational function. (General cognitive development is also obviously important in symbolic development, but it is not formally incorporated into the Model.)

IMPLICATIONS AND APPLICATION

The Model described here has a number of clear practical implications. One cannot take for granted that children will detect a symbolic relation, no matter how obvious it is to older individuals. There are no fully transparent symbols. Only through experience do young children come to appreciate the abstract, representational relation that holds between a symbol and referent, regardless of how physically similar they may be.

Educational materials are often designed with the assumption that three-dimensional materials—"manipulables"—will help children acquire abstract concepts (e.g., various blocks are often used to teach number concepts and arithmetic). It is assumed that the relation between the object symbols and the concepts will be obvious or readily figured out. My research indicates that this assumption cannot be made blithely—and will not always be valid. Hence, the utility of any such educational aids cannot simply be taken for granted.

Similarly, anatomically explicit dolls are commonly used in investigations of suspected child abuse on the assumption that the self–doll relation will be obvious to young children and will help them provide more complete and accurate testimony. Recent research in my laboratory and others questions this assumption. There is increasing evidence that, as predicted by dual representation, very young children do not find it natural or easy to use a doll as a representation of themselves.[12]

In conclusion, children start early to acquire the variety of symbols needed for full participation in their culture. However, the representational nature of any given symbol may not be clear to them. Understanding and using a symbol depends on the interaction of many factors, including characteristics of the symbol and its referent, the child's prior experience with symbols, and the information given to the child about the nature and meaning of the symbol.

Acknowledgments—The research summarized in this review was supported by Research Grant HD-25271 and Training Grant HD-07205 from the National Institute for Child Health and Human Development. I thank Reneé Baillargeon, Gerald Clore, Larry Jones, and Don Marzolf for helpful comments on earlier versions of the manuscript. I also thank Kathy Anderson for her invaluable contributions to this research.

Notes

1. Address correspondence to Judy DeLoache, Department of Psychology, University of Illinois, 603 East Daniel, Champaign, IL 61820.

2. For theories on the development of symbolization, see, e.g., H. Werner and H. Kaplan, *Symbol Formation* (Wiley, New York, 1967); L.5. Vygotsky, *Mind in Society*, M. Cole, V. John-Steiner, S. Scribner, and E. Souberman, Eds. (Harvard University Press, Cambridge, MA, 1978). For summaries of research on particular symbols, see, e.g., J. Goodnow, *Children Drawing* (Harvard University Press, Cambridge, MA, 1977); U. Goswarni and P. E. Bryant, *Phonological Skills and Learning to Read* (Erlbaum, Hove, England, 1990); R. Gelman and C.R. Callistel, *The Child's Understanding of Number* (Harvard University Press, Cambridge, MA, 1978). For recent reviews of research on the development of representation, see C. Pratt and A. Garton, Eds., *The Development and Use of Representation in Children* (Wiley, Chichester, England, 1993); R.R. Cocking and K.A. Renninger. Eds., *The Development and Meaning of Psychological Distance* (Erlbaum, Hillsdale, NJ, 1993).

3. J.S. DeLoache, Rapid change in the symbolic functioning of very young children, *Science, 238*, 1556–1557 (1987); J.S. DeLoache, Symbolic functioning in very young children: Understanding of pictures and models, *Child Development, 62*, 736–752 (1991).

4. J.S. DeLoache, D.V. Kolstad, and K.N. Anderson, Physical similarity and young children's understanding of scale models, *Child Development, 62*, 111–126 (1991).

5. G.A. Dow and H.L. Pick, Young children's use of models and photographs as spatial representations, *Cognitive Development, 7*, 351–363 (1992).

6. D.P. Marzolf and J.S. DeLoache, Transfer in young children's understanding of spatial representations. *Child Development, 65*, 1-15 (1994).

7. J.S. DeLoache, Young children's understanding of the correspondence between a scale model and a larger space, *Cognitive Development, 4*, 121–129 (1989).

8. S.K. Langer, *Philosophy in a New Key* (Harvard University Press, Cambridge, MA, 1942), p. 75.

9. Described in J.S. DeLoache and N.M. Burns, Symbolic development in young children: Understanding models and pictures, in Pratt and Garton, note 1.

10. J.S. DeLoache, K.F. Miller. K.S. Rosengren, and N. Bryant, *Symbolic development in young children: Honey, I shrunk the troll*, paper presented at the meeting of the Psychonomic Society, Washington, DC (November 1994).

11. J.S. DeLoache and D.P. Marzolf, When a picture is not worth a thousand words, *Cognitive Development, 7*, 317–329 (1992).

12. J.S. DeLoache, The use of dolls in interviewing young children, in *Memory and Testimony in the Child Witness*, M.S. Zaragoza, J.R. Graham, G.C N. Hall, R. Hirschman, and Y.S. Ben-Porath, Eds. (Sage. Thousand Oaks, CA, 1995); J.S. De-Loache and D.P. Marzolf, The use of dolls to interview young children: Issues of symbolic representation, *Journal of Experimental Child Psychology* (in press).

Young Natural-Number Arithmeticians

Rochel Gelman[1]
Rutgers Center for Cognitive Science and the Department of Psychology, Rutgers University

Abstract

When preschoolers count to check their arithmetic predictions, their counts are better than when they simply count a set of items on count-only tasks. This is so even for 2½- and 3-year-olds dealing with small values. Such results lend support to the view that learning about verbal counting benefits from a nonverbal count-arithmetic system and challenge theories that place understanding of verbal counting at 4½ or 5 years. That preschoolers readily engage in predicting-and-checking number tasks has implications for educational programs.

Keywords

informal cognition; preschool arithmetic; early counting; cognitive development; abstraction; preschool children

The idea that preschoolers (2 to about 5 years) are budding arithmeticians with respect to the natural (i.e., counting) numbers will strike many as odd. After all, mathematical ideas are not "out there" for inspection. They are abstract ideas, the kind that many assume preschoolers lack. I differ from several theorists who share the view that children younger than 4 or 5 do not understand the cardinal counting principle—the last word in a count represents the cardinal numerosity of the collection—let alone its relationship to addition and subtraction (e.g., Carey, 2004; Fuson, 1988; Mix, Huttenlocher, & Levine, 2002; Piaget, 1952). My viewpoint gains support from arithmetic counting tasks. Young children's success on such tasks is consistent with the theme that the meaning of the counting procedure is tied to its relation to principles of natural-number arithmetic, as opposed to the idea (expressed by other theorists) that addition and subtraction is an induction that follows after an understanding of counting is achieved. Given the understanding of counting, the children can notice that the repeated placement of one item into a collection increases its value.

For some theorists, children's understanding of the count numbers requires a conceptual change. For example, Carey argues that the first few count words (*one, two, three*, etc.) are initially treated like the quantities one, some, more, a lot, all, and so on. When children switch to treating count terms above *four* and *five* as unique representations of successively larger cardinal values, they can move on to the idea that each successive count word in the list represents one more than the previous word.

Mix et al. (2002) propose a gradual march from associations of number words to small collections of homogeneous items to associations of number words to larger collections and then to collections of heterogeneous items, and so on. Finally, the child achieves the abstract concept of natural number. Learning about the relation of counting to addition and subtraction follows. Fuson (1988) offers a closely related view. Piaget (1952) requires a qualitative shift from preoperational mental structures to concrete-operational ones, the latter supporting the use of one-to-one correspondences to assess equivalence or nonequivalence of sets, no matter what the set sizes are.

The list of abstraction abilities demonstrated by young children is ever grow-ing, and includes the abilities to assign pairs of look-alike photos, such as a statue and an animal, to their different ontological categories; to reason about unseen causal conditions; to answer questions about the insides of novel items; to attrib-ute mental states to people; and so on (see Gelman & Lucariello, 2002). Still, all this is about people, objects, and events that occur in the natural world, not about arithmetic, which is *really* abstract. Or is it? My inclusion of ideas about the natu-ral numbers and their relation to addition and subtraction was motivated by the ease with which a sample of 5-year-olds who failed a battery of conservation pretests, including those for number, length, and liquid and quantity amounts, responded to training. The conservation tasks assess whether a child understands that a given quantity does not change in amount when it is rearranged or moved, as when one of 2 rows of N items is spread out to look longer than the other, one of 2 sticks is moved to extend beyond the other, one ball of clay is pounded into a flat disk, or one glass of water is poured into a thin, tall beaker (see below for fur-ther details). Children younger than 6 years of age typically failed to conserve on any of these tasks. Yet they had no trouble choosing two of three rows of objects that had the same or different number. Similarly, they did very well on length problems for which they had to choose two of three sticks that were either the same or different lengths as the experimenter continually altered their con-figuration (Gelman, 1969). The children also achieved high levels of success on posttests of conservation of number and length, as well as of liquid and mass amount. It seemed most unlikely that training instilled a new set of mental struc-tures that would support belief in equivalence despite the contradiction of per-ceptual data. More plausibly, the children were ready to conserve number across irrelevant transformations as well as conserve the pretested other quantities.

My search was on for ways to show early number knowledge and other abstract abilities. As supporting data came in, I started to move toward a domain-specific view of cognitive development, with the assumption that the presence of a small set of implicit mental structures support learning on the fly. The idea that the mind initially has a small set of skeletal structures, each with their own prin-ciples, contrasts with the initial-blank-slate view held by associationists and Piaget. Despite their skeletal format, they are mental structures, and we know from cognitive psychology that when one already has a domain-specific mental structure, it is rather easy to learn more about content that fits that structure. The mind will use these different structures to actively engage and assimilate environmental data that share their internal relations.

How does this bear on the acquisition of verbal knowledge of counting and arithmetic? It is known that a nonverbal numerical-reasoning system that sup-ports counting, addition, and subtraction is available to young children, infants, and animals (Barth, La Mont, Lipton, & Spelke, 2005; Cordes & Gelman, 2005). This supports Gelman and Gallistel's (1986) proposal that implicit principles of nonverbal enumeration facilitate identifying and learning about both the words

112

for counting and rules for how to use them. The nonverbal principles—one and only one unique tag for each to-be-counted item, stable ordering of the tags, and use of the last tag to represent the cardinal value—correspond to the use rules of verbal counting. So, given a counting list that maps to nonverbal counting principles, the stage is set for the child's nonverbal structure to identify and start to assimilate the count list to a relevant structure. Since verbal counts and numerical estimates do not stand alone—that is, they gain their meaning from their relation to a mental structure of arithmetic reasoning that includes principles of addition, subtraction, and ordering—assessment of understanding of the language of counting might best be tapped in arithmetic counting tasks as opposed to tasks that only assess counting ability.

SOME EARLY RESEARCH

Piaget (1952) designed tasks that reflected his goal of contributing results to the efforts of logicians like Russell and Von Neumann to show that arithmetic could be derived from set theory. The number-conservation task taps the idea that any two sets that can be placed in one-to-one correspondence are equal—whatever their arrangement or set size. In the conservation task, even preschool children agree that when the items in two rows are opposite each other, the numbers are the same. But, when the items in one row are spread out, preschoolers deny the conservation of equivalence, typically saying the spread-out row has more. Failures on the task contributed to Piaget's conclusion that preschoolers lack a concept of natural number. For him, early counting is just rote learning.

I found it hard to entertain the idea that the conservation-training experience I offered could generate a new set of mental structures. The children must have known quite a bit already. A series of magic tasks (detailed in Fig. 1 and summarized in Gelman & Gallistel, 1986) provided the first lines of evidence. In phase 1, a child saw two plates with varying numbers of items on them, such as toy mice or strawberries. One plate was dubbed "the winner" and the other "the loser." The set-up (phase 2), which was modeled after a shell game, followed as a series of trials in which the plates were covered and shuffled as the child watched. Then the child made guesses about which cover concealed the "winner" plate. The experimenter avoided talk about number or quantity. Phase 3 began after both of the plates were uncovered by the child, who now saw the effect of a surreptitious addition or subtraction of one or more items or a change in how close together the items were on a plate. Changes in number in the subtraction conditions were greeted with surprise, search, and talk about the missing items. For example, J.E., who expected three mice on one plate and two on the other but saw two on both plates during phase 3, told us that we "took one. Cuz, there's two now . . . where is it?" J.S., who expected two and encountered three, explained the unexpected addition as follows: "Something might pop out of these little bumps" (on the inside of the cans used to cover the plates) as a possible source of the additional mouse. Changes in length or density were accepted—for example, "because it's still three."

As the hiding-and-guessing trials in phase 2 proceeded, children began to volunteer that number mattered—for example: "That's the winner, three—one, two, three," or "one, two—loser." Of particular interest was the use of rule-governed

Fig. 1. The three phases of the number-magic tasks. In phase 1 (left), two plates with toy red strawberries on them were labeled the "winner" and the "loser," and children were rewarded with prizes for identifying the "winner." In phase 2 (center), the plates were covered and the covers were shuffled; children then pointed to the cover that they thought hid the winner-plate; if they were incorrect on the first try, they were allowed to pick the second cover; they were always rewarded whenever they identified the winner. At various points during phase 2, children were asked why a given plate was a winner or loser. At first, they seldom said anything; but as we continued, most of the 3-, 4-, and 5-year-olds in the study talked about number correctly during this phase. Children also became sufficiently interested in their collection of prizes to stop watching closely as the experimenter shuffled the covers, allowing the displays to be surreptitiously altered in number of strawberries or in non-numerical values like length, color, and so on. Across experiments, changes in the number or arrangement of items in phase 3 (right) were noticed by almost all children in some way. Additionally, in almost all children, including the 2½-year-olds, changes in number elicited strong emotional reactions, search for missing items, and verbal statements about the number change. (The right panel shows a child with both sets of fingers in her mouth; before this, she was smiling, having found the "winner.")

but idiosyncratic count lists, as when D.S., who was 2½ years old, encountered three mice instead of the expected two; he volunteered "umm, one, two" for the two-mouse plate and "one, two, six" for the three-mouse plate and then the same "one, two, six" count at a later point in phase 3. Analyses in Gelman and Gallistel (1986) of errors across counting and magic experiments revealed that children who used idiosyncratic count lists (e.g., "one, two, six" instead of "one, two, three") across trials made many fewer counting errors than those who used the conventional count sequence.

SOME RECENT RESEARCH

Bisanz, Sherman, Rasmussen, and Ho (2005) confirmed and extended our conclusion that young children correctly negotiate arithmetic problems when the total number is equal to or less than four. But many, including Carey (2004), counter that judgments of numerical order and equality for very young children are mediated by mechanisms that work only for this range (Carey, 2004). When we tried to use our magic paradigm with larger sets, we had to use larger cans to cover the displays with larger numbers of items. They were so large that children dropped them or put them on their heads or faces to play games like "hats," "masks," etc. A different task was needed. Zur and Gelman (2004) hit upon one that was inspired by a familiar ditty: *There were six in the bed and the little one said "roll over," and they all rolled over, one fell out, and there were five in the bed, and the little one said "roll over"*—and so on. To start, we worked mainly with 4-year-olds. Then a suitable variant of the arithmetized counting task was run with 3-year-olds.

To begin one set of trials, the experimenter handed the child objects—say, nine "donuts" made from felt—to place in a "bakery" and asked: "How many donuts are in the bakery?" The child answered, and the adult continued: "I have 3 three pennies to buy donuts. Predict, how many will be left." Charmingly, children assumed that one penny buys one donut. The purchase complete, the experimenter continued: "Check how many you have now." Children now counted, and almost always they were correct. When rare counting errors occurred, a recount was almost always correct, even for the largest values. The achieved checking value served as the first value for the next cycle of prediction and checking: "Okay, so now you have six donuts. Here comes a delivery of two donuts. Predict how many will be in the donut shop," and so on.

Using videotapes, we verified that children almost always predicted without counting but counted aloud when checking. They did not try to make their counts conform to their predictions and acted as if verbal counting was definitive. We assumed that their prediction would benefit from their nonverbal number knowledge and the mapping from this to number words. This is consistent with the proposal that preschoolers can perform both approximate and precise counting-arithmetic tasks (Barth et al., 2005; Cordes & Gelman, 2005).

The task was developed in the context of a classroom. When it was clear that the children in the class succeeded as a group, even on totals of 15, we tested each of them individually. A year later we tested a novice group of same-aged children. As expected, there was some effect of experience. Still, even the children who came naive to the task did well. Figure 2 plots the Zur and Gelman (2004) data for one problem set, showing the averages and ranges of the children's predictions as a function of the correct answers. Predictions increased

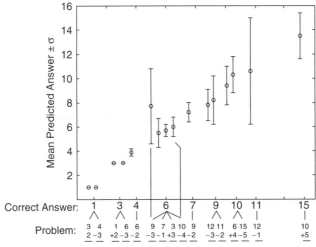

Fig. 2. The relationship between the correct answers for arithmetic problems and the prediction averages and ranges (denoted by bars) given by 14 children with ages ranging from 3.11 to 5.4 years (average age=4.7). Note the tendency to give the same prediction for different problems having the same arithmetic result (e.g., the problems with an answer of 6), a clue that implicit rules of arithmetic were available.

systematically even when the correct answers were high—between 10 and 15! Further, predictions for problems with the same answer tended to cluster together (e.g., 3 + 3, 7 − 1, and 10 − 4). This is consistent with our assumption that predictions are mediated by the mapping of a nonverbal arithmetic system to a verbal one. The 3-year-olds did rather well at predicting and checking when answers were as large as 5. Eighty percent of the predictions were in the right direction; 92% of the checking trials were correct. Thus, we have more evidence for the proposal that the arithmetized counting system is applied to small numbers as well as to larger ones.

An unexpected result led us to propose that preschool children implicitly recognize the inverse principle (if a + b = c, then c − b = a, and vice versa): There was a reliable tendency for them to do better on the second of a pair of inverse problems—as they did on the problem 10 − 6 when they had already encountered the problem 6 + 4, as opposed to when they had seen 5 + 4. This corroborates and extends Bryant, Christie, and Rendu's (1999) demonstration of 5- to 6-year-olds' success on the inverse principle with problems of the form a + b − b.

There is other evidence that young children have some implicit knowledge of arithmetic before they master the counting list of their language. Recall that 2 1/2-year-olds in a magic task understood the effect of addition and subtraction on numerical ordering (Barth et al., 2005, report related findings). A similar conclusion follows from Sarnecka and S. Gelman's (2005) clever use of addition and subtraction questions in their study of 4-year-olds' knowledge of counting and quantifier terms. These researchers added to (or subtracted from) a can they first said had either a specific number (e.g., "six") or a nonspecific quantity (e.g., "a lot"). When asked whether the amount following an addition or subtraction was different, the children said "yes" for the number-word can and "no" for the quantifier one. When a can was shaken, the same children said that neither value had changed. This effect of framing questions in an arithmetic format provides more support for the position that young children know that the meaning of count words is related to addition and subtraction. The results also fit with evidence that early language learners take number words to refer only to cardinal values and not to imprecise quantities that can be referred to with quantifiers like "some" and "all" (Hodent, Bryant, & Houdé 2005; Hurewitz, Papafragou, Gleitman, & Gelman, 2006). The Hodent et al. (2005) study follows up the finding that when French-speaking children are provided arithmetic stories that represent 1 + 1 = 1 and 1 + 1 = 3, they say the former is "not okay" and the latter is "okay." Hodent et al. reasoned that this could reflect the ambiguity of *un* in French, where it represents both the first count word (i.e., "one") and the indefinite singular in the pair *un–des* ("a"–"some"). To control for this possibility, there were conditions in which 2-year-old French speakers were shown two items that were then covered. Next, one item was added to the hidden display. Subsequently, uncovered test trials included displays of two, three, or four items. Now, the children declared that the outcome of three was "okay" but that the displays with two or four items were "not okay." Hurewitz, Papafragou, Gleitman, and Gelman (2006) show that that, when presented with displays that can be interpreted as either "two" or "four" or as either "some" or "all," very young children do better at labeling the displays when requested to use a number than they do when asked to label the displays with quantifiers.

Sarnecka and S. Gelman's (2005) study with older preschoolers continues this pattern of evidence, favoring the position that children know that the operations of adding and subtracting systematically increase and decrease the value of cardinality, even if they cannot reliably count the number of items involved. So too does Hartnett and Gelman's (1998) study on 5- to 8-year-olds' understanding of the successor principle. These children were more likely to say that adding 1—as opposed to counting further—could go on indefinitely. Why? Although they knew that adding would increase the number, they did not know the words for those numbers, as illustrated by explanations two children gave: "You just can't put it in the newspaper like, we thought of some new numbers"; and "There aren't real numbers [meaning known terms] but you could make them up."

It would be a mistake to assume that the eventual command of the verbal counting system guarantees ready understanding of all number concepts and other mathematical ideas. Indeed, many adults lack an understanding of the numbers used in the discourse of commerce, like 12.56 million or 2 trillion dollars, or that the birthrate of a given country is 1.9 and not the whole number 2, probably because they have no reason to have developed a quantitative representation of such large sums of money or rational numbers (fractions). Learning about fractions in either fractional or decimal format turns out to be extremely difficult, even for many adults. In fact, the relative ease of working with the counting numbers turns out to be a key source of difficulty regarding rational numbers. This is because the principles underlying each kind of number differ dramatically. Each natural number has a unique next. By contrast, there is an infinite number of rational numbers between each pair of rationals. The fact that a unit fraction's value increases as the value of its denominator decreases is a major source of trouble for students who believe numbers are what one gets when one counts (Hartnett & Gelman, 1998).

CONCLUSION AND FURTHER DIRECTIONS

When children as young as 2½ years participate in tasks that evoke arithmetic reasoning, they reveal knowledge that counting determines cardinality. Still, their failure on stand-alone counting tasks must be explained, for both pedagogical and theoretical reasons. Acquisition of the specific language of the cardinal count words and the particular notation system for arithmetic needs to be researched. On the practical side, when we take the predicting-and-checking tasks used in our research to the classroom, children enjoy and readily engage in the activities, including when they predict and check the number of seeds they will find inside different fruits. Further, on the assumption that part of the difficulty of understanding fractions is due to the lack of extensive experience with measurement tools and their corresponding variations in unit size, we have moved to offering relevant experiences in our preschool science program.

Recommended Reading

Butterworth, G. (1999). *The mathematical brain*. London: Macmillan.
Dehaene, S. (1997). *The number sense: How the mind creates mathematics*. New York: Oxford University Press.

Gelman, R., & Butterworth, B. (2005). Number and language: How are they related? *Trends in Cognitive Sciences, 9*, 6–10.

McCrink, K., & Wynn, K. (2004). Large-number addition and subtraction by 9-month-old infants. *Psychological Science, 15*, 776–782.

Acknowledgments—Partial support for the preparation of this paper came from National Science Foundation Grants LIS-720410 and REC-0529579.

Note

1. Address correspondence to Rochel Gelman, Rutgers Center for Cognitive Science, 152 Frelinghuysen Road, Piscataway, New Brunswick, NJ 08854-8020; e-mail: rgelman@ruccs.rutgers.edu.

References

Barth, H., La Mont, K., Lipton, J., & Spelke, E.S. (2005). Abstract number and arithmetic in preschool children. *Proceedings of the National Academy of Sciences, U.S.A., 102*, 14116–14121.

Bisanz, J., Sherman, J.L., Rasmussen, C., & Ho, E. (2005). Development of arithmetic skills and knowledge in preschool children. In J. Campbell (Ed.), *The handbook of mathematical cognition* (pp. 143–162). New York: Psychology Press.

Bryant, P., Christie, C., & Rendu, A. (1999). Children's understanding of the relation between addition and subtraction: Inversion, identity, and decomposition. *Journal of Experimental Child Psychology, 74*, 194–212.

Carey, S. (2004). On the origin of concepts. In J. Miller (Ed.), *Daedalus*. Cambridge, MA: MIT Press.

Cordes, S., & Gelman, R. (2005). The young numerical mind: What does it count? In J. Campbell (Ed.), *The handbook of mathematical cognition*. New York: Psychology Press.

Fuson, K. (1988). *Children's counting and concepts of numbers*. New York: Springer-Verlag.

Gelman, R.S. (1969). Conservation acquisition: A problem of learning to attend to relevant attributes. *Journal of Experimental Child Psychology, 7*, 167–187.

Gelman, R., & Gallistel, C.R. (1986). *The child's understanding of number*. Cambridge, MA: Harvard University Press.

Gelman, R., & Lucariello, J. (2002). Learning in cognitive development. In H. Pashler & C.R. Gallistel (Eds.), *Stevens' Handbook of Experimental Psychology* (3rd ed., Vol. 3). New York: Wiley.

Hartnett, P.M., & Gelman, R. (1998). Early understandings of numbers: Paths or barriers to the construction of new understandings? *Learning and Instruction: The Journal of the European Association for Research in Learning and Instruction, 8*, 341–374.

Hodent, C., Bryant, P., & Houdé, O. (2005). Language-specific effects on number computation in toddlers. *Developmental Science, 8*, 420–423.

Hurewitz, F., Papafragou, A., Gleitman, L., & Gelman, R. (2006). Asymmetries in the acquisition of numbers and quantifiers. *Language learning and development, 2*, 77–96.

Mix, K.S., Huttenlocher, J., & Levine, S.C. (2002). *Quantitative development in infancy and early childhood*. New York: Oxford University Press.

Piaget, J. (1952). *The child's concept of number*. New York: Norton.

Sarnecka, L., & Gelman, S. (2005). Six does not just mean a lot: Quantitative development in infancy and early childhood. *Cognition, 92*, 239–352.

Zur, O., & Gelman, R. (2004). Doing arithmetic in preschool by predicting and checking. *Early Childhood Quarterly Review, 19*, 121–137.

This article has been reprinted as it originally appeared in *Current Directions in Psychological Science*. Citation information for this article as originally published appears above.

What and When of Cognitive Aging

Timothy A. Salthouse[1]

University of Virginia

Abstract

Adult age differences have been documented on a wide variety of cognitive variables, but the reasons for these differences are still poorly understood. In this article, I describe several findings that will need to be incorporated into eventual explanations of the phenomenon of cognitive aging. Despite common assumptions to the contrary, age-related declines in measures of cognitive functioning (a) are relatively large, (b) begin in early adulthood, (c) are evident in several different types of cognitive abilities, and (d) are not always accompanied by increases in between-person variability.

Keywords

aging; cognition; reasoning; memory; speed

The phenomenon of cognitive aging has been noticed almost as long as the phenomenon of physical aging, but it is still not well understood. This is unfortunate because cognitive functioning can affect one's quality of life, and even the ability to live independently. Furthermore, cognitive functioning in early adulthood may be related to the development of pathologies such as Alzheimer's disease in later adulthood.

One way to conceptualize understanding is that it is equivalent to knowing answers to the questions of what, when, why, where, and how. In this article, I summarize some of the progress that has been achieved in describing the phenomenon of cognitive aging in terms of the questions of what and when. Although not much is yet known about why (what is ultimately responsible), where (in the nervous system), and how (via what mechanisms) age-related cognitive changes occur, a key assumption of my research is that answering these other questions will be easier as the characterization of what and when becomes more precise.

WHAT AND WHEN

It is often assumed that age-related effects on cognitive functioning are small, are limited to aspects of memory, begin relatively late in adulthood, and possibly affect only some people, so that any age-related declines are accompanied by increases in between-person variability. However, recent research in my laboratory and elsewhere suggests that these assumptions may all be incorrect. Evidence relevant to these issues can be illustrated with data aggregated across several recent studies in my laboratory (Salthouse, 2001a, 2001b; Salthouse, Atkinson, & Berish, 2003; Salthouse & Ferrer-Caja, 2003; Salthouse, Hambrick, & McGuthry, 1998; Salthouse et al., 2000). Participants in these studies were recruited through newspaper advertisements, appeals to community groups, and referrals from other participants. Nearly all of the participants reported themselves to be in good to excellent health, and they averaged approximately 16 years of education.

Four tests were common to most of these studies. A vocabulary test involved the examinee selecting the best synonyms of target words, in each case from a set of five alternatives. A speed test required the participant to classify pairs of line patterns as the same or different as rapidly as possible. Reasoning was assessed with the Raven's Progressive Matrices, in which each test item consists of a matrix of geometric patterns with one missing cell, and the task for the participant is to select the best completion of the missing cell from a set of alternatives. Finally, a memory test involved three auditory presentations of the same list of unrelated words, with the participant instructed to recall as many words as possible after each presentation. Data for the vocabulary, speed, and reasoning tests are based on 1,424 adults, and those for the memory test are based on 997 adults.

Because the raw scores for the four tests are in different units, all of the scores have been converted to z scores (by subtracting each score from the mean for that test and then dividing by the standard deviation) so that the age trends can be directly compared. The means for the z scores are plotted as a function of age in Figure 1. The bars above and below each point are standard errors, which represent the precision of the estimate (i.e., the smaller the bars, the more precise the estimate). Six important observations about the data in this figure can be noted.

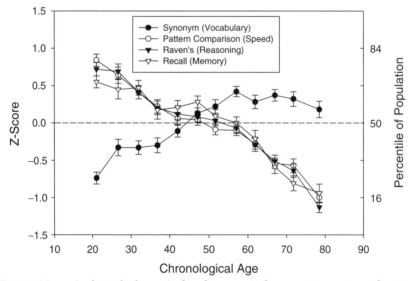

Fig. 1. Means (and standard errors) of performance in four cognitive tests as a function of age. Each data point is based on between 52 and 156 adults.

First, scores on the vocabulary test were higher with increased age until about the mid-50s, after which they either remained stable or declined slightly. Findings such as these have been interpreted as indicating that knowledge accumulates with increased age, but compelling explanations for why this age function is curvilinear are not yet available (Salthouse, 2003).

Second, similar negative age trends are evident in the measures of speed, reasoning, and memory. Although not represented in the figure, the correlations between age and these variables were also similar, as they were $-.47$, $-.48$, and $-.43$, respectively, for the speed, reasoning, and memory variables.

Third, the age-related effects on the speed, reasoning, and memory variables are fairly large. Not only are the age correlations for these variables greater than most correlations involving individual differences reported in the behavioral sciences, but the average performance for adults in their early 20s was near the 75th percentile in the population, whereas the average for adults in their early 70s was near the 20th percentile.

Fourth, the relations between age and the speed, reasoning, and memory variables are primarily linear. This observation is relevant to potential interpretations of the effects because the absence of obvious discontinuities in the functions suggests that transitions such as retirement, or menopause for women, are probably not responsible for much, if any, of the effects.

Fifth, the data in the figure indicate that age-related effects are clearly apparent before age 50. For some variables, there may be an acceleration of the influences at older ages, but age-related differences are evident in early adulthood for each variable.

And sixth, the age-related declines in these samples are not accompanied by increases in between-person variability. One way to express the relation between age and between-person variability is in terms of the correlation between age and the between-person standard deviation for the individuals in each 5-year age group. For the data in Figure 1, these correlations were $-.18$ for vocabulary, $-.80$ for speed, $-.74$ for reasoning, and .13 for memory. If anything, therefore, the trend in these data is for increased age to be associated with a smaller range of scores. Instead of a pattern of increased variability that might be attributable to some people maintaining high levels of performance and others experiencing large declines, the data show a nearly constant variability that is more consistent with a downward shift of the entire distribution of speed, reasoning, and memory scores with increased age.

Many of the patterns apparent in Figure 1 have been reported in a number of individual studies (see the earlier citations), and are also evident in data from nationally representative samples used to establish norms for standardized tests such as the third edition of the Wechsler Adult Intelligence Scale (Wechsler, 1997) and the Woodcock-Johnson III Tests of Cognitive Abilities (Woodcock, McGrew, & Mather, 2001). Results such as these suggest the following answers to the questions of the what and when of cognitive aging. With respect to what, many different types of cognitive variables are affected by increased age, and with respect to when, age-related differences appear to begin in early adulthood, probably in the 20s.

WHY ARE THE EFFECTS NOT MORE NOTICEABLE
IN EVERYDAY LIFE?

The research I have summarized suggests that age-related cognitive declines are fairly broad, begin early in adulthood, and are cumulative across the life span. A question frequently raised when findings such as these are mentioned is, why are there not greater negative consequences of the age-related cognitive declines? I suspect that there are at least four reasons.

First, cognitive ability is only one factor contributing to successful functioning in most activities. Other factors such as motivation, persistence, and various personality characteristics are also important, and they either may be unrelated to age or may follow different age trajectories than measures of cognitive functioning.

Second, very few situations require individuals to perform at their maximum levels because humans tend to modify their environments to reduce physical and cognitive demands. An analogy to physical ability and physical demands may be relevant here because there are well-documented age-related declines in strength, stamina, and speed, but these declines are seldom noticed in everyday life because of the relatively low physical requirements of most situations.

Third, many people may adapt to age-related changes by altering the nature and pattern of their activities. Examples of this type of adaptation are apparent in driving, because as they grow older, many adults make adjustments such as driving at different times and under different conditions, and possibly avoiding certain maneuvers, such as left turns. Accommodations such as these do not eliminate the declines, but they may serve to minimize their detrimental consequences.

And fourth, the greater experience and knowledge associated with increased age probably reduces the need for the type of novel problem solving that declines with age. Continuous age-related increases in knowledge may not be apparent in standardized tests because the tests are designed to be applicable to the general population, and much of the individual's knowledge may be increasingly idiosyncratic as he or she pursues progressively more specialized vocational and avocational interests. Nevertheless, very high levels of performance might be apparent among older adults, given the right combination of individuals and tasks. Research in my laboratory suggests, for example, that older adults demonstrate a high level of performance if they regularly work crossword puzzles and the task is solving crossword puzzles. In four recent studies, adults recruited because of their crossword-puzzle experience were asked to perform a number of activities, including spending 15 min attempting to solve a crossword puzzle taken from the *New York Times*. As can be seen in Figure 2, in general, the highest average level of crossword performance in every sample was achieved by adults in their 60s and 70s.

It could be argued that successful performance in solving crossword puzzles is primarily dependent on accumulated knowledge rather than on novel problem solving or abstract reasoning. This may be the case, but I suspect that the same is true in many real-world activities. That is, much of what we typically do may be more dependent on successful access and retrieval of what we already know than on our ability to solve novel problems or reason with unfamiliar material.

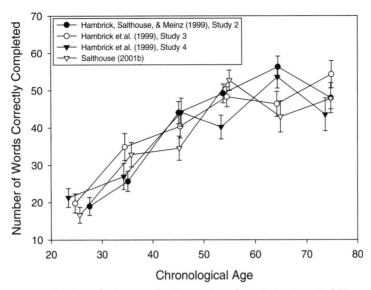

Fig. 2. Means (and standard errors) for the number of words in a *New York Times* crossword puzzle correctly answered in 15 min as a function of age. Between 195 and 218 adults participated in each study. The crossword puzzles required either 76 or 78 words for their solutions.

INVESTIGATING THE WHY, WHERE, AND HOW OF COGNITIVE AGING

Although the phenomenon of cognitive aging is fairly well documented in terms of the questions of what and when, there is much less consensus with respect to the answers to, or even the best methods of investigating, the questions of why, where, and how. In fact, it can be argued that much of the current theoretical debate in the field of cognitive aging is not focused on distinguishing among alternative explanations, but rather is concerned with which approach is likely to be most productive in investigating causes of age-related differences in cognitive functioning. Several of the major issues can be described in terms of the following dichotomies, although it should be recognized that these are simplifications, and that this list is by no means exhaustive.

Micro Versus Macro

One theoretical issue is whether the primary focus should be on determining which specific aspects (e.g., theoretical processes or components) of cognition are most (or least) affected by aging, or whether several variables should be examined simultaneously to determine the extent to which the age-related effects on a particular variable are unique to that variable or are shared with other variables. Advocates of the former, micro, perspective point out that most cognitive tasks can be assumed to involve multiple processes, and thus an overall measure of performance in nearly any task is likely to represent an unknown mixture of theoretically distinct processes that may be difficult to interpret.

Advocates of the latter, macro, perspective emphasize that a large number of cognitive variables have been found to be related to age, and that analyses have revealed that age-related influences on different types of cognitive variables are not statistically independent of one another. Researchers favoring the macro perspective have therefore argued that the age-related effects on particular cognitive tasks may be symptoms of a broader phenomenon, and consequently that it may not be very meaningful to attempt to provide a distinct explanation for the age differences in each variable.

Proximal Versus Distal

A second theoretical issue is whether researchers should concentrate on specifying characteristics (e.g., strategy, efficiency of specific hypothesized processes, adherence to particular sets of beliefs) associated with the performance differences of adults of different ages at the time of assessment (proximal factors), or whether researchers should try to identify factors occurring earlier in life that may have contributed to any differences observed at the current time (distal factors). The key question in this connection is whether it is more important to specify precisely how the performance of people of different ages differs at the current time or to investigate the role of earlier life experiences in producing those differences.

Moderation Versus Manipulation

A third issue relevant to the investigation of causes of cognitive aging arises from the fact that true experiments are not possible because the critical variable of age cannot be randomly assigned. Researchers differ in which of two approximations to true experiments they think will be most fruitful. On one side are those who say the focus should be on determining if particular characteristics (moderators) are associated with differences in the age-related trends on various cognitive variables. Their approach is to compare the age-related trends of preexisting groups (e.g., people sharing various lifestyle characteristics). On the other side are researchers who say that the most will be learned by attempting to alter people's current level of performance by some type of intervention. Using this approach, they hope to identify manipulations that influence the relation between age and level of performance.

Difference Versus Change

One of the perennial issues in developmental research is whether the results of cross-sectional comparisons can be considered informative about age-related changes, or whether all inferences about aging must be based on directly observed longitudinal changes. There is little dispute that people of different ages who are tested at the same point in time may also differ in other characteristics, and thus results of cross-sectional comparisons might not directly reflect effects of aging. There is also considerable agreement that there are several possible influences on longitudinal changes, including effects related to practice or learning from one occasion to the next and effects associated with changes in the society or culture in which the individual lives. However, there is much less consensus about the best method of distinguishing between "age" and "nonage" influences in each type of design. On the one hand, researchers favoring cross-sectional methods feel that it is plausible to assume that people who are of different ages and observed at the same point in time were similar in most important respects when they were at the same age, so that it is reasonable to make inferences about maturational changes on the basis of cross-sectional differences. On the other hand, researchers favoring longitudinal methods frequently assume that the maturational component of change can be distinguished from other components of change, such as practice effects and effects of sociocultural change, either because the latter are small relative to maturational effects or because they can be separated by statistical or other means.

It is probably healthy for a field to pursue different approaches to explanation when the level of understanding is relatively limited. However, it is probably also the case that progress toward answering the why, where, and how of cognitive aging will not be reached until there is some agreement among different theoretical perspectives on the best methods of addressing those questions.

CONCLUSION

To summarize, recent research in my laboratory and elsewhere has provided considerable information about the what and when of cognitive aging. We are also beginning to learn about the implications of this phenomenon for functioning outside of the research laboratory, but, perhaps because of different perspectives on the best methods of investigation, much less is currently known about the why, where, and how of this phenomenon.

Recommended Reading

Craik, F.I.M., & Salthouse, T.A. (2000). *Handbook of aging and cognition* (2nd ed.). Mahwah, NJ: Erlbaum.

Salthouse, T.A. (1991). *Theoretical perspectives in cognitive aging*. Mahwah, NJ: Erlbaum.

Acknowledgments—This research was supported by National Institute on Aging Grants AG06826 and AG19627 to the author.

Note

1. Address correspondence to Timothy A. Salthouse, Department of Psychology, P.O. Box 400400, University of Virginia, Charlottesville, VA 22904-4400; e-mail: salthouse@virginia.edu.

References

Hambrick, D.Z., Salthouse, T.A., & Meinz, E.J. (1999). Predictors of crossword puzzle proficiency and moderators of age-cognition relations. *Journal of Experimental Psychology: General, 128*, 131–164.

Salthouse, T.A. (2001a). Attempted decomposition of age-related influences on two tests of reasoning. *Psychology and Aging, 16*, 251–263.

Salthouse, T.A. (2001b). Structural models of the relations between age and measures of cognitive functioning. *Intelligence, 29*, 93–115.

Salthouse, T.A. (2003). Interrelations of aging, knowledge, and cognitive performance. In U. Staudinger & U. Lindenberger (Eds.), *Understanding human development: Lifespan psychology in exchange with other disciplines* (pp. 265–287). Berlin, Germany: Kluwer Academic.

Salthouse, T.A., Atkinson, T.M., & Berish, D.E. (2003). Executive functioning as a potential mediator of age-related cognitive decline in normal adults. *Journal of Experimental Psychology: General, 132,* 566–594.

Salthouse, T.A., & Ferrer-Caja, E. (2003). What needs to be explained to account for age-related effects on multiple cognitive variables? *Psychology and Aging, 18,* 91–110.

Salthouse, T.A., Hambrick, D.Z., & McGuthry, K.E. (1998). Shared age-related influences on cognitive and non-cognitive variables. *Psychology and Aging, 13,* 486–500.

Salthouse, T.A., Toth, J., Daniels, K., Parks, C., Pak, R., Wolbrette, M., & Hocking, K. (2000). Effects of aging on the efficiency of task switching in a variant of the Trail Making Test. *Neuropsychology, 14,* 102–111.

Wechsler, D. (1997). *Wechsler Adult Intelligence Scale–third edition.* San Antonio, TX: Psychological Corp.

Woodcock, R.W., McGrew, K.S., & Mather, N. (2001). *Woodcock-Johnson III Tests of Cognitive Abilities.* Itasca, IL: Riverside.

Section 3: Critical Thinking Questions

1. Several of the articles in this section show that conclusions about cognitive development seem to depend on the task used to assess it. Gelman's work illustrates this explicitly when she reports conclusions from two different counting tasks. Do you think that the two tasks are measuring the same kind of cognitive skill? Can you think of any kind of empirical research that might be designed to help answer that question? Select a task from one of the other articles that was used to measure some cognitive competency. Can you identify any requirements of that task that seem peripheral to the competency being studied? Can you think of some way to modify the task to avoid this problem?

2. Yet another contrast of interest within developmental psychology concerns whether competencies develop within each specialized arena independently (domain specific) or across cognition in general (domain general). Consider two or more of the specific domains studied in the articles in this section (e.g., memory, language, dual representation, number concepts). Do you see parallel changes across domains? Might development in one of these domains help to explain development in the other (or the reverse)? Might there be some broader developmental progression that underlies advances in each of the domains? Can you think of what kinds of data you would want to evaluate these possibilities?

This article has been reprinted as it originally appeared in *Current Directions in Psychological Science*. Citation information for this article as originally published appears above.

Section 4: Family Environments

As recently as a half century ago, the term "family" in the United States conjured up an image of a father working long hours to earn the entire family income, a mother tending home and children, and two or more siblings who shared the same family throughout childhood. Family constellations have changed strikingly since then. Dual-earner families are common; children, even infants, spend many hours in day care; same-sex partners have and raise children; blended families follow varied living arrangements, sometimes differing from day to day. The articles in this section only begin to sample the variety of contemporary family structures and the research studying their impact on development.

The first article, by David Reiss, addresses biological factors in family effects. He begins by cautioning that a statistical correlation between parent behaviors and child outcomes need not necessarily mean that parental behaviors play a *causal* role in child outcomes. Instead, the correlations might reflect one or more possible genetic mechanisms. For example, the child's own inherited qualities may evoke certain kinds of responses from parents (e.g., warmth) and simultaneously lead to the expression of certain child qualities. Reiss also discusses direct transmission of traits genetically, explains the rationale for twin research, and enumerates implications for interventions.

Taking an approach that places more weight on the child's environmental experiences, Grazyna Kochanska discusses the way in which the individual child's moral development—specifically the conscience—is affected by the relationship between parent and child. In particular, she studies the degree to which there is a positive, close, mutually binding, cooperative relationship that includes responsiveness and shared positive affect, referred to as a mutually responsive orientation (MRO). Children who experience MRO are more apt to trust their parents, to embrace parental values, and thus to be willing and even eager to cooperate with parental rules, even in the parent's absence.

Nancy Marshall addresses the impact of nonparental child care, which, as noted above, has become increasingly more common in recent decades. Using Bronfenbrenner's ecological perspective, Marshall highlights the need to consider the many levels of the environment in which a child is nested. For example, Marshall considers the relevance of government policies which affect the availability of community day care programs, in turn, influencing the kind of experiences encountered by a given child. Marshall reviews methods for conceptualizing and assessing day care quality, and reports data that link day care variables to child outcomes.

In the fourth article, Charlotte Patterson compares children's outcomes as a function of whether their parents are heterosexual versus lesbian or gay. Among the studies described is one in which data were collected from both lesbian and heterosexual families in which the children were conceived via the same sperm bank. Data revealed no significant differences in social competence in children from the two kinds of families, although they did reveal better outcomes when the relationships between parents and children were characterized by warmth and affection. Findings from an adolescent sample similarly showed that adolescents' well being was not related to the gender of parents' partners but it was related to the quality of the family relationship.

Finally, Gene Brody identifies a number of pathways by which siblings may influence developmental outcomes. First, siblings may influence one another by acting as teachers and guides (e.g., teaching younger siblings to read or to skate or modeling social behaviors). Second, siblings may affect how much time parents have for any given child, and may affect parents' expectations for each child (e.g., a girl with a brother may be less likely to be asked to take on traditionally masculine roles). Third, children may perceive that a sibling receives differential treatment which may have emotional and behavioral consequences for the child. Empirical findings are discussed that support the hypothesis that sibling effects occur via all three routes.

The Interplay Between Genotypes and Family Relationships: Reframing Concepts of Development and Prevention

David Reiss[1]

Center for Family Research, Department of Psychiatry and Behavioral Sciences, George Washington University

Abstract

Children's genotypes and their social relationships are correlated throughout their development. Heritable characteristics of children evoke strong and specific responses from their parents; frequently, these same heritable characteristics also influence the children's adjustment. Moreover, parental heritable traits that influence their parenting are also transmitted to children and influence their children's adjustment. Thus, genetically influenced evocative processes from children and parental-transmission mechanisms influence the covariances between measures of family relationships and child development. These findings suggest new targets for preventing adverse development: altering parental responses to heritable characteristics of children and influencing the genetically influenced ontogeny of parenting.

Keywords

genotype; relationships; parenting; prevention

Conventional models of psychological development acknowledge that genetic and social factors both play a role. Older models assumed that these two influences were independent from each other and that differences among individuals in personality development, cognitive development and psychological development could be explained by adding their effects together. More recently, it has become clear that, in many cases, the social environment interacts with genetic influences. For example, the genetic risk for schizophrenia seems to be fully expressed only when children at genetic risk grow up in families with high conflict, emotional restriction, and chaotic intergenerational boundaries (Tienari et al., 2004). Such a perspective still allows social and genetic variables to be thought of as relatively distinct: Genetic factors render individuals susceptible to adverse social environments; then, at some point—perhaps in early childhood or much later in development—unfavorable social factors elicit behavioral difficulties.

Recent data suggest that genetic and social influences are even more intertwined, however. From early development through adulthood, genetic and social factors are *correlated*; that is, individuals' genotypes are associated with many specific characteristics of their environment. This association occurs in two ways. First, as can be inferred from twin, sibling, and adoption studies, heritable characteristics of children can evoke highly specific responses from the social environment. For example, certain heritable characteristics of children evoke warmth and involvement from their parents. More importantly, the same genetic factors that evoke parental warmth also contribute to a child's social responsibility, including adherence to community norms and helping and sharing behaviors. In the research of my colleagues and I, almost all of the covariance between maternal warmth and child social responsibility is due to these genetic influences common to both parenting and child development (Reiss, Neiderhiser, Hetherington, & Plomin, 2000).

The second way such associations may occur is that heritable traits that influence a mother's or father's parenting may be genetically transmitted to their children. Those same traits in children may make them vulnerable to psychopathology. For example, a recent twin study suggests that heritable factors influence maternal smoking during pregnancy and, when transmitted to children, increase the childrens' likelihood of having conduct problems. These data raise questions about whether fetal exposure to tobacco products is the main cause of their postnatal conduct problems (Maughan, Taylor, Caspi, & Moffitt, 2004).

In behavioral genetics, associations between individuals' genotypes and their environment are called *genotype–environment correlations*. When a correlation is due to the effects of heritable features stimulating responses from the environment, it is called an *evocative* genotype–environment correlation. When it is due to genes transmitted by parents to their children, the term is *passive* genotype–environment correlation. Use of the word *genotype* in this type of research signifies the cumulative effect of all genetic influences on a particular trait, as examined in studies that usually use twin, sibling, or adoption designs.

GENOTYPE–ENVIRONMENT CORRELATIONS AND MECHANISMS OF DEVELOPMENT

Parent–Child Relationships May Amplify Genetic Influences

Rowe (1981) first reported data suggesting evocative genotype–parenting correlations. Monozygotic (i.e. derived from a single egg and genetically identical) twins' reports of how accepted they were by their parents were correlated more than twice as highly as the reports of dizygotic (i.e. from different eggs and 50% genetically related) twins. Figure 1 illustrates how monozygotic–dizygotic comparisons are used to make inferences about such correlations. Rowe's finding was subsequently replicated many times using different methods of assessing parent–child relationships: interviews of parents (Goodman & Stevenson, 1991), parental self-reports, and direct observation of parent–child relationships (O'Connor, Hetherington, Reiss, & Plomin, 1995). These findings do not reflect parental bias due to their knowledge of whether their twins were monozygotic or dizygotic, since the findings also hold where monozygotic twins have been misdiagnosed as dizygotic (Goodman & Stevenson, 1991).

Adoption studies have confirmed the importance of evocative genotype–parenting correlations: The behavior of an adoptive parent toward his or her child can be predicted from patterns of behavior in the birth parent. For example, two separate studies predicted adoptive parents' degree of harsh discipline and hostility toward their children from the level of aggressive behavior in the birth

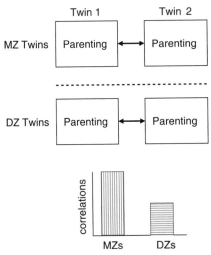

Fig. 1. Diagram showing how inferences about genetic influences on variation of a measured variable, in this case parenting, may be drawn from twin data. Boxes represent measured variable in a comparison of monozygotic (MZ) and dizygotic (DZ) child twins; the arrows represent correlations. The bar graph at the bottom of the figure represents example findings. The example finding shows MZ child twins correlate much more strongly than DZ child twins, enabling the inference that heritable characteristics of the child influence parenting (Reiss, Neiderhiser, Hetherington, & Plomin, 2000).

parents. These studies suggest that inherited externalizing (including aggressive and delinquent) behavior in the children evoked the response in the adoptive parents (Ge et al., 1996; O'Connor, Deater-Deckard, Fulker, Rutter, & Plomin, 1998).

Heritable evoked parental responses have been reported from age 1 through late adolescence. For example, one study compared nonadoptive siblings, who share 50% of their individual-differences genes, with siblings adopted from different birth parents. Data gathered at age 1 and again at age 2 suggested that children's genotypes greatly influenced how much intellectual stimulation their parents provided to them: Parental behavior correlated much higher toward the nonadoptive siblings than toward the adoptive siblings (Braungart, Plomin, Fulker, & DeFries, 1992). Other studies have reported on genetic influences on parenting at age 3, in middle childhood, and in adolescence. One longitudinal twin study suggested that heritable evocative effects increase across adolescence; this increase across age was particularly marked for fathers (Elkins, McGue, & Iacono, 1997).

To study heritable evocative effects, the Nonshared Environment in Adolescent Development study (NEAD; Reiss et al., 2000) combined a twin design with a stepfamily design. We drew genetic inferences from comparisons among monozygotic twins, dizygotic twins, full siblings, half siblings (e.g., a mother brings a child from a previous marriage and has a child with her new husband) and unrelated siblings (i.e., each parent brings a child from a previous marriage).

NEAD showed that heritable evocative effects may be quite specific. For example, genetic factors that evoke maternal warmth are distinct from those that evoke paternal warmth.

Additional findings reveal that heritable effects go beyond evocative effects on parents. The same genetic factors in a child that evoke particular parenting responses also influence many dimensions of their own adjustment during childhood and adolescence. Inferences about these influences are drawn by comparing *cross correlations* across sibling types (see Fig. 2). For example, a mother's harsh parenting towards sibling A can be correlated with the level of antisocial behavior of sibling B. Genetic influences on covariance are inferred when these cross correlations decline systematically from monozygotic twins at the highest to dizygotic twins and full siblings in the middle to unrelated siblings at the lowest.

NEAD found that over 70% of the covariance between a mother's hostile parenting and her adolescents' antisocial behavior was accounted for by genetic influences common to both. These findings have been confirmed by several subsequent studies (e.g., Burt, Krueger, McGue, & Iacono, 2003). NEAD found sizable genetic contributions to many other covariances including mothers' hostile

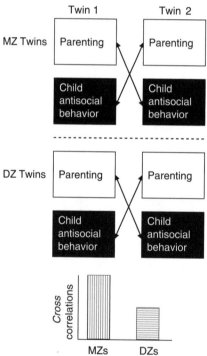

Fig. 2. Example cross correlation of parenting and child adjustment across sibling types. Parenting in one twin cross correlates with antisocial behavior in the other, more highly for monozygotic (MZ) twins than for dizygotic (DZ) twins. This suggests that the covariation between parenting and child antisocial behavior can be attributed to genetic influences common to both variables (Reiss et al., 2000).

parenting with impairment in adolescents' cognitive performance, fathers' warmth with adolescents' social responsibility, and fathers' hostility with adolescents' depression. NEAD, using longitudinal data collected from earlier and later adolescence, found that, in many cases, the child's heritable impact on parental response preceded the development of the behavior in question. For example, genetic influence on hostile parenting preceded the evolution of antisocial behavior.

Evocative genotype–parenting correlations may amplify more direct genetic influences on the child's problem behavior. Indeed, it is possible that parental responses to their children's heritable characteristics—responses to which the parents themselves are insensible—are critical for transforming heritable influences on children's temperaments into problems requiring clinical attention. To verify this hypothesis and test its significance for preventive intervention, my colleagues and I are currently conducting a prospective adoption study. We are following birth- and adoptive parents and adopted toddlers from age 9 months. This Early Growth and Development Study (EGADS) will allow us to pinpoint exactly what heritable noxious behaviors in the child evoke adverse parental responses and the consequence of these parental responses for subsequent child development.

The Heritable Development of Parenting

Evidence for passive genotype–parenting correlation requires evidence that (a) the parents' genes influence their parenting and (b) genetic factors that influence parenting are transmitted to their children and influence important dimensions of the children's adjustment. Evidence of this kind provides clues to childhood origins of parenting styles. For example, suppose it is observed that the same genetic factors that influence lack of warmth in mothers also influence depressive symptoms in their children. This would suggest that genetic factors link childhood internalizing with reduced maternal warmth, thereby offering clues about how genetically influenced parenting patterns unfold over the long term. Evidence for these passive effects comes from two sources.

First, studies using twins who are parents have shown genetic influences on dimensions of parenting. Our Twin Mom study investigated a sample of monozygotic and dizygotic twins who were mothers of adolescents. It showed that mothers' reports of their own warmth, hostility, and monitoring of the whereabouts of their children were more highly correlated for monozygotic than for dizygotic twins. A similar pattern of findings was shown using observer ratings for mothers' warmth and for children's ratings of their mothers' monitoring (Neiderhiser et al., 2004).

Second, adoption studies have found evidence for passive genetic links between parenting and the adjustment of children both in early childhood and in later adolescence. The correlation between parenting and child adjustment in birth families reflects evocative genotype–parenting correlations, environmental mechanisms, and passive genotype–parenting correlations. The last type are missing in adoptive families. Thus, by comparing correlations between parenting and child adjustment between the two groups it is possible to estimate—by elimination—the strength of passive genotype–parenting correlations. For example, one adoption study assessed parents' ratings of cohesiveness, lack of conflict, and open expression of feelings in their family during the time their children were 1 to 5 years old. For boys but not for girls, these ratings predicted teacher ratings of child delinquency and aggression at age 7, but only for boys raised by their own birth parents (Braungart-Rieker, Rende, Plomin, & DeFries, 1995). The correlations between parenting and teacher-rated aggression were insignificant in adoptive families. The correlations between adolescent problems and ratings of the quality of family relationships by their mothers were higher in families in which parents reared their own children than in adoptive families (McGue, Sharma, & Benson, 1996).

Taken together, these finding suggest that genotypic differences among parents influence their parenting and that these genotypic differences are transmitted to children, in whom they are manifested by psychiatric symptoms. We are currently investigating whether there are specific genetic links between childhood behavioral characteristics and patterns of parenting. For example, might internalizing problems in childhood be genetically linked to parental withdrawal and lack of support? Might childhood externalizing be genetically linked to aggressive and hostile parenting styles?

Highlighting Relationship Influences

Genetically informed studies highlight two sorts of family relationships that are linked with child psychological development independently of children's genotypes. Parent–child relationships are the first sort of such relationships identified by behavioral genetic data. For example, NEAD found that maternal rapport and affection was linked to adolescent autonomy and sociability. This is the case no matter what the child's genotype. Moreover, siblings within the same family are similar in their autonomy and sociability whether they are dizygotic or monozygotic twins or unrelated siblings. In contrast to parent hostility, the amount of maternal warmth received is also similar across both types of twins and unrelated siblings. Thus, taken together, our data suggest that mothers are relatively consistent in the positive feelings they show to children in their family and that all children benefit, no matter their genotype (Reiss et al., 2000).

Second, behavioral genetic data have highlighted nonparental family relationships that appear to influence childrens' development independently of their genotype. For example, NEAD showed that hostility and conflict in sibling relationships was strongly associated with adolescent antisocial behavior and depression. Conflict and hostility were highly reciprocal in adolescent siblings and put both siblings at equal risk for psychiatric symptoms independently of their genotypes. Moreover, NEAD showed a strong association between marital conflict and parent–child conflict on the one hand and sibling hostility on the other. More importantly, these links across family subsystems were independent of child genotype. Thus, in adolescence, hostility between siblings may be an indirect route through which family discord increases the vulnerability of children regardless of their genotype (Reiss et al., 2000).

Because it included the partners of the sisters who were the biological parents of the adolescent children, the Twin Mom study was able to yield valuable data on the role of adult genotypes in marital relationships. The study found that although genetic factors had a substantial influence on marital quality, as reported by both the twin siblings and their husbands, genetic factors explained little of the covariance between marital satisfaction and levels of wives' depressive symptoms. Rather, in this association, the dynamics of the marital relationships may play a central role (Spotts et al., 2004). These findings extend non- genetic studies of adult development that appeared to show that good marriages protect against depression and other behavior difficulties. However, nongenetic studies may miss heritable features of individuals that lead to both sustained, high-quality marriages and invulnerability to depression. Yet if the Twin Moms data is replicated, heritable features will seem unlikely to play a significant role in how marriages protect the marital partners.

IMPLICATIONS: NEW TARGETS FOR PREVENTION

Data on genotypes and family relationships offer three novel opportunities to design preventive interventions to forestall the development of serious problem behaviors and psychopathology.

First, findings suggesting that parent–child relationships amplify maladaptive genetic influences offer some of the most promising leads in preventing the expression of unfavorable genetic influences on many domains of child and adolescent adjustment. EGADS is designed to specify particular targets for intervention: parents' responses to heritable difficulties in their children. Numerous studies show that highly focused interventions can produce sustained changes in how parents respond to challenging children (Bakermans-Kranenburg, van Ijzendoorn, & Juffer, 2003). EGADS is designed to ascertain whether such interventions might suppress the parental amplification process and thus diminish adverse genetic influences.

Second, findings on passive genotype correlations provide a new target for interventions: promoting favorable parenting. The discovery of genetic links between childhood behavior and parenting suggests some childhood and adolescent origins of parenting behavior that should be addressed in efforts to prevent risky parental behavior such as drug abuse during pregnancy or hostile and abusive parenting subsequently. For example, efforts to prevent the early emergence of conduct problems may prevent later serious antisocial behavior as well as abusive parenting.

Finally, studies of genotype–environment correlation suggest new psychosocial targets for preventing psychological and behavioral disorders: siblings and marriages. Techniques already developed for clinical interventions with maladaptive sibling relationships and with marriages might be refashioned for preventing psychological disorders in the siblings or marital partners.

Recommended Reading

Maughan, B., Taylor, A., Caspi, A., & Moffitt, T.E. (2004). (See References)
Reiss, D., Pedersen, N.L., Cederblad, M., Lichtenstein, P., Hansson, K., Neiderhiser, J.M., et al. (2001). Genetic probes of three theories of maternal adjustment: I. Recent evidence and a model. *Family Process, 40,* 247–259.
Rutter, M., Pickles, A., Murray, R., & Eaves, L. (2001). Testing hypotheses on specific environmental causal effects on behavior. *Psychological Bulletin, 127,* 291–324.

Note

1. Address correspondence to David Reiss, Center for Family Research, Department of Psychiatry and Behavioral Sciences, George Washington University, 2300 K Street, NW, Washington, DC 20037; e-mail: cfrdxr@gwumc.edu.

References

Bakermans-Kranenburg, M.J., van Ijzendoorn, M.H., & Juffer, F. (2003). Less is more: Meta-analyses of sensitivity and attachment interventions in early childhood. *Psychological Bulletin, 129*, 195–215.

Braungart, J.M., Plomin, R., Fulker, D.W., & DeFries, J.C. (1992). Genetic mediation of the home environment during infancy: A sibling adoption study of the HOME. *Developmental Psychology, 28*, 1048–1055.

Braungart-Rieker, J., Rende, R.D., Plomin, R., & DeFries, J.C. (1995). Genetic mediation of longitudinal associations between family environment and childhood behavior problems. *Development & Psychopathology, 7*, 233–245.

Burt, S., Krueger, R.F., McGue, M., & Iacono, W. (2003). Parent–child conflict and the comorbidity among childhood externalizing disorders. *Archives of General Psychiatry, 60*, 505–513.

Elkins, I.J., McGue, M., & Iacono, W.G. (1997). Genetic and environmental influences on parent–son relationships: Evidence for increasing genetic influence during adolescence. *Developmental Psychology, 33*, 351–363.

Ge, X., Conger, R.D., Cadoret, R.J., Neiderhiser, J.M., Yates, W., Troughton, E., & Stewart, M.A. (1996). The developmental interface between nature and nurture: A mutual influence model of child antisocial behavior and parent behaviors. *Developmental Psychology, 32*, 574–589.

Goodman, R., & Stevenson, J. (1991). Parental criticism and warmth towards unrecognized monozygotic twins. *Behavior and Brain Sciences, 14*, 394–395.

Maughan, B., Taylor, A., Caspi, A., & Moffitt, T.E. (2004). Prenatal smoking and early childhood conduct problems: Testing genetic and environmental explanations of the association. *Archives of General Psychiatry, 61*, 836–843.

McGue, M., Sharma, A., & Benson, P. (1996). The effect of common rearing on adolescent adjustment: Evidence from a U.S. adoption cohort. *Developmental Psychology, 32*, 604–613.

Neiderhiser, J.M., Reiss, D., Pedersen, N.L., Lichtenstein, P., Spotts, E.L., Hansson, K., Cederblad, M., & Elthammar, O. (2004). Genetic and environmental influences on mothering of adolescents: A comparison of two samples. *Developmental Psychology, 40*, 335–351.

O'Connor, T.G., Deater-Deckard, K., Fulker, D., Rutter, M., & Plomin, R. (1998). Genotype-environment correlations in late childhood and early adolescence: Antisocial behavioral problems and coercive parenting. *Developmental Psychology, 34*, 970–981.

O'Connor, T.G., Hetherington, E.M., Reiss, D., & Plomin, R. (1995). A twin-sibling study of observed parent–adolescent interactions. *Child Development, 66*, 812–829.

Reiss, D., Neiderhiser, J., Hetherington, E.M., & Plomin, R. (2000). *The relationship code: Deciphering genetic and social patterns in adolescent development*. Cambridge, MA: Harvard University Press.

Rowe, D.C. (1981). Environmental and genetic influences on dimensions of perceived parenting: A twin study. *Developmental Psychology, 17*, 203–208.

Spotts, E.L., Neiderhiser, J.M., Ganiban, J., Reiss, D., Lichtenstein, P., Hansson, K., Cederblad, M., & Pedersen, N. (2004). Accounting for depressive symptoms in women: A twin study of associations with interpersonal relationships. *Journal of Affective Disorders, 82*, 101–111.

Tienari, P., Wynne, L.C., Sorri, A., Lahti, I., Laksy, K., Moring, J., Naarala, M., Nieminen, P., & Wahlberg, K. (2004). Genotype-environment interaction in schizophrenia spectrum disorder. *British Journal of Psychiatry, 184*, 216–222.

This article has been reprinted as it originally appeared in *Current Directions in Psychological Science*. Citation information for this article as originally published appears above.

Mutually Responsive Orientation Between Mothers and Their Young Children: A Context for the Early Development of Conscience

Grazyna Kochanska[1]

Department of Psychology, University of Iowa, Iowa City, Iowa

Abstract

Some parent-child dyads establish a mutually responsive orientation (MRO), a relationship that is close, mutually binding, cooperative, and affectively positive. Such relationships have two main characteristics—mutual responsiveness and shared positive affect—and they foster the development of conscience in young children. Children growing up with parents who are responsive to their needs and whose interactions are infused with happy emotions adopt a willing, responsive stance toward parental influence and become eager to embrace parental values and standards for behavior. The concurrent and longitudinal beneficial effects of MRO for early development of conscience have been replicated across studies, for a broad range of developmental periods from infancy through early school age, and using a wide variety of behavioral, emotional, and cognitive measures of conscience in the laboratory, at home, and in school. These findings highlight the importance of the early parent-child relationship for subsequent moral development.

Keywords

relationships; mutuality; conscience

How do young children become aware of rules, values, and standards of behavior accepted within their families and cultures? How do they gradually come to internalize those values and make them their own? Why do some children adopt societal norms wholeheartedly and with ease, and become conscientious citizens, whereas others do not?

The emergence of an individual conscience, a reliable internal guidance system that regulates conduct without the need for external control, is the endpoint of the process of integrating a child into a broader network of values. How this process works continues to be debated as one of the perennial and central issues in human socialization (Grusec, 1997).

Research on conscience was once dominated by a cognitive approach, focused on children's abstract understanding of societal rules, measured by their ability to reason about hypothetical moral dilemmas. Moral development was seen as a product of cognitive maturation, aided by peer interactions, but fundamentally unrelated to parental influence. In contrast, other theories acknowledged parental contributions. Parents and other socializing agents were seen as critical in several versions of learning theory. Those approaches emphasized the importance of parental discipline and modeling as instruments that modify and shape children's behavior. Somewhat later, attributional theories underscored the importance of children's perceptions of parental discipline, and revealed surprising, often paradoxical effects of salient parental rewards and punishments.

More recently, many scholars have come to appreciate an approach grounded in psychoanalytic and neo-psychoanalytic theories. Although Freud's views on the early development of conscience as linked to the Oedipus or Electra complex have long been discarded, his general emphasis on the role of early emotions and early relationships in emerging morality has proven insightful. That approach has been strongly reinvigorated and modernized by John Bowlby and the burgeoning research on attachment. From that perspective, moral emotions, moral conduct, and moral thought are all components of an internal guidance system, or conscience, whose foundations are established in early childhood in the context of socialization in the family. The early parent-child relationship, which encompasses but is not limited to control and discipline, can substantially foster or undermine that process (Emde, Biringen, Clyman, & Oppenheim, 1991).

THE RELATIONSHIP PERSPECTIVE: MUTUALLY RESPONSIVE ORIENTATION

In 1951, Robert Sears argued for a shift in psychological research from studying individuals to studying dyads. Over the past two or three decades, the science of relationships has blossomed in personality, social, and developmental psychology (Collins & Laursen, 1999; Reis, Collins, & Berscheid, 2000). Several scholars have proposed that when relationship partners—whether two adults or a parent and a child—are responsive and attuned to each other, are mutually supportive, and enjoy being together, they form an internal model of their relationship as a cooperative enterprise, and develop an eager, receptive stance toward each other's influence and a compelling sense of obligation to willingly comply with the other. For example, Clark (1984) referred to "communal relationships" in adults as contexts in which the partners are invested in each other's well-being, are empathic and responsive to each other, and experience an internal sense of mutual obligation.

In developmental research, those resurging perspectives afford a productive vantage point for exploring social development. Socialization is seen as a process jointly constructed by parents and children over time (Collins & Laursen, 1999; Collins, Maccoby, Steinberg, Hetherington, & Bornstein, 2000; Maccoby, 1999; Reis et al., 2000). Maccoby (1999) referred to parent-child mutuality as a positive socialization force that engenders a spirit of cooperation in the child. Attachment scholars believe that children raised in a loving, responsive manner become eager to cooperate with their caregivers and to embrace their values.

To describe such relationships between parents and children, my colleagues and I have proposed a construct of *mutually responsive orientation* (MRO). MRO is a positive, close, mutually binding, and cooperative relationship, which encompasses two components: *responsiveness* and *shared positive affect*. Responsiveness refers to the parent's and the child's willing, sensitive, supportive, and developmentally appropriate response to one another's signals of distress, unhappiness, needs, bids for attention, or attempts to exert influence. Shared positive affect refers to the "good times" shared by the parent and the child—pleasurable, harmonious, smoothly flowing interactions infused with positive emotions experienced by both.

We further proposed that children who grow up in mutually responsive dyads, compared with those who do not, become more eager to embrace their parents' values and more likely to develop a strong conscience. Their eager stance to embrace parental values reflects an internal sense of obligation to respond positively to parental influence, and emerges from a history of mutually gratifying, mutually accommodating experiences. A child who has developed a mutually responsive relationship with the parent comes to trust the parent and to expect that the parent will be responsive and supportive; at the same time, the child comes to feel motivated to cooperate willingly with the parent, to embrace the parent's values, and to adopt parental standards for behavior and make them his or her own. In this view, the parent-child relationship influences the child's conscience mainly through a gradually evolving shared working model of the relationship as a mutually cooperative enterprise rather than through the cumulative history of parental discipline as the instrument of behavior modification.

MOTHER-CHILD MRO AND CHILDREN'S CONSCIENCE: EMPIRICAL EVIDENCE

In two large studies, we measured the qualities of the mother-child relationship and the child's emerging conscience for more than 200 mother-child dyads. To assess the strength of MRO for the individual dyads, we observed the mothers and children interacting in multiple lengthy, naturalistic yet carefully scripted contexts at home and in the laboratory. The situations we observed included care-giving routines, preparing and eating meals, playing, relaxing, and doing household chores. We coded each mother's responsiveness to her child's numerous signals of needs, signs of physical or emotional distress or discomfort, bids for attention, and social overtures. We also assessed shared positive affect by coding the flow of emotion expression for both the mother and the child over the course of each interaction, focusing particularly on the times when they both displayed positive emotion. We obtained these measures repeatedly, following the same families over a period of several years.

In the individual dyads, the degree of MRO was significantly consistent across separate sessions close in time, and significantly stable over several years. This indicates that our observational markers captured a robust quality of the relationships that unfolded along a fairly stable dyadic trajectory.

Using a broad variety of laboratory paradigms, we also observed rich manifestations of the young children's conscience: moral emotions, moral conduct, and moral cognition. These assessments took place at many points in the children's development—starting in their 2nd year and continuing until early school age. The children's moral emotions, including guilt, discomfort, concern, and empathy, were observed when they were led to believe that they had violated a standard of conduct, or when they witnessed others' distress. While they were unsupervised, either alone or with peers, their moral conduct was assessed in many types of situations in which they faced strong temptations to break various rules and were coaxed to violate standards of behavior. Their moral cognition was measured by presenting them with age-appropriate, hypothetical moral dilemmas and asking them to express their thoughts and feelings about rules and transgressions, and consider moral decisions. We also asked their mothers and teachers to evaluate the children's moral emotions and conduct displayed in environments outside the laboratory—at home and at school.

Both studies supported the view that children who grow up in a context of a highly mutually responsive relationship with their mothers develop strong consciences (Kochanska, 1997; Kochanska, Forman, & Coy, 1999; Kochanska & Murray, 2000). The strength of the replicated findings was striking, given the broad range of the children's ages and the wide variety of conscience measures used.

In both studies, the links between MRO and the development of conscience were both concurrent and longitudinal. The concurrent links were found for both toddlers and preschoolers. The longitudinal findings were robust: MRO in infancy predicted conscience development in the 2nd year, and MRO in toddlerhood predicted children's conscience at preschool age and again at early school age. The history of MRO in the first 2 years predicted conscience at age 5. In short, the beneficial effect of MRO on the development of conscience was evident across diverse measures of conscience involving emotions, conduct, and cognition. It was also evident whether conscience was assessed by observations in the laboratory or reports from mothers and teachers. These results have been replicated by other researchers (Laible & Thompson, 2000).

HOW DOES MRO EXERT ITS IMPACT?

What causal mechanisms may be responsible for these well-established empirical findings? Using statistical approaches (sequences of multiple regressions, as well as structural equations modeling, or SEM) to analyze the causal factors that accounted for the associations in our data, we determined that MRO exerts its influence through at least two mechanisms.

The first mechanism involves promoting the child's positive mood. Early MRO between the parent and the child contributes to the child's positive, happy disposition, and that, in turn, increases his or her broad eagerness to behave prosocially. This finding is consistent with a large body of research in social and developmental psychology (Eisenberg & Fabes, 1998). Adults and children who are in a positive mood have often been found to be more prosocial, altruistic, cooperative, rule abiding, and socially responsive than those who are in neutral or negative moods.

The second mechanism involves promoting the child's responsive stance toward parental influence. We have found that in playlike teaching situations, children in mutually responsive relationships are attuned to their mothers and eagerly follow their lead (Forman & Kochanska, 2001; Kochanska et al., 1999). In discipline situations, they show what we called *committed compliance*—willing, eager, wholehearted cooperation with the parent (Kochanska, Coy, & Murray, 2001). Such a generalized responsive stance may be an intermediate step between simple cooperation with the parent and genuine internalization of parental rules, evident even in the parent's absence. We believe it reflects the child's emerging working model of a cooperative, reciprocal, mutually accommodating relationship in which partners naturally do things for one another without abrogating their autonomy.

FUTURE RESEARCH DIRECTIONS

MRO and Qualities of Individuals

It takes two to develop dyadic MRO. Although the relationship between a parent and child—like any relationship—is more than a simple sum of their characteristics, those characteristics may nevertheless foster or impede the formation of MRO. Recent advances in research on the role of genetics in behavior and on the biological foundations of children's temperament are beginning to be reflected in scientific work in what has been traditionally conceived as the domain of relationships. For example, Deater-Deckard and O'Connor (2000), studying identical and fraternal twins, and biological and adoptive siblings, found that parent-child MRO was driven, in part, by the child's genetically based qualities. In addition, a child's biologically based traits, such as being prone to anger or joy, or being hard or easy to soothe, may facilitate or undermine the evolution of the child's relationships within particular dyads. Being responsive to and having enjoyable interactions with a child may be more challenging if the child is temperamentally difficult than if he or she is easygoing and mellow.

Mothers' traits, some also biologically based, may be important as well. We have found that the more empathic mothers are, the better able they are to form MRO with their children (Kochanska, 1997). A large body of research indicates that depression and high levels of negative emotion in mothers reduce their responsiveness and positive behavior when interacting with their young children.

More complex interplay between biological and relationship factors also deserves future research attention. Our findings indicate that MRO may be particularly beneficial for children with certain temperaments, particularly fearless, thrill-seeking children whose behavior is not easily modified by actual or anticipated punishments and threats. Other interactions between temperament and relationships are also possible.

MRO as a Developmentally Changing System

A mutually responsive relationship between a parent and an infant differs from a mutually responsive relationship between a parent and a preschooler, or between a parent and an adolescent. The contexts and currency of parent-child interactions change. In infancy, those contexts include mostly the contexts of caregiving, play, and daily routines, and the currency of exchange is often nonverbal. Gradually, the contexts expand to include parent-child discussions of events and ideas, and the exchanges are increasingly verbal (Laible & Thompson, 2000). The child's and the parent's relative contributions to the relationship change over time, and so do their cognitive representations, perceptions, and expectations of the relationship and of each other. Psychologists' understanding of the child's side of MRO lags considerably behind their understanding of the parent's side of MRO. How MRO can be assessed in a manner that is developmentally sensitive and yet captures stable qualities of the parent-child dyad over time is one of the future challenges.

MRO and Internal Representations

In research to date, MRO has been inferred from parents' and children's observed behavior and affect during interactions. This outer layer, however, only partially captures the essence of a relationship. Scholars studying relationships have adopted Bowlby's premise that, over time, the parent and the child gradually form inner representations, or internal working models, of their relationship (Collins & Laursen, 1999). Those evolving models include generalized memories of each other's behavior, implicit beliefs and feelings about each other and the relationship, and a sense of what the relationship is like and what to expect from one another. Those generalized products of an individual's experience serve to organize and bias his or her future information processing, behavior, and emotions. In the case of MRO, the parent's and child's internal models entail mutual cooperation and implicit reciprocity, and the child's internal model is thought to underlie his or her willingness to embrace parental rules. Those inner representations, however, are difficult to access and to study. To develop sensitive yet rigorous methodologies that will provide insights into the representational aspect of MRO is an important future challenge.

MRO and the Family System

The relationship between a parent and child is itself nested in a network of family relationships. The importance of studying development in the context of the entire family system has been increasingly acknowledged. In particular, future research should study mother-child and father-child MRO, both separately and as a triadic interconnected system. More generally, family-level variables such as stress, conflict, support, and affective ambience may be significant dimensions of the context in which mutually responsive relationships with the child may flourish or fail.

Recommended Reading

Collins, W.A., & Laursen, B. (Eds.). (1999). (See References)
Kochanska, G. (1997). (See References)
Kochanska, G., & Murray, K.T. (2000). (See References)

Acknowledgments—This research has been sponsored by grants from the National Institute of Mental Health (RO1 MH63096, KO2 MH01446) and National Science Foundation (DBS-9209559, SBR-9510863) to the author. I gratefully acknowledge the comments of Nazan Aksan, David Forman, and Robert Siegler, and contributions of numerous students, staff, and the families who participated in the studies.

Note

1. Address correspondence to Grazyna Kochanska, Department of Psychology, University of Iowa, Iowa City, IA 52242-1447.

References

Clark, M.S. (1984). Record keeping in two types of relationships. *Journal of Personality and Social Psychology, 47*, 549–557.

Collins, W.A., & Laursen, B. (Eds.). (1999). *Minnesota Symposia on Child Psychology: Vol. 30. Relationships as developmental contexts.* Hillsdale, NJ: Erlbaum.

Collins, W.A., Maccoby, E.E., Steinberg, L., Hetherington, E.M., & Bornstein, M.H. (2000). Contemporary research on parenting: The case for nature and nurture. *American Psychologist, 55,* 218–232.

Deater-Deckard, K., & O'Connor, T.G. (2000). Parent-child mutuality in early childhood: Two behavioral genetic studies. *Developmental Psychology, 36,* 561–570.

Eisenberg, N., & Fabes, R.A. (1998). Prosocial development. In W. Damon (Series Ed.) & N. Eisenberg (Vol. Ed.), *Handbook of child psychology: Vol. 3. Social, emotional, and personality development* (pp. 701–778). New York: Wiley.

Emde, R.N., Biringen, Z., Clyman, R.B., & Oppenheim, D. (1991). The moral self of infancy: Affective core and procedural knowledge. *Developmental Review, 11,* 251–270.

Forman, D.R., & Kochanska, G. (2001). Viewing imitation as child responsiveness: A link between teaching and discipline domains of socialization. *Developmental Psychology, 37,* 198–206.

Grusec, J.E. (1997). A history of research on parenting strategies and children's internalization of values. In J.E. Grusec & L. Kuczynski (Eds.), *Parenting and children's internalization of values: A handbook of contemporary theory* (pp. 3–22). New York: Wiley.

Kochanska, G. (1997). Mutually responsive orientation between mothers and their young children: Implications for early socialization. *Child Development, 68,* 94–112.

Kochanska, G., Coy, K.C., & Murray, K.T. (2001). The development of self-regulation in the first four years of life. *Child Development, 72,* 1091–1111.

Kochanska, G., Forman, G., & Coy, K.C. (1999). Implications of the mother-child relationship in infancy for socialization in the second year of life. *Infant Behavior and Development, 22,* 249–265.

Kochanska, G., & Murray, K.T. (2000). Mother-child mutually responsive orientation and conscience development: From toddler to early school age. *Child Development, 71,* 417–431.

Laible, D.J., & Thompson, R.A. (2000). Mother-child discourse, attachment security, shared positive affect, and early conscience development. *Child Development, 71,* 1424–1440.

Maccoby, E.E. (1999). The uniqueness of the parent-child relationship. In W.A. Collins & B. Laursen (Eds.), *Minnesota Symposia on Child Psychology: Vol. 30. Relationships as developmental contexts* (pp. 157–175). Hillsdale, NJ: Erlbaum.

Reis, H.T., Collins, W.A., & Berscheid, E. (2000). Relationships in human behavior and development. *Psychological Bulletin, 126,* 844–872.

This article has been reprinted as it originally appeared in *Current Directions in Psychological Science*. Citation information for this article as originally published appears above.

The Quality of Early Child Care and Children's Development

Nancy L. Marshall[1]
Wellesley College

Abstract

The past half-century saw dramatic changes in families that altered the daily experiences of many young children. As more mothers of young children entered the labor force, increasing numbers of young children spent substantial hours in various child-care settings. These changes gave rise to a large body of research on the impact of the quality of early child care on children's development. However, a full understanding of the role of the quality of early child care requires consideration of the interplay among child care, family, work-place, and society. This article places what we know about the quality of early child care and children's development in this larger ecological context, and suggests directions for future research and practice.

Keywords

child care; maternal employment; child development; child-care services

The past half-century saw dramatic changes in families that altered the daily experiences of many young children. In 1970, only 24% of mothers with a young child (birth through age 3) were in the labor force; by 2000, this figure had risen to 57%. This growth in maternal employment was accompanied by changes in children's daily experiences. By 2000, 80% of children under the age of 6 were in some form of nonparental care, spending an average of 40 hours a week in such care (National Research Council and Institute of Medicine, 2003).

Research on children's experiences saw a parallel change that was equally dramatic. Early research in the field focused primarily on the question of whether child care (or maternal employment) per se was good or bad for children; current research asks questions about the relation between children's development and variations in the quality and quantity of child care that they experience. The field also now recognizes varying types of child care, including center-based care, licensed or regulated home-based care by nonrelatives (family- child-care homes), and other home-based care, such as care by relatives or in-home sitters. There have been methodological advances as well. Early research was more likely to study small samples and examine correlations between child care and children's outcomes at a single point in time; current research is more likely to involve large samples at multiple sites, to use experimental or quasi-experimental designs, and to follow participants over time.

Perhaps the most important advance in child-care research has been theoretical. Early research tended to study the effects of child care in isolation from other significant aspects of children's lives. Current research is more likely to be grounded in ecological systems theory, which considers children's development in the context of the child-care system as well as the family system, and recognizes the links between these systems and the larger society.

In this article, I focus on one segment of current research on early child care—the links between the quality of child care and children's development—drawing on ecological systems theory to provide an overview of recent advances and to suggest directions for future research.

ECOLOGICAL SYSTEMS THEORY AND EARLY CHILD CARE

Ecological systems theory places child development in an ecological perspective, in which an individual's experience is nested within interconnected systems (Bronfenbrenner, 1989). *Microsystems,* such as families or child-care settings, are characterized by face-to-face connections among individuals. *Mesosystems* consist of two or more microsystems and the linkages or processes that combine or connect them. These mesosystems exist within the larger context of the exosystem, those settings in which the child does not directly participate but that influence the lives of parents and other adults in the child's world, such as a parent's workplace, educational institutions that train child-care teachers and providers, and government agencies that set regulations for child-care facilities or establish welfare-reform policies. The mesosystems and exosystems operate within the context of a *macrosystem* of societal and cultural beliefs and practices. Note that these systems are not static, but may change over time.

The Mesosystem of Family ← → Child Care

Children inhabit both families and child-care microsystems, and these systems are linked. Parents select particular types of child care, of varying quality, for children of different ages—and these decisions vary with family structure, parental characteristics, geographical location, and other factors. Singer, Fuller, Keiley, and Wolf (1998) argued that child-care researchers must consider these *selection effects* if they are to accurately model the impact of child care on children's development over time.[2]

Through their selection of particular child-care arrangements, parents have an indirect impact on their children's development (in addition to their direct impact within the family system). But this linkage between the family system and child-care system operates in both directions: The child-care system can also influence the family system. For example, Ahnert, Rickert, and Lamb (2000) described a particular mesosystem characterized by shared care; in this mesosystem, mothers adapted their interactions with their toddlers in response to the toddlers' experiences in child care.

The Exosystem

The family ← → child-care mesosystem operates within the larger context of the exosystem of parental employment—one of the primary functions of child care is to enable parents, particularly mothers, to work outside the home. Historically, the child-care system has developed in response to characteristics of parents' employment. For instance, the current child-care system includes child-care centers, which tend to have operating hours that match those of parents who are working weekdays, as well as family-child-care homes and kith-and-kin care, which are more likely to meet the needs of parents who are working evenings, weekends, or variable hours. However, in industries that operate around the clock, particularly those with highly skilled workers such as hospitals, we are more likely to see on-site child-care centers, sick-child care,[3] and other accommodations to parents' employment needs.

Another important aspect of the exosystem is government policies and regulations that affect both the demand for child care (such as welfare-reform efforts that require low-income mothers to seek employment) and the affordability of child care. Although the United States provides some child-care subsidies for families, many low- and moderate-income families do not have effective access to subsidies.[4] Given the links between the quality of care and the cost of care, it is not surprising that children in low-income families who are not in the higher-quality, government-subsidized programs tend to receive lower-quality child care than children in middle-income families (cf. Phillips, Voran, Kisker, Howes, & Whitebook, 1994). In this way, the exosystem of government policies and regulations provides an important context for the operation of the family ←→ child-care mesosystem.

THE QUALITY OF EARLY CHILD CARE AND CHILDREN'S DEVELOPMENT

Using ecological systems theory as a framework, I turn now to the question of the relation between the quality of early child care and children's development. I begin with a discussion of the concept of quality, and then move on to an overview of what researchers currently know about the role of the quality of early child care in children's lives.

What Is Quality?

The underlying assumption of all definitions of quality is that a high-quality early-child-care setting is one that supports optimal learning and development. However, quality has been measured in a variety of ways across different studies. Measures of child-care quality can be categorized as either structural or process indicators. Structural characteristics include the child:staff ratio (the number of children per teacher or provider), the group size (number of children in the setting), and the education and specialized training of teachers, providers, or directors. The features of structural quality can be regulated, and most states set minimum standards for at least some aspects of structural quality, at least in center-based care. Studies that assess structural quality are most useful in evaluating the impact of features that can be regulated.

Although understanding the links between structural indicators of quality and children's development is important, we also need to understand the mechanisms by which structural quality affects children's development, which requires examining what actually happens in the early-care setting (i.e., the process). How do adults and children interact? What materials are available for the children, and how do adults support children's use of those materials? Process quality refers to the nature of the care that children experience—the warmth, sensitivity, and responsiveness of the caregivers; the emotional tone of the setting; the activities available to children; the developmental appropriateness of activities; and the learning opportunities available to children. Unlike the features of structural quality, process quality is not subject to state or local regulations, and it is harder to measure. One of the more commonly used measures, the Early Childhood Environment Rating Scale (ECERS; Harms, Clifford, & Cryer, 1998), assesses multiple aspects of process quality. Such multidimensional process measures tell us much more about the quality of care that children receive than do structural measures alone.

Structural Indicators of Quality and Children's Development

What do we know about the links between the structural indicators of quality in early child care and children's development? The research to date has found that better ratios (fewer children per adult) and more education or training for teachers are associated with higher language, cognitive, and social skills of the children cared for (National Research Council and Institute of Medicine, 2003). However, many of the studies that have examined structural indicators have employed small samples (fewer than 100 children) or have not considered selection effects in their analyses, so studies that do not have these limitations are of particular importance. In an interesting study that assessed the links between structural quality, process quality, and children's outcomes, the NICHD Early Child Care Research Network (2002) found that the relation between caregiver training and child-staff ratio, on the one hand, and children's cognitive and social competence, on the other hand, was mediated by process quality—that is, higher levels of caregiver training and lower ratios of children to adults in child-care settings were associated with higher levels of process quality, which were, in turn, associated with children's greater cognitive and social competence.

Process Quality and Children's Development

Among studies published in the past 15 years, those that employed an ecological model[5] consistently found that higher process quality is related to greater language and cognitive competence, fewer behavior problems, and more social skills, particularly when multidimensional measures of quality, such as the ECERS, are used or quality is assessed at more than one point in time. For example, the Cost, Quality and Child Outcomes Study (Peisner-Feinberg, Burchinal, & Clifford, 2001) found that higher process quality in preschool classrooms predicted fewer behavior problems 1 year later, and predicted higher language and math scores in kindergarten and second grade, although the magnitude of these associations declined over time. This same study also found a link between the child-care and family systems, such that the association between child-care quality and children's school performance was moderated by mothers' education; specifically, the association was stronger for children whose mothers had less education.

BEYOND SELECTION EFFECTS

I began this article with a discussion of the importance of considering children's development from an ecological systems perspective, which considers the family

← → child-care mesosystem as a context for children's development. Many studies of child care now consider the role of selection effects by statistically controlling for family characteristics. However, other linkages within the mesosystem must also be considered if one is to adequately understand the role of child-care quality in children's development. For instance, aspects of the family system, such as the mother's education or depression, parenting practices, and family income, may have independent effects on children's development. In fact, in a study of 1,100 children, the NICHD Early Child Care Research Network (2001) found that although the quality of early child care consistently predicted socio-emotional and cognitive-linguistic outcomes during the first 3 years of life, family factors were more consistent predictors of children's development than quality of child care, or any other child-care factors examined.

Research on the family ← → child-care mesosystem is familiar territory for many psychologists. However, Bronfenbrenner's ecological systems theory calls attention to other influences on children's development—the exosystem of parental employment and government policy and the macrosystem of societal beliefs about the desirability of maternal employment and the desired outcomes for children. For example, there is a complex interplay between parental employment, government policy, child care, and children's development for low-income families. Government policy and the macrosystem of societal beliefs promote employment for low-income parents. However, low-income parents tend to have less education and fewer marketable skills compared with other parents, and are likely to be employed in sectors of the labor market where jobs are part-time or contingent (temporary), allow little flexibility for managing family demands, and offer few benefits. Work schedules are also likely to include hours outside of the typical Monday-through-Friday daytimes when child-care centers normally operate. Although government subsidies are available to some low-income families, most do not receive subsidies. As a result, children from low-income families are likely to be placed in lower-cost and lower-quality center care or informal care that is itself often of lower quality (cf. Henly & Lyons, 2000). Viewing this "choice" as a selection effect leads one to interpret it as parental preference—but an ecological perspective suggests a different interpretation: Regardless of their individual preferences, low-income families' choices are constrained by the operation of the exosystem of the workplace and government policy.

FUTURE DIRECTIONS

Current state-of-the-art research has provided clear evidence that the quality of early child care matters to children's development. Children who attend higher-quality child-care settings have greater language and cognitive competence and greater social competence than children who receive lower-quality child care. However, several studies have documented the prevalence of mediocre or inadequate child care in the United States (National Research Council and Institute of Medicine, 2003, pp. 53–54). In addition, the high-quality care that does exist is not equitably distributed—lower-income children are less likely than higher-income children to have access to it.

The next step is to answer the question: How can we best raise the quality of early child care for all children? Ecological systems theory draws our attention to the importance of placing this question in the context of family processes, parental employment, governmental policies, and societal beliefs and goals when developing theoretical models and models for practice. We must integrate our societal goals of supporting healthy families, economic self-sufficiency, and women's employment with our goals of supporting healthy development and school readiness for children, if we expect to advance research and practice in the area of early-child-care quality and children's development.

Recommended Reading

Lamb, M.E. (1998). Nonparental child care: Context, quality, correlates. In W. Damon, I.E. Sigel, & K.A. Renninger (Eds.), *Handbook of child psychology: Vol. 4. Child psychology in practice* (5th ed., pp. 73–134). New York: John Wiley & Sons.

National Research Council and Institute of Medicine, Committee on Integrating the Science of Early Childhood Development, Board on Children, Youth, and Families. (2000). *From neurons to neighborhoods: The science of early child development* (J.P. Shonkoff & D.A. Phillips, Eds.). Washington, DC: National Academy Press.

National Research Council and Institute of Medicine, Division of Behavioral and Social Sciences and Education, Board on Children, Youth, and Families, Committee on Family and Work Policies. (2003). (See References)

Phillips, D.A., Voran, M.N., Kisker, E., Howes, C., & Whitebook, M. (1994). (See References)

Notes

1. Address correspondence to Nancy L. Marshall, Center for Research on Women, Wellesley College, 106 Central St., Wellesley, MA 02481.

2. *Selection effects* refers to the effects of family-level and community-level factors on decisions about the selection of child care.

3. Sick-child care consists of backup child-care arrangements for children who are mildly ill and cannot go to their regular child care or school, but do not require full-time parental care.

4. Middle-income families may receive subsidies through the child-care deductions in the federal tax code and through employers' Dependent Care Assistance Plans that allow eligible families to pay for child care with pretax dollars. Low-income families may receive subsidies through federal Head Start programs or through state-administered Transitional Assistance for Needy Families (TANF) programs, as well as other state and local programs.

5. The ecological model might be explicitly specified, or implicitly indicated through statistically controlling for key selection effects, such as the effects of family income or education.

References

Ahnert, L., Rickert, H., & Lamb, M.E. (2000). Shared caregiving: Comparisons between home and child care settings. *Developmental Psychology, 36*, 339–351.

Bronfenbrenner, U. (1989). Ecological systems theory. *Annals of Child Development, 6*, 187–249.

Harms, T., Clifford, R.M., & Cryer, D. (1998). *Early Childhood Environment Rating Scale: Revised edition*. New York: Teachers College Press.

Henly, J.R., & Lyons, S. (2000). The negotiation of child care and employment demands among low-income parents. *Journal of Social Issues, 56*, 683–706.

National Research Council and Institute of Medicine, Division of Behavioral and Social Sciences and Education, Board on Children, Youth, and Families, Committee on Family and Work Policies. (2003). *Working families and growing kids: Caring for children and adolescents* (E. Smolensky & J.A. Gootman, Eds.). Washington, DC: National Academies Press. Retrieved August 14, 2003, from http://www.nap.edu/openbook/0309087031/html/R1.html.

NICHD Early Child Care Research Network. (2001). Nonmaternal care and family factors in early development: An overview of the NICHD Study of Early Child Care. *Applied Developmental Psychology, 22,* 457–492.

NICHD Early Child Care Research Network. (2002). Child-care structure $\leftarrow \rightarrow$ process $\leftarrow \rightarrow$ outcome: Direct and indirect effects of child-care quality on young children's development. *Psychological Science, 13,* 199–206.

Peisner-Feinberg, E.S., Burchinal, M.R., & Clifford, R.M. (2001). The relation of preschool child-care quality to children's cognitive and social developmental trajectories through second grade. *Child Development, 72,* 1534–1553.

Phillips, D.A., Voran, M.N., Kisker, E., Howes, C., & Whitebook, M. (1994). Child care for children in poverty: Opportunity or inequity? *Child Development, 65,* 472–492.

Singer, J.D., Fuller, B., Keiley, M.K., & Wolf, A. (1998). Early child-care selection: Variation by geographic location, maternal characteristics, and family structure. *Developmental Psychology, 34,* 1129–1144.

Children of Lesbian and Gay Parents

Charlotte J. Patterson[1]
University of Virginia

Abstract

Does parental sexual orientation affect child development, and if so, how? Studies using convenience samples, studies using samples drawn from known populations, and studies based on samples that are representative of larger populations all converge on similar conclusions. More than two decades of research has failed to reveal important differences in the adjustment or development of children or adolescents reared by same-sex couples compared to those reared by other-sex couples. Results of the research suggest that qualities of family relationships are more tightly linked with child outcomes than is parental sexual orientation.

Keywords

sexual orientation; parenting; lesbian; gay; child; socialization

Does parental sexual orientation affect child development, and if so, how? This question has often been raised in the context of legal and policy proceedings relevant to children, such as those involving adoption, child custody, or visitation. Divergent views have been offered by professionals from the fields of psychology, sociology, medicine, and law (Patterson, Fulcher, & Wainright, 2002). While this question has most often been raised in legal and policy contexts, it is also relevant to theoretical issues. For example, does healthy human development require that a child grow up with parents of each gender? And if not, what would that mean for our theoretical understanding of parent–child relations (Patterson & Hastings, in press)? In this article, I describe some research designed to address these questions.

EARLY RESEARCH

Research on children with lesbian and gay parents began with studies focused on cases in which children had been born in the context of a heterosexual marriage. After parental separation and divorce, many children in these families lived with divorced lesbian mothers. A number of researchers compared development among children of divorced lesbian mothers with that among children of divorced heterosexual mothers and found few significant differences (Patterson, 1997; Stacey & Biblarz, 2001).

These studies were valuable in addressing concerns of judges who were required to decide divorce and child custody cases, but they left many questions unanswered. In particular, because the children who participated in this research had been born into homes with married mothers and fathers, it was not obvious how to understand the reasons for their healthy development. The possibility that children's early exposure to apparently heterosexual male and female role models had contributed to healthy development could not be ruled out.

When lesbian or gay parents rear infants and children from birth, do their offspring grow up in typical ways and show healthy development? To address this question, it was important to study children who had never lived with heterosexual parents. In the 1990s, a number of investigators began research of this kind.

An early example was the Bay Area Families Study, in which I studied a group of 4- to 9-year-old children who had been born to or adopted early in life by lesbian mothers (Patterson, 1996, 1997). Data were collected during home visits. Results from in-home interviews and also from questionnaires showed that children had regular contact with a wide range of adults of both genders, both within and outside of their families. The children's self-concepts and preferences for same-gender playmates and activities were much like those of other children their ages. Moreover, standardized measures of social competence and of behavior problems, such as those from the Child Behavior Checklist (CBCL), showed that they scored within the range of normal variation for a representative sample of same-aged American children. It was clear from this study and others like it that it was quite possible for lesbian mothers to rear healthy children.

STUDIES BASED ON SAMPLES DRAWN FROM KNOWN POPULATIONS

Interpretation of the results from the Bay Area Families Study was, however, affected by its sampling procedures. The study had been based on a convenience sample that had been assembled by word of mouth. It was therefore impossible to rule out the possibility that families who participated in the research were especially well adjusted. Would a more representative sample yield different results?

To find out, Ray Chan, Barbara Raboy, and I conducted research in collaboration with the Sperm Bank of California (Chan, Raboy, & Patterson, 1998; Fulcher, Sutfin, Chan, Scheib, & Patterson, 2005). Over the more than 15 years of its existence, the Sperm Bank of California's clientele had included many lesbian as well as heterosexual women. For research purposes, this clientele was a finite population from which our sample could be drawn. The Sperm Bank of California also allowed a sample in which, both for lesbian and for heterosexual groups, one parent was biologically related to the child and one was not.

We invited all clients who had conceived children using the resources of the Sperm Bank of California and who had children 5 years old or older to participate in our research. The resulting sample was composed of 80 families, 55 headed by lesbian and 25 headed by heterosexual parents. Materials were mailed to participating families, with instructions to complete them privately and return them in self-addressed stamped envelopes we provided.

Results replicated and expanded upon those from earlier research. Children of lesbian and heterosexual parents showed similar, relatively high levels of social competence, as well as similar, relatively low levels of behavior problems on the parent form of the CBCL. We also asked the children's teachers to provide evaluations of children's adjustment on the Teacher Report Form of the CBCL, and their reports agreed with those of parents. Parental sexual orientation was not related to children's adaptation. Quite apart from parental sexual orientation, however, and consistent with findings from years of research on children of heterosexual parents, when parent–child relationships were marked by warmth and affection, children were more likely to be developing well. Thus, in this sample drawn from a known population, measures of children's adjustment were unrelated to parental sexual orientation (Chan et al., 1998; Fulcher et al., 2005).

Even as they provided information about children born to lesbian mothers, however, these new results also raised additional questions. Women who conceive children at sperm banks are generally both well educated and financially comfortable. It was possible that these relatively privileged women were able to protect children from many forms of discrimination. What if a more diverse group of families were to be studied? In addition, the children in this sample averaged 7 years of age, and some concerns focus on older children and adolescents. What if an older group of youngsters were to be studied? Would problems masked by youth and privilege in earlier studies emerge in an older, more diverse sample?

STUDIES BASED ON REPRESENTATIVE SAMPLES

An opportunity to address these questions was presented by the availability of data from the National Longitudinal Study of Adolescent Health (Add Health). The Add Health study involved a large, ethnically diverse, and essentially representative sample of American adolescents and their parents. Data for our research were drawn from surveys and interviews completed by more than 12,000 adolescents and their parents at home and from surveys completed by adolescents at school.

Parents were not queried directly about their sexual orientation but were asked if they were involved in a "marriage, or marriage-like relationship." If parents acknowledged such a relationship, they were also asked the gender of their partner. Thus, we identified a group of 44 12- to 18-year-olds who lived with parents involved in marriage or marriage-like relationships with same-sex partners. We compared them with a matched group of adolescents living with other-sex couples. Data from the archives of the Add Health study allowed us to address many questions about adolescent development.

Consistent with earlier findings, results of this work revealed few differences in adjustment between adolescents living with same-sex parents and those living with opposite-sex parents (Wainright, Russell, & Patterson, 2004; Wainright & Patterson, 2006). There were no significant differences between teenagers living with same-sex parents and those living with other-sex parents on self-reported assessments of psychological well-being, such as self-esteem and anxiety; measures of school outcomes, such as grade point averages and trouble in school; or measures of family relationships, such as parental warmth and care from adults and peers. Adolescents in the two groups were equally likely to say that they had been involved in a romantic relationship in the last 18 months, and they were equally likely to report having engaged in sexual intercourse. The only statistically reliable difference between the two groups—that those with same-sex parents felt a greater sense of connection to people at school—favored the youngsters living with same-sex couples. There were no significant differences in self-reported substance use, delinquency, or peer victimization between those reared by same- or other-sex couples (Wainright & Patterson, 2006).

Although the gender of parents' partners was not an important predictor of adolescent well-being, other aspects of family relationships were significantly associated with teenagers' adjustment. Consistent with other findings about adolescent development, the qualities of family relationships rather than the gender of parents' partners were consistently related to adolescent outcomes. Parents who reported having close relationships with their offspring had adolescents who reported more favorable adjustment. Not only is it possible for children and adolescents who are parented by same-sex couples to develop in healthy directions, but—even when studied in an extremely diverse, representative sample of American adolescents—they generally do.

These findings have been supported by results from many other studies, both in the United States and abroad. Susan Golombok and her colleagues have reported similar results with a near-representative sample of children in the United Kingdom (Golombok et al., 2003). Others, both in Europe and in the United States, have described similar findings (e.g., Brewaeys, Ponjaert, Van Hall, & Golombok, 1997).

The fact that children of lesbian mothers generally develop in healthy ways should not be taken to suggest that they encounter no challenges. Many investigators have remarked upon the fact that children of lesbian and gay parents may encounter anti-gay sentiments in their daily lives. For example, in a study of 10-year-old children born to lesbian mothers, Gartrell, Deck, Rodas, Peyser, and Banks (2005) reported that a substantial minority had encountered anti-gay sentiments among their peers. Those who had had such encounters were likely to report having felt angry, upset, or sad about these experiences. Children of lesbian and gay parents may be exposed to prejudice against their parents in some settings, and this may be painful for them, but evidence for the idea that such encounters affect children's overall adjustment is lacking.

CONCLUSIONS

Does parental sexual orientation have an important impact on child or adolescent development? Results of recent research provide no evidence that it does. In fact, the findings suggest that parental sexual orientation is less important than the qualities of family relationships. More important to youth than the gender of their parent's partner is the quality of daily interaction and the strength of relationships with the parents they have.

One possible approach to findings like the ones described above might be to shrug them off by reiterating the familiar adage that "one cannot prove the null hypothesis." To respond in this way, however, is to miss the central point of these studies. Whether or not any measurable impact of parental sexual orientation on children's development is ever demonstrated, the main conclusions from research to date remain clear: Whatever correlations between child outcomes and parental sexual orientation may exist, they are less important than those between child outcomes and the qualities of family relationships.

Although research to date has made important contributions, many issues relevant to children of lesbian and gay parents remain in need of study. Relatively few studies have examined the development of children adopted by lesbian or gay parents or of children born to gay fathers; further research in both areas would be welcome (Patterson, 2004). Some notable longitudinal studies have been reported, and they have found children of same-sex couples to be in good mental health. Greater understanding of family relationships and transitions over time would, however, be helpful, and longitudinal studies would be valuable. Future research could also benefit from the use of a variety of methodologies.

Meanwhile, the clarity of findings in this area has been acknowledged by a number of major professional organizations. For instance, the governing body of the American Psychological Association (APA) voted unanimously in favor of a statement that said, "Research has shown that the adjustment, development, and psychological well-being of children is unrelated to parental sexual orientation and that children of lesbian and gay parents are as likely as those of heterosexual parents to flourish" (APA, 2004). The American Bar Association, the American Medical Association, the American Academy of Pediatrics, the American Psychiatric Association, and other mainstream professional groups have issued similar statements.

The findings from research on children of lesbian and gay parents have been used to inform legal and public policy debates across the country (Patterson et al., 2002). The research literature on this subject has been cited in amicus briefs filed by the APA in cases dealing with adoption, child custody, and also in cases related to the legality of marriages between same-sex partners. Psychologists serving as expert witnesses have presented findings on these issues in many different courts (Patterson et al., 2002). Through these and other avenues, results of research on lesbian and gay parents and their children are finding their way into public discourse.

The findings are also beginning to address theoretical questions about critical issues in parenting. The importance of gender in parenting is one such issue. When children fare well in two-parent lesbian-mother or gay-father families, this suggests that the gender of one's parents cannot be a critical factor in child development. Results of research on children of lesbian and gay parents cast doubt upon the traditional assumption that gender is important in parenting. Our data suggest that it is the quality of parenting rather than the gender of parents that is significant for youngsters' development.

Research on children of lesbian and gay parents is thus located at the intersection of a number of classic and contemporary concerns. Studies of lesbian- and gay-parented families allow researchers to address theoretical questions that had previously remained difficult or impossible to answer. They also address oft-debated legal questions of fact about development of children with lesbian and gay parents. Thus, research on children of lesbian and gay parents contributes to public debate and legal decision making, as well as to theoretical understanding of human development.

Recommended Reading

Golombok, S., Perry, B., Burston, A., Murray, C., Mooney-Somers, J., Stevens, M., & Golding, J. (2003). (See References)
Patterson, C.J., Fulcher, M., & Wainright, J. (2002). (See References)
Stacey, J., & Biblarz, T.J. (2001). (See References)
Wainright, J.L., & Patterson, C.J. (2006). (See References)
Wainright, J.L., Russell, S.T., & Patterson, C.J. (2004). (See References)

Note

1. Address correspondence to Charlotte J. Patterson, Department of Psychology, P.O. Box 400400, University of Virginia, Charlottesville, VA 22904; e-mail: cjp@virginia.edu.

References

American Psychological Association (2004). Resolution on sexual orientation, parents, and children. Retrieved September 25, 2006, from http://www.apa.org/pi/lgbc/policy/parentschildren.pdf

Brewaeys, A., Ponjaert, I., Van Hall, E.V., & Golombok, S. (1997). Donor insemination: Child development and family functioning in lesbian mother families. *Human Reproduction, 12,* 1349–1359.

Chan, R.W., Raboy, B., & Patterson, C.J. (1998). Psychosocial adjustment among children conceived via donor insemination by lesbian and heterosexual mothers. *Child Development, 69,* 443–457.

Fulcher, M., Sutfin, E.L., Chan, R.W., Scheib, J.E., & Patterson, C.J. (2005). Lesbian mothers and their children: Findings from the Contemporary Families Study. In A. Omoto & H. Kurtzman (Eds.), *Recent research on sexual orientation, mental health, and substance abuse* (pp. 281–299). Washington, DC: American Psychological Association.

Gartrell, N., Deck., A., Rodas, C., Peyser, H., & Banks, A. (2005). The National Lesbian Family Study: 4. Interviews with the 10-year-old children. *American Journal of Orthopsychiatry, 75,* 518–524.

Golombok, S., Perry, B., Burston, A., Murray, C., Mooney-Somers, J., Stevens, M., & Golding, J. (2003). Children with lesbian parents: A community study. *Developmental Psychology, 39,* 20–33.

Patterson, C.J. (1996). Lesbian mothers and their children: Findings from the Bay Area Families Study. In J. Laird & R.J. Green (Eds.), *Lesbians and gays in couples and families: A handbook for therapists* (pp. 420–437). San Francisco: Jossey-Bass.

Patterson, C.J. (1997). Children of lesbian and gay parents. In T. Ollendick & R. Prinz (Eds.), *Advances in clinical child psychology* (Vol. 19, pp. 235–282). New York: Plenum Press.

Patterson, C.J. (2004). Gay fathers. In M.E. Lamb (Ed.), *The role of the father in child development* (4th ed., pp. 397–416). New York: Wiley.

Patterson, C.J., Fulcher, M., & Wainright, J. (2002). Children of lesbian and gay parents: Research, law, and policy. In B.L. Bottoms, M.B. Kovera, & B.D. McAuliff (Eds.), *Children, social science and the law* (pp. 176–199). New York: Cambridge University Press.

Patterson, C.J., & Hastings, P. (in press). Socialization in context of family diversity. In J. Grusec & P. Hastings (Eds.), *Handbook of socialization*. New York: Guilford Press.

Stacey, J., & Biblarz, T.J. (2001). (How) Does sexual orientation of parents matter? *American Sociological Review, 65,* 159–183.

Wainright, J.L., & Patterson, C.J. (2006). Delinquency, victimization, and substance use among adolescents with female same-sex parents. *Journal of Family Psychology, 20,* 526–530.

Wainright, J.L., Russell, S.T., & Patterson, C.J. (2004). Psychosocial adjustment and school outcomes of adolescents with same-sex parents. *Child Development, 75,* 1886–1898.

Siblings' Direct and Indirect Contributions to Child Development

Gene H. Brody[1]

Department of Child and Family Development and Center for Family Research, University of Georgia

Abstract

Since the early 1980s, a growing body of research has described the contributions of sibling relationships to child and adolescent development. Interactions with older siblings promote young children's language and cognitive development, their understanding of other people's emotions and perspectives, and, conversely, their development of antisocial behavior. Studies address the ways in which parents' experiences with older children contribute to their rearing of younger children, which in turn contributes to the younger children's development. Finally, by virtue of having a sibling, children may receive differential treatment from their parents. Under some conditions, differential treatment is associated with emotional and behavioral problems in children.

Keywords

siblings; interaction; development; differential treatment

The first studies of the contributions that older siblings make to their younger brothers' and sisters' development were conducted in Britain around the turn of the 20th century by Sir Francis Galton, a cousin of Charles Darwin. Sibling research, however, only recently has begun to address many of the issues that concern families. Parents, clinicians, and now researchers in developmental psychology recognize the significance of the sibling relationship as a contributor to family harmony or discord and to individual children's development. Since the early 1980s, a growing interest in the family has prompted research on those aspects of sibling relationships that contribute to children's cognitive, social, and emotional adjustment. These contributions can be direct, occurring as a result of siblings' encounters with one another, or indirect, occurring through a child's impact on parents that influences the care that other brothers and sisters receive. Differential treatment by parents is a third way in which having a sibling may contribute to child development. Children may be treated differently by their parents than their siblings are, or at least believe that they are treated differently. The development of this belief has implications for children's and adolescents' mental health. In this article, I present an overview of the ways in which siblings' direct and indirect influences and parental differential treatment contribute to child development.

SIBLINGS' DIRECT CONTRIBUTIONS TO DEVELOPMENT

Currently, research suggests that naturally occurring teaching and caregiving experiences benefit cognitive, language, and psychosocial development in both older and younger siblings. Studies conducted in children's homes and in laboratories show that older siblings in middle childhood can teach new cognitive concepts and language skills to their younger siblings in early childhood. Across the middle childhood years, older siblings become better teachers as they learn how to simplify tasks for their younger siblings. The ability to adjust their teaching behaviors to their younger siblings' capacities increases as older siblings develop the ability to take other people's perspectives (Maynard, 2002). Older siblings who assume teaching and caregiving roles earn higher reading and language achievement scores, gain a greater sense of competence in the caregiving role, and learn more quickly to balance their self-concerns with others' needs than do older siblings who do not assume these roles with their younger siblings (Zukow-Goldring, 1995). When caregiving demands on the older sibling become excessive, however, they may interfere with the older child's time spent on homework or involvement in school activities. Caregiving responsibilities during middle childhood and adolescence can compromise older siblings' school performance and behavioral adjustment (Marshall et al., 1997).

Children who are nurtured by their older siblings become sensitive to other people's feelings and beliefs (Dunn, 1988). As in all relationships, though, nurturance does not occur in isolation from conflict. Sibling relationships that are characterized by a balance of nurturance and conflict can provide a unique opportunity for children to develop the ability to understand other people's emotions and viewpoints, to learn to manage anger and resolve conflict, and to provide nurturance themselves. Indeed, younger siblings who experience a balance of nurturance and conflict in their sibling relationships have been found to be more socially skilled and have more positive peer relationships compared with children who lack this experience (Hetherington, 1988).

Sibling relationships also have the potential to affect children's development negatively. Younger siblings growing up with aggressive older siblings are at considerable risk for developing conduct problems, performing poorly in school, and having few positive experiences in their relationships with their peers (Bank, Patterson, & Reid, 1996). The links between older siblings' antisocial behavior and younger siblings' conduct problems are stronger for children living in disadvantaged neighborhoods characterized by high unemployment rates and pervasive poverty than for children living in more advantaged neighborhoods (Brody, Ge, et al., 2003). Younger siblings who live in disadvantaged neighborhoods have more opportunities than do children living in more affluent areas to practice the problematic conduct that they learn during sibling interactions as they interact with peers who encourage antisocial behavior.

The importance of the sibling relationship is probably best demonstrated by older siblings' ability to buffer younger siblings from the negative effects of family turmoil. Younger siblings whose older siblings provide them with emotional support (caring, acceptance, and bolstering of self-esteem) during bouts of intense, angry interparental conflict show fewer signs of behavioral or emotional problems than do children whose older siblings are less supportive (Jenkins, 1992).

SIBLINGS' INDIRECT CONTRIBUTIONS

Conventional wisdom suggests that parents' experiences with older children influence their expectations of subsequent children and the child-rearing strategies that parents consider effective. Similarly, the experiences that other adults, particularly teachers, have with older siblings may influence their expectations and treatment of younger siblings. Research has confirmed the operation of these indirect effects on younger siblings' development. Whiteman and Buchanan (2002) found that experiences with earlier-born children contributed to parents' expectations about their younger children's likelihood of experiencing conduct problems, using drugs, displaying rebellious behavior, or being helpful and showing concern for others. Teachers are not immune from the predisposing effects of experiences with older siblings. As a result of having an older sibling in class or hearing about his or her accomplishments or escapades, teachers develop expectations regarding the younger sibling's academic ability and conduct even before the younger child becomes their student (Bronfenbrenner, 1977). Some parents and teachers translate these expectations into parenting and teaching practices they subsequently use with younger siblings that influence the younger children's beliefs about their academic abilities, interests, and choice of friends; children often choose friends whom they perceive to be similar to themselves.

Rather than viewing behavioral influence as flowing in one direction, from parents to children, developmental psychologists now recognize that these influences are reciprocal. The behaviors that children use during everyday interactions with their parents partially determine the behaviors that the parents direct toward their children. Children with active or emotionally intense personalities receive different, usually more negative, parenting than do children with calm and easygoing personalities. Some studies suggest that older siblings' individual characteristics may contribute indirectly to the quality of parenting that younger siblings receive. For example, East (1998) discovered that negative experiences with an earlier-born child lead parents to question their ability to provide good care for their younger children and to lower their expectations for their younger children's behavior.

In our research, my colleagues and I explored the specific ways in which older siblings' characteristics contribute to the quality of parenting that younger siblings receive, which in turn contributes to younger siblings' development of conduct problems and depressive symptoms. The premise of the study was simple. Rearing older siblings who are doing well in school and are well liked by other children provides parents with opportunities for basking in their children's achievements. (Basking is a phenomenon in which one's psychological well-being increases because of the accomplishments of persons to whom one is close.) Using a longitudinal research design in which we collected data from families for 4 years, we found that academically and socially competent older siblings contributed to an increase in their mothers' self-esteem and a decrease in their mothers' depressive symptoms. Positive changes in mothers' psychological functioning forecast their use of adjustment-promoting parenting practices with younger siblings. Over time, these practices forecast high levels of self-control and low levels of behavior problems and depressive symptoms in the younger siblings (Brody, Kim, Murry, & Brown, 2003). We expect future research to clarify further the indirect pathways through which siblings influence one another's development, including the processes by which children's negative characteristics affect their parents' child-rearing practices. A difficult-to-rear older sibling, for example, may contribute over time to decreases in his or her parents' psychological well-being, resulting in increased tension in the family. Under these circumstances, the parents' negativity and distraction decrease the likelihood that a younger sibling will experience parenting that promotes self-worth, academic achievement, and social skills.

PARENTAL DIFFERENTIAL TREATMENT

Any discussion of siblings' contributions to development would be incomplete without acknowledging parental differential treatment. Having a sibling creates a context in which parental behavior assumes symbolic value, as children use it as a barometer indicating the extent to which they are loved, rejected, included, or excluded by their parents. Children's and adolescents' beliefs that they receive less warmth and more negative treatment from their parents than do their siblings is associated with poor emotional and behavioral functioning (Reiss, Neiderhiser, Hetherington, & Plomin, 2000).

Not all children who perceive differential treatment develop these problems, however. Differential parental treatment is associated with poor adjustment in a child only when the quality of the child's individual relationship with his or her parents is distant and negative. The association between differential treatment and adjustment is weak for children whose parents treat them well, even when their siblings receive even warmer and more positive treatment (Feinberg & Hetherington, 2001). Children's perceptions of the legitimacy of differential treatment also help determine its contribution to their adjustment. Children who perceive their parents' differential behavior to be justified report fewer behavior problems than do children who consider it to be unjust, even under conditions of relatively high levels of differential treatment. Children and adolescents who perceive differential treatment as unfair experience low levels of self-worth and have high levels of behavior problems (Kowal, Kramer, Krull, & Crick, 2002). Children justify differential treatment by citing ways in which they and their siblings differ in age, personality, and special needs. Sensitive parenting entails treating children as their individual temperaments and developmental needs require. Nevertheless, it is important that children understand why parents treat siblings differently from one another so that they will be protected from interpreting the differences as evidence that they are not valued or worthy of love.

FUTURE DIRECTIONS

Considerable work is needed to provide a comprehensive understanding of the processes through which siblings influence one another's cognitive development, language development, psychological adjustment, and social skills. Current studies can best be considered "first generation" research. They describe associations between older and younger siblings' behaviors and characteristics. Some studies have demonstrated that the prediction of younger siblings' outcomes is more accurate if it is based on older siblings' characteristics plus parenting, rather than parenting alone (Brody, Kim, et al., 2003). More research is needed to isolate influences other than parenting, such as shared genetics, shared environments, and social learning, before siblings' unique contributions to development can be specified. The next generation of research will address the ways in which sibling relationships contribute to children's self-images and personal identities, emotion regulation and coping skills, explanations of positive and negative events that occur in family and peer relationships, use of aggression, and involvement in high-risk behaviors.

Recommended Reading

Brody, G.H. (1998). Sibling relationship quality: Its causes and consequences. *Annual Review of Psychology, 49*, 1–24.
Feinberg, M., & Hetherington, E.M. (2001). (See References)
Kowal, A., Kramer, L., Krull, J.L., & Crick, N.R. (2002). (See References)
Maynard, A.E. (2002). (See References)
Whiteman, S.D., & Buchanan, C.M. (2002). (See References)

Acknowledgments—I would like to thank Eileen Neubaum-Carlan for helpful comments. Preparation of this article was partly supported by grants from the National Institute of Child Health and Human Development, the National Institute of Mental Health, and the National Institute on Alcohol Abuse and Alcoholism.

Note

1. Address correspondence to Gene H. Brody, University of Georgia, Center for Family Research, 1095 College Station Rd., Athens, GA 30602-4527.

References

Bank, L., Patterson, G.R., & Reid, J.B. (1996). Negative sibling interaction patterns as predictors of later adjustment problems in adolescent and young adult males. In G.H. Brody (Ed.), *Sibling relationships: Their causes and consequences* (pp. 197–229). Norwood, NJ: Ablex.
Brody, G.H., Ge, X., Kim, S.Y., Murry, V.M., Simons, R.L., Gibbons, F.X., Gerrard, M., & Conger, R. (2003). Neighborhood disadvantage moderates associations of parenting and older sibling problem attitudes and behavior with conduct disorders in African American children. *Journal of Consulting and Clinical Psychology, 71*, 211–222.
Brody, G.H., Kim, S., Murry, V.M., & Brown, A.C. (2003). Longitudinal direct and indirect pathways linking older sibling competence to the development of younger sibling competence. *Developmental Psychology, 39*, 618–628.
Bronfenbrenner, U. (1977). Toward an experimental ecology of human development. *American Psychologist, 32*, 513–531.
Dunn, J. (1988). Connections between relationships: Implications of research on mothers and siblings. In R.A. Hinde & J. Stevenson-Hinde (Eds.), *Relationships within families: Mutual influences* (pp. 168–180). New York: Oxford University Press.
East, P.L. (1998). Impact of adolescent childbearing on families and younger siblings: Effects that increase younger siblings' risk for early pregnancy. *Applied Developmental Science, 2*, 62–74.
Feinberg, M., & Hetherington, E.M. (2001). Differential parenting as a within-family variable. *Journal of Family Psychology, 15*, 22–37.
Hetherington, E.M. (1988). Parents, children, and siblings: Six years after divorce. In R.A. Hinde & J. Stevenson-Hinde (Eds.), *Relationships within families: Mutual influences* (pp. 311–331). New York: Oxford University Press.
Jenkins, J. (1992). Sibling relationships in disharmonious homes: Potential difficulties and protective effects. In F. Boer & J. Dunn (Eds.), *Children's sibling relationships: Developmental and clinical issues* (pp. 125–138). Hillsdale, NJ: Erlbaum.

Kowal, A., Kramer, L., Krull, J.L., & Crick, N.R. (2002). Children's perceptions of the fairness of parental preferential treatment and their socioemotional well-being. *Journal of Family Psychology, 16*, 297–306.

Marshall, L., Garcia-Coll, C., Marx, F., McCartney, K., Keefe, N., & Ruh, J. (1997). After-school time and children's behavioral adjustment. *Merrill-Palmer Quarterly, 43*, 497–514.

Maynard, A.E. (2002). Cultural teaching: The development of teaching skills in Maya sibling interactions. *Child Development, 73*, 969–982.

Reiss, D., Neiderhiser, J.M., Hetherington, E.M., & Plomin, R. (2000). *The relationship code: Deciphering genetic and social influences on adolescent development.* Cambridge, MA: Harvard University Press.

Whiteman, S.D., & Buchanan, C.M. (2002). Mothers' and children's expectations for adolescence: The impact of perceptions of an older sibling's experience. *Journal of Family Psychology, 16*, 157–171.

Zukow-Goldring, P.G. (1995). Sibling caregiving. In M.H. Bornstein (Ed.), *Handbook of parenting: Vol. 3. Status and social conditions of parenting* (pp. 177–208). Mahwah, NJ: Erlbaum.

Section 4: Critical Thinking Questions

1. Why was it important for Patterson and her colleagues to use families identified via a sperm bank to study developmental outcomes in children with heterosexual versus lesbian parents? How would you answer this question from the perspective of David Reiss? Grazyna Kochanska? What kinds of data do you imagine that each of these investigators would have collected if they had been collaborators on that research project?

2. In the article on early child care, Marshall demonstrates the value of taking a systems perspective on child development in the context of nonparental child care. Using Bronfenbrenner's ecological theory in particular, she highlights the importance of the meso- and exosystem variables. Do you think that this approach already includes consideration of genetic variables such as those discussed by Reiss or sibling effects such as those discussed by Brody? If so, where would you place them, and if not, what would you add to the systems model? Do you think their potential impact is already accounted for in the empirical work discussed by Marshall, and if not, what would you suggest might be added in future research on the effects of nonparental child care?

This article has been reprinted as it originally appeared in *Current Directions in Psychological Science*. Citation information for this article as originally published appears above.

Section 5: Social Groups

The prior section makes it clear that an individual's family of origin has an important influence on development. However, the child's family is not the only important social group with which individuals identify and interact. The articles in this section discuss social groups beyond the family (e.g., groups defined by gender, race), including how they acquire significance and the ways in which they influence behaviors.

Carol Martin and Diane Ruble focus on groups defined by gender. Consistent with cognitive-developmental approaches to gender such as Kohlberg's, they argue that children first come to identify their own gender, and then, as a consequence, selectively attend to information in the environment that is relevant to their own sex. Children then develop rigid gender beliefs, expecting themselves and others to behave in gender traditional ways. Once they understand that gender remains constant even in the face of superficial changes (e.g., in clothes) or even in the face of nontraditional behaviors, they then become more flexible.

In the second article, Bigler and Liben describe a more general model, "Developmental Intergroup Theory" (DIT), designed to be applicable to a range of groups (e.g., gender, race, ethnicity). They identify factors that render some human qualities particularly salient for defining social groups (e.g., groups that are perceptually easy to distinguish; groups that are labeled and treated differently by adults). They also identify cognitive-developmental mechanisms that support children's attempts to attach meaning to social groups, and the processes by which stereotypes and prejudice may result. They argue that environments may be designed to reduce the strength of group divisions, and hence to diminish prejudice.

Melanie Killen also draws on ideas from intergroup theory, but her focus is explicitly on how children reason about the morality of excluding another person based on that person's group membership. For example, how does someone judge the morality of telling another child that she may not join a play group because she is girl? Based on her empirical findings, Killen rejects a stage model approach to moral development in which exclusion reasoning is assumed to vary systematically with age but not context. Instead, she argues for a social-domain theory approach in which reasoning about exclusion is affected not only by the participant child's age, but also by the context in which exclusion occurs and by the qualities of the excluded child.

The fourth article by Sandra Graham explores the role of the ethnic context on peer victimization in school. Graham finds that with greater ethnic diversity, students feel less victimized and vulnerable. Her research also shows that when there is relatively less diversity within a class—but not total homogeneity—students who are members of the majority group are more likely to blame themselves when they are victimized. In addition to providing insights into victimization itself, this article demonstrates the more general importance of examining the ecology of the school when studying individual children's feelings and attributions.

Cillessen and Rose likewise address peer relationships, but rather than focus on victims, they focus on the positive end of the peer scale—popular children. They distinguish between two kinds of popularity. *Sociometric* popularity refers to youth who display prosocial behaviors and little aggression, and are explicitly named as children with whom others like to interact. *Perceived* popularity refers to youth who are *thought* to be popular, but who are not actually named by others as preferred playmates. Although not liked, other children seem to wish to emulate them. The article argues for the importance of distinguishing and studying both types of youth in the study of peer relationships and in the design of interventions.

Children's Search for Gender Cues: Cognitive Perspectives on Gender Development

Carol Lynn Martin[1]
Arizona State University

Diane Ruble
New York University

Abstract

Young children search for cues about gender—who should or should not do a particular activity, who can play with whom, and why girls and boys are different. From a vast array of gendered cues in their social worlds, children quickly form an impressive constellation of gender cognitions, including gender self-conceptions (gender identity) and gender stereotypes. Cognitive perspectives on gender development (i.e., cognitive developmental theory and gender-schema theory) assume that children actively search for ways to make sense of the social world that surrounds them. Gender identity develops as children realize that they belong to one gender group, and the consequences include increased motivation to be similar to other members of their group, preferences for members of their own group, selective attention to and memory for information relevant to their own sex, and increased interest in activities relevant to their own sex. Cognitive perspectives have been influential in increasing understanding of how children develop and apply gender stereotypes, and in their focus on children's active role in gender socialization.

Keywords

gender development; gender stereotypes; cognitive theories

Erin, a 4-year-old, explained to her aunt about a drawing she had done: "The ones with eyelashes are girls; boys don't have eyelashes."

In an Italian restaurant, a four-year-old noticed his father and another man order pizza and his mother order lasagna. On his way home in the car, he announced that he had figured it out: "Men eat pizza and women don't." (Bjorklund, 2000, p. 361)

Children are gender detectives who search for cues about gender—who should or should not engage in a particular activity, who can play with whom, and why girls and boys are different. Cognitive perspectives on gender development assume that children are actively searching for ways to find meaning in and make sense of the social world that surrounds them, and they do so by using the gender cues provided by society to help them interpret what they see and hear. Children are wonderfully skilled in using these cues to form expectations about other people and to develop personal standards for behavior, and they learn to do this very quickly and often with little direct training. By the age of 5, children develop an impressive constellation of stereotypes about gender (often amusing and incorrect) that they apply to themselves and others. They use these stereotypes to form impressions of others, to help guide their own behavior, to direct their attention, and to organize their memories.

The first cognitive theory of gender development was Kohlberg's (1966) cognitive developmental approach, which was based on the ideas of Piaget. Kohlberg's theory emphasized the active role of the child in gender development, and proposed that children's understanding of gender concepts influences their behavior, and that this influence becomes more pronounced once children reach a relatively sophisticated understanding of gender—knowing that a person's sex is stable and unchanging. In the 1970s, a new group of cognitive approaches to gender emerged—gender-schema theories. Gender-schema theory is based on the idea that children form organized knowledge structures, or *schemas*, which are gender-related conceptions of themselves and others, and that these schemas influence children's thinking and behavior. Although similar to Kohlberg's theory in the assumption that children play an active role in gender development, gender-schema theory assumes a more basic understanding of gender is all that is required to motivate children's behavior and thinking. Gender-schema theory was further elaborated with contributions from developmental and social psychologists (Liben & Bigler, 2002; for reviews, see Martin, Ruble, & Szkrybalo, 2002). Over time, these two cognitive perspectives—that is, cognitive developmental and gender-schema theories—have been influential in promoting the idea that children actively construct gender on the basis of both the nature of the social environment and how they think about the sexes. Other perspectives also have incorporated cognitive mechanisms to account for gender development (e.g., Bussey & Bandura, 1999).

MAJOR THEMES OF COGNITIVE THEORIES OF GENDER DEVELOPMENT

We believe that cognitive theories of gender development are characterized by three central features.

The Emergence of Gender Identity and Its Consequences

A central tenet of cognitive approaches is that there are immediate consequences of children's recognition that there are two gender groups and that they belong to one of them. These consequences are both evaluative and motivational-informational.

Evaluative Consequences   Considerable research with diverse kinds of social groups suggests that an individual evaluates a group positively as soon as he or she identifies, even in a very minimal way, with that group (see Ruble et al., in press). For instance, children as young as 3 years of age have been shown to like their own sex more than the other. Similarly, young children attribute more positive characteristics to their own sex than to the other (see Ruble & Martin, 1998). One of the most powerful developmental phenomena is children's striking tendency to segregate by sex when they can choose play partners (Maccoby, 1998). Young children seldom play exclusively with members of the other sex. Evaluative consequences of group identification are particularly likely when group membership is salient (e.g., when groups differ in appearance) and when it is made functionally significant by authority figures; both of these conditions are true for gender (Bigler, Jones, & Lobliner, 1997).

Motivational and Informational Consequences   The emergence of gender identity and growing understanding of the stability of social group membership affects children's motivation to learn about gender, to gather information about their gender group, and to act like other group members (Ruble & Martin, 1998). For example, experimental studies using novel toys find that at an age when children have achieved gender identity, they pay more attention to and remember more information relevant to toys they believe are appropriate for their own gender group than for toys they believe to be for the other sex (Bradbard, Martin, Endsley, & Halverson, 1986).

Once they recognize their gender group, children make broad assumptions about similarities within the gender groups and about differences between girls and boys. In numerous studies, children have been found to use the sex of a person to form impressions and make judgments about him or her (e.g., judgments about whether they would like the person, what the person may like to do, and what the person is like). For instance, using gender stereotypes, a girl may not approach a new neighbor who is a boy because she suspects that he will not share her interests. By acting on their assumptions about what other members of their gender like to do, children further differentiate the sexes.

Active, Self-Initiated View of Gender Development

When cognitive theorists refer to the motivational consequences of self-identification as a boy or girl, they mean something quite specific. Gender identification produces a new motivation that is initiated by and emanates from the child. This motivation involves the child's deliberate efforts to learn about a social category that he or she is actively constructing as part of a process of finding meaning in the social world.

Perhaps the clearest evidence for this kind of active construction is found when the process goes awry and children draw faulty conclusions about gender distinctions and show distorted perception of and memory for gender-role-inconsistent information. There are numerous examples of such errors in the literature. In one study, after being shown equal numbers of pictures of people engaged in gender-stereotypic activities (e.g., a girl sewing) and gender-inconsistent activities (e.g., a boy cooking), children were three times more likely to misremember the inconsistent than the stereotypic pictures. For example, instead of remembering that they had been shown a picture of a *girl* sawing wood, children reported having seen a picture of a *boy* sawing wood (Martin & Halverson, 1983). Children also seem to want to generate or exaggerate male-female differences, even if none exist. In our own studies, it has been difficult to generate neutral stimuli because children appear to seize on any element that may implicate a gender norm so that they may categorize it as male or female. Experimental research also suggests that young children are quick to jump to conclusions about sex differences, even on the basis of only a single instance. For example, when 3-year-olds were told that a particular boy likes a sofa and a particular girl likes a table, they generalized this information to draw the conclusion that another girl would also like the table (Bauer & Coyne, 1997).

Developmental Patterns

A major feature of cognitive theories of gender is an emphasis on developmental changes in understanding of gender, which may be accounted for by children's changing cognitive abilities (e.g., abilities to classify on multiple dimensions) and their evolving understanding of concepts. Because of such changes, the relative strength (rigidity) of children's gender-related beliefs and behaviors is predicted to wax and wane across development. The early learning of gender categories and associated attributes (stereotypes) appears to set off a sequence of events that results in, first, very rigid beliefs (that only boys or only girls can do or be something), which are followed by more flexible, realistic beliefs (that either sex can do almost anything). Specifically, considerable evidence suggests that gender stereotyping shows a developmental pattern that can be characterized by three ordered phases (Trautner et al., 2003):

- First, children begin learning about gender-related characteristics. This phase takes place mainly during the toddler and preschool years.
- Second, the newly acquired gender knowledge is consolidated in a rigid either-or fashion, reaching its peak of rigidity between 5 and 7 years.
- Third, after this peak of rigidity, a phase of relative flexibility follows.

This phase pattern (see Fig. 1) received striking support by an analysis of data collected on a sample of children over a period of 6 years (Trautner et al., 2003). The children reached peak rigidity in their gender stereotypes at age 5 to 6, then showed a dramatic increase in flexibility 2 years later (i.e., at age 7 or 8). Moreover, although the children varied considerably in their maximal levels of rigidity at age 5 to 6, there was little difference in levels of flexibility by age 8.

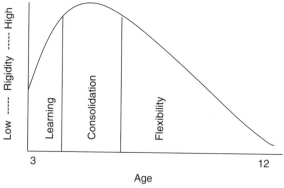

Fig. 1. A model of phase changes in the rigidity of children's gender stereotypes as a function of age.

168

These findings provide strong support for a cognitive perspective by showing that all children take basically the same path of waxing and waning of stereotype rigidity across development, despite variations in when the path begins and what level it reaches. Although this developmental sequence of gender stereotyping is no doubt associated with more general cognitive processes and abilities, such as understanding of gender constancy and categorization and classifications skills, the exact mechanisms underlying changes in gender stereotyping are not yet fully understood.

Gender-related preferences and behaviors show more mixed developmental patterns than stereotyping (Liben & Bigler, 2002; Ruble & Martin, 1998), with some showing clear rigidity in preschool (Maccoby, 1998) and others showing little developmental change in rigidity (Serbin, Powlishta, & Gulko, 1993). These differences are probably due to varying influences of socialization, biological, and cognitive developmental factors.

On the basis of an extensive review of the literature, we have recently suggested the following developmental hypothesis: The consequences of gender identity may differ at different levels of understanding. Specifically, lower levels of understanding (recognizing one's sex) may serve to orient children to the importance of gender, thereby increasing their in-group biases and their motivation to attend to information about gender, whereas higher levels of understanding (recognizing the invariance of the category) may heighten children's behavioral responsiveness to gender-related social norms (Martin et al., 2002). A parallel hypothesis has received support in research on ethnic-related identity and consequences, but the hypothesis remains to be tested for gender (Ruble et al., in press).

THE EARLY ORIGINS OF GENDER

Researchers have been fascinated for years with questions about the early origins of gendered behavior and thinking. The two most pressing issues are, at what age do children begin to think of themselves and other people in terms of gender, and how do these gender cognitions influence their behavior and thinking?

Development of Gender-Based Perceptual Discriminations

In the quest to understand the earliest origins of gender development, researchers have been conducting studies with infants and toddlers. The latest research on this topic has yielded surprising findings: Six-month-old infants can distinguish the voices of women and men, and most 9-month-olds are able to discriminate between photographs of men and women. Even more surprising is that between the ages of 11 and 14 months, infants learn to recognize the associations between women's and men's photographs and their voices (e.g., that men's faces "go with" low voices), showing that they can form associations across sensory modalities. These studies suggest that by the time children can talk, they have in place perceptual categories that distinguish "male" from "female" (for a review, see Martin et al., 2002).

Linking Thought and Behavior

If cognitions play a role in guiding behavior, one would expect that the onset of gender-related cognitions precedes behavior that reflects sex differences. Developmental trends tend to support this pattern, but not always. For instance, girls show preferences for dolls and boys for transportation toys at a very early age, before gender cognitions develop. Yet most sex differences do not become apparent until after age 2, when children have at least rudimentary gender cognitions.

Do young children's gender cognitions actually influence behavior? Specifically, do children who recognize their gender identity or know gender stereotypes behave in more gender-differentiated ways than children who do not recognize gender identity or know gender stereotypes? Establishing clear causal linkages between knowing about gender and acting on the basis of that knowledge has been challenging (Martin et al., 2002). In natural settings, it is difficult to assess the role of cognition because patterns of behavior are also influenced by children's prior experiences. Nevertheless, a few longitudinal analyses have shown that once children know gender stereotypes, their personal preferences become more gender typed (Miller, Trautner, & Ruble, in press).

These links have also been studied in the laboratory by giving novel toys or activities gender-related labels, either directly (e.g., "I think that boys like this toy better than girls") or subtly (e.g., "this is a test to see how good you would be at mechanics or operating machinery"). Such studies have shown that children pay more attention to toys and activities that they believe are for their own sex than to toys and activities they think are for the other sex. Similarly, children have better memory for, perform better with, and have greater expectations of success with toys and activities they think are for their own sex. Essentially, these studies illustrate that when a toy or activity is stereotyped, with either overt or covert cues, children respond according to whether the toy or activity is appropriate for their own sex.

FUTURE DIRECTIONS

In conclusion, several lines of evidence support cognitive theories of gender development. First, children's growing knowledge about and identification with gender categories has evaluative and motivational consequences. For instance, knowledge of gender stereotypes is linked to behavior, especially in carefully designed experimental and correlational studies. Second, children show developmental changes in stereotyping that parallel other cognitive developmental changes. Third, knowledge about gender categories may be found in primitive forms in infancy, well before the emergence of many gender-typed behaviors.

However, many fundamental questions remain to be tackled by future research. For example, it is not yet known at what age children begin to identify with gender in some form. Is it possible that toddlers have developed gender preferences based on primitive gender identities by the time they are able to talk? Researchers also do not know what processes underlie the waxing and waning of rigidity and flexibility in gender beliefs and behaviors. Do socialization processes interact with cognitive-developmental factors to determine when children attend to gender information and adopt rigid beliefs about it?

Recently, interest in integrating multiple perspectives on gender has been heightened by research on children and adults who either have a mismatch between their biological sex and their gender identity or are born with ambiguous genitalia. Collaborative efforts with biologically oriented theorists could address such important issues as whether there is a critical or sensitive period for gender identity and how social, biological, and cognitive factors affect its development. How, for example, do the gender-identification processes unfold for children born with ambiguous genitalia? What cues might children use to lead them to conclude that their gender is different from their biological sex? Are there interpersonal and mental health consequences of whether or not they forge a clear identity as one sex or the other? Such questions have been asked for decades, and have critical implications for health and mental health, but convincing answers have remained elusive.

Recommended Reading

Liben, S.L., & Bigler, R.S. (2002). (See References)
Martin, C.L., Ruble, D.N., & Szkrybalo, J. (2002). (See References)
Ruble, D.N., & Martin, C.L. (1998). (See References)
Ruble, D.N., & Martin, C.L. (2002). Conceptualizing, measuring, and evaluating the developmental course of gender differentiation: Compliments, queries, and quandaries. *Monographs of the Society for Research in Child Development, 67*(2, Serial No. 269), 148–166.

Acknowledgments—Preparation of this article was supported by grants from the MacArthur Foundation, the Russell Sage Foundation, and the National Institute of Mental Health (R01 37215).

Note

1. Address correspondence to Carol Martin, Department of Family and Human Development, Arizona State University, Tempe, AZ 85287-2502; e-mail: cmartin@asu.edu.

References

Bauer, P.J., & Coyne, M.J. (1997). When the name says it all: Preschoolers' recognition and use of the gendered nature of common proper names. *Social Development, 6,* 271–291.
Bigler, R.S., Jones, L.C., & Lobliner, D.B. (1997). Social categorization and the formation of intergroup attitudes in children. *Child Development, 68,* 530–543.
Bjorklund, D.F. (2000). *Children's thinking: Developmental function and individual differences.* Belmont, CA: Wadsworth.
Bradbard, M.R., Martin, C.L., Endsley, R.C., & Halverson, C.F. (1986). Influence of sex stereotypes on children's exploration and memory: A competence versus performance distinction. *Developmental Psychology, 22,* 481–486.
Bussey, K., & Bandura, A. (1999). Social-cognitive theory of gender development and differentiation. *Psychological Review, 106,* 676–713.
Kohlberg, L.A. (1966). A cognitive-developmental analysis of children's sex role concepts and attitudes. In E. Maccoby (Ed.), *The development of sex differences* (pp. 82–173). Stanford, CA: Stanford University Press.
Liben, S.L., & Bigler, R.S. (2002). The developmental course of gender differentiation: Conceptualizing, measuring and evaluating constructs and pathways. *Monographs of the Society for Research in Child Development, 67*(2, Serial No. 269), 1–147.

Maccoby, E.E. (1998). *The two sexes: Growing up apart, coming together*. Cambridge, MA: Belknap Press.

Martin, C.L., & Halverson, C.F. (1983). The effects of sex-stereotyping schemas on young children's memory. *Child Development, 54*, 563–574.

Martin, C.L., Ruble, D.N., & Szkrybalo, J. (2002). Cognitive theories of early gender development. *Psychological Bulletin, 128*, 903–933.

Miller, C.F., Trautner, H.M., & Ruble, D.N. (in press). The role of gender knowledge in children's gender-typed preferences. In C. Tamis-LeMonda & L. Balter (Eds.), *Child psychology: A handbook of contemporary issues*. Philadelphia: Psychology Press.

Ruble, D.N., Alvarez, J., Bachman, M., Cameron, J., Fuligni, A., Garcia-Coll, C., & Rhee, E. (in press). The development and implications of children's social self or the "we." In M. Bennett & F. Sani (Eds.), *The development of the social self*. East Sussex, England: Psychological Press.

Ruble, D.N., & Martin, C.L. (1998). Gender development. In W. Damon (Ed.), *Handbook of child psychology: Vol. 3* (pp. 933–1016). New York: Wiley.

Serbin, L.A., Powlishta, K.K., & Gulko, J. (1993). The development of sex typing in middle childhood. *Monographs of the Society for Research in Child Development, 58*(2, Serial No. 232).

Trautner, H.M., Ruble, D.N., Cyphers, L., Kirsten, B., Behrendt, R., & Hartmann, P. (2003). *Rigidity and flexibility of gender stereotypes in childhood: Developmental or differential?* Manuscript submitted for publication.

This article has been reprinted as it originally appeared in *Current Directions in Psychological Science*. Citation information for this article as originally published appears above.

Developmental Intergroup Theory: Explaining and Reducing Children's Social Stereotyping and Prejudice

Rebecca S. Bigler[1]

University of Texas, Austin

Lynn S. Liben

The Pennsylvania State University

Abstract

Social stereotyping and prejudice are intriguing phenomena from the standpoint of theory and, in addition, constitute pressing societal problems. Because stereotyping and prejudice emerge in early childhood, developmental research on causal mechanisms is critical for understanding and controlling stereotyping and prejudice. Such work forms the basis of a new theoretical model, developmental intergroup theory (DIT), which addresses the causal ingredients of stereotyping and prejudice. The work suggests that biases may be largely under environmental control and thus might be shaped via educational, social, and legal policies.

Keywords

stereotyping; intergroup; children; prejudice

Young children are often perceived as being untainted by the negative social biases that characterize adults, but many studies reveal that stereotyping and prejudice exist by the age of 4. Contemporary theories explain how cognitive processes predispose children to acquire and maintain social stereotypes and prejudice (see Aboud, 2005; Martin, Ruble, & Szkrybalo, 2002). However, they fail to account for why some dimensions of human variation rather than others (e.g., gender but not handedness) become foundations for social stereotyping and prejudice, and they skirt the issue of whether biases are inevitable and, if not, how they might be prevented. A new theoretical model of social stereotyping and prejudice, *developmental intergroup theory* (DIT; Bigler & Liben, 2006), addresses both these issues. The theory's name reflects its grounding in two complementary theoretical approaches: *intergroup theory*, referring to social identity (Tajfel & Turner, 1986) and self-categorization theories (Turner, Hogg, Oakes, Reicher, & Wetherell, 1987), and *cognitive-developmental theory*, referring to Piagetian and contemporary approaches to cognitive development. We describe empirical foundations and then mechanisms by which children single out groups as targets of stereotyping and prejudice, associate characteristics with groups (i.e., stereotypes), and develop affective responses (i.e., prejudices). Elsewhere (Bigler & Liben, 2006) we focus on how DIT handles developmental differences (e.g., how the development of multiple classification skills during childhood affects stereotyping; see Bigler & Liben, 1992) and individual differences (e.g., the consequences of individual differences in attitudes; see Liben & Signorella, 1980). Here, we focus on how DIT conceptualizes group-level effects.

EMPIRICAL FOUNDATIONS

Causes of stereotypes and prejudice are difficult to study in the everyday world both because messages about social groups are pervasive and because it is impossible or unethical to assign individuals experimentally to most relevant groups (e.g., gender, race, social class). DIT thus draws heavily on research that circumvents these constraints by creating and manipulating *novel* social groups (e.g., Bigler, 1995; Bigler, Jones, & Lobliner, 1997; Bigler, Brown, & Markell, 2001). As in classic intergroup studies, group membership and environmental conditions are experimentally manipulated, permitting conclusions about causal effects of various factors on the development of stereotyping and prejudice.

In a typical study, participants are 6- to 11-year-old summer-school students who are unacquainted with each other when school begins. They are initially given tasks measuring factors (e.g., cognitive-developmental level, self-esteem) hypothesized to affect intergroup attitudes. Novel groups are created, usually by assigning children to wear different colored tee shirts. Characteristics of the groups (e.g., proportional size, purported traits) and their treatment within the classroom (e.g., labeling, segregation) are then manipulated. After several weeks, children's intergroup attitudes are assessed. One study, for example, tested children's intergroup attitudes as a function of adults' labeling and functional use of color groups (Bigler et al., 1997). In experimental classrooms, teachers used color groups to organize classroom desks, bulletin boards, and activities. In control classrooms, teachers ignored the color groups. After several weeks, children completed measures of their perceptions of trait variability within and between color groups, evaluated group competence and performance, and were assessed for behavioral biases and peer preferences. In-group biases developed only in experimental classrooms.

COMPONENT PROCESSES OF DIT

Three core processes (double-bordered rectangles in Fig. 1) are hypothesized to contribute the formation of social stereotyping and prejudice: (a) establishing the psychological salience (EPS) of different person attributes, (b) categorizing encountered individuals by salient dimensions, and (c) developing stereotypes and prejudices (DSP) of salient social groups.

Establishing the Psychological Salience of Person Attributes

Virtually all explanations of social stereotyping rest on categorization. However, there are almost endless bases on which humans might be parsed into groups. How and why are some of the available bases for classification—and not others—used by children to sort individuals? The first component of DIT addresses why some attributes become salient for categorization.

Drawing from constructive theories, we assume that individuals are motivated to understand their physical and social worlds and thus actively seek to determine which of the available bases for classifying people are important. Given the vast diversity of potentially important categories and the complexity of the cues that mark such categories, we reject the idea that evolution "hard

174

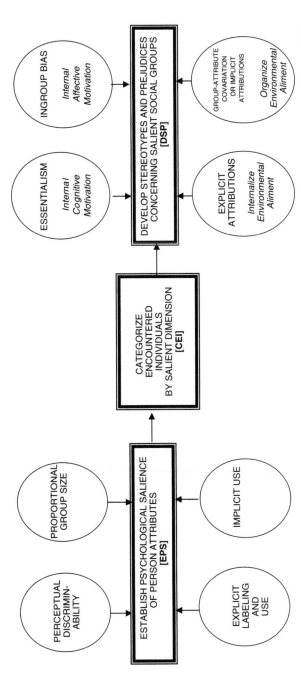

Fig. 1. The key processes involved in the formation of social stereotypes and prejudice in developmental intergroup theory (abbreviated from Bigler & Liben, 2006). Rectangles represent the three key processes contributing to the formation of social stereotyping and prejudice: (a) establishment of the psychological salience of different person attributes, (b) categorization of encountered individuals by salient dimensions, and (c) development of stereotypes and prejudices of salient social groups. Ovals represent the factors that shape the operation of core processes, including four factors that shape the establishment of psychological salience (perceptual discriminability, proportional group size, explicit labeling and use, and implicit use) and four factors that shape the development of stereotypes and prejudice (essentialism, ingroup bias, explicit attributions, and implicit attributions).

wired"specific dimensions as salient bases for classification. We instead suggest that evolution led to a flexible cognitive system that motivates and equips children to infer—from environmental data—which bases of classification are important within a given context.

One relevant factor is the child's tendency to note perceptually salient dimensions of objects and people (Fig. 1., top left oval feeding EPS). Research indicates that young children tend to focus on perceptually salient attributes in person-perception tasks: Perceptually salient features such as race, gender, age, and attractiveness typically become the basis for their social stereotyping, whereas perceptually indistinct features (e.g., some nationalities and political affiliations) typically do not (e.g., Rutland, 1999). Cultural environments may be explicitly structured to make some classification schemes perceptually salient (e.g., requiring Jews to wear yellow stars in Nazi Germany or socializing males and females to wear different hair styles and clothing).

Further, we argue that proportional group size (Fig. 1., top right oval feeding EPS) affects the psychological salience of social groups for children (as for adults; Brewer & Brown, 1998). Proportionally smaller (minority) groups are more distinctive than proportionally larger (majority) groups, thus making minority groups more likely to become the targets of stereotypes and prejudice.

DIT also proposes that the psychological salience of grouping criteria (e.g., gender, color, reading ability) increases when adults label groups or group members, either as a matter of routine (e.g., beginning the day by stating "Good morning girls and boys" [or, "reds and blues"]) or in the service of organizing the environment (e.g., assigning different desks or bulletin boards to each group; Fig. 1., bottom left oval feeding EPS). This outcome holds even when groups are distinguished in a completely neutral (as opposed to stereotypic) manner (e.g., asking children to sit alternately by gender).

We also posit that implicit mechanisms increase the salience of social categories (Fig. 1., bottom right oval feeding EPS). Unlike explicit mechanisms in which categories are directly labeled, implicit mechanisms present some social grouping without explanation, thereby providing a cognitive puzzle for children to solve. One particularly powerful example is de facto segregation. Although segregation has long been linked to stereotyping and prejudice, the explanatory mechanism traditionally offered is unfamiliarity. Under this view, intergroup contact promotes familiarity, thereby increasing intergroup liking (Pettigrew & Tropp, 2000). We propose an additional inferential, constructive process in which children observe the characteristics along which humans are sorted. They notice perceptual similarities among those who live, work, and socialize together and then infer that the social divisions they observe must have been caused by meaningful, inherent differences between groups.

Thus, rather than explaining children's tendency to classify others along some dimension because of reinforcement or imitation, we suggest that children see a dimension used and then construct hypotheses about its importance. Consider a father directing his child to "Ask that lady if we are in the correct line." In traditional social learning theory, this event would not be expected to shape the child's gender stereotyping: The statement involves neither reward nor punishment, nor conveys the father's gender attitudes. In DIT, however, it would be

Table 1. *Key factors hypothesized to affect the formation of social stereotypes and prejudice in Developmental Intergroup Theory (DIT) and studies offering relevant empirical data*

DIT factor	Relevant empirical work	Key manipulations	Major conclusions
Perceptual discriminability	Bigler, 1995; Bigler et al., 1997	Groups were perceptually marked or unmarked.	Higher bias when groups were perceptually marked
Proportional group size	Brown & Bigler, 2002	Groups were equal or unequal in size.	Higher bias when groups were unequal in size
Explicit labeling and use	Bigler et al., 1997, 2001; Patterson & Bigler, 2006	Groups were labeled or ignored by teachers.	Higher bias when groups were labeled by teachers
Implicit use	Bigler, 2004	Groups were segregated or integrated within classrooms.	Higher bias when groups were segregated
Explicit attributions	Patterson, 2007	Groups were labeled as excelling or not at tasks.	Higher bias when groups were linked to positive traits
Implicit attributions	Bigler et al., 2001; Brown & Bigler, 2002	Groups were associated with positive or negative traits via classroom posters.	Higher bias when groups were linked to positive traits

expected to make gender salient, thereby inspiring the child to devise hypotheses about gender's importance. Studies consistent with our hypothesized mechanisms are identified in Table 1.

Categorizing Encountered Individuals by Salient Dimensions

Because children categorize stimuli as they attempt to structure knowledge and reduce cognitive complexity (Mervis & Rosch, 1981), we propose that they will classify encountered individuals into groups using those dimensions that are psychological salient. The degree and way in which the categorization process operates will be affected by the individual child's classification skill (which undergoes age-related change) and environmental experience (e.g., the number of encounters with exemplars). The mere act of categorization triggers processes involved in the construction of social stereotypes.

Developing Stereotypes and Prejudices Concerning Salient Social Groups

The process of categorization is hypothesized to result in constructivist, cognitive-developmental processes (enumerated later) that attach meaning to social groups in the form of beliefs (i.e., stereotypes) and affect (i.e., prejudice). DIT outlines the factors that guide children's acquisition of the content of their social stereotypes and the nature of their affective responses to social groups.

We propose that both internally and externally driven processes lead children to attach meaning to psychologically salient groups. The former are constructive processes through which children actively interpret and recall objects and events in the external world in relation to their current cognitive and affective schemata. Internally driven processes involve the self-generation (rather than passive learning) of links between social categories and (a) attributes (e.g., traits, behaviors, roles) and (b) affect (e.g., liking). In these processes, children go above and beyond the veridical information available in the environment to infer beliefs about the attributes associated with particular social categories. For example, cognitive-developmental psychologists have suggested that some categories, particularly those found in the natural world, are structured by *essentialist* thinking (see Gelman, 2003). Essentialism is the belief that members of a category share important, non-obvious qualities (Fig. 1., top left oval feeding DSP). Thus, children are likely to presume that visible markers of group membership denote other, unseen, inherent qualities (e.g., believing that African Americans and European Americans have different blood types, see Gelman, 2003). Obviously, such beliefs are based not on empirical evidence; instead they reflect the imposition of an internalized group schema onto the world.

With respect to prejudice, the processes are conceptualized as ones in which children actively generate more positive affective links to in-groups than to out-groups. Among adults, the mere act of categorizing individuals into social groups is often sufficient to produce intergroup prejudice and discrimination (Tajfel & Turner, 1986). Children, too, show prejudice within many intergroup contexts, viewing their in-group as superior to out-groups, despite the fact that such beliefs are neither modeled by adults nor objectively true (Fig. 1., top right oval feeding DSP). When stereotype content is acquired via self-generative or constructive processes, children fabricate category–attribute links that favor their own group (Bigler et al., 1997).

Children's cognitive processes are applied to what they encounter in the world. Children are exposed to explicit statements linking social groups to attributes—for example, "African Americans are hostile" and "girls are shy" (Fig. 1., bottom left oval feeding DSP). Explicit remarks are powerful because they operate at two levels simultaneously by employing labels that inherently mark the social groups as important and by providing information about attributes associated with the group. Although public remarks like these have undoubtedly diminished, they still occur, especially among peers. That is, children may "teach" attributions that they have detected (a process described next) or invented, as in the popular children's rhyme: "Girls go to college to get more knowledge; boys go to Jupiter to get more stupider." They may also explicitly teach prejudice without reference to attributes (e.g., "I hate girls").

In addition, children's environments (both macro- and micro-level) are characterized by covariations between social categories and attributes. Illustratively, the occupation of President of the United States shows a perfect correlation to race and gender: All Presidents have been White men. This high-profile correlation is likely to be detected by children, even when it is not explicitly pointed out. The nonverbal behavior that adults direct toward members of social groups or show in response to the presence of group members (e.g., Whites becoming nervous or socially withdrawn in the presence of African Americans) is another source of implicit information likely to cause prejudice. Importantly, these nonverbal behaviors are likely to be unconscious and, as a consequence, adults are unlikely to explain their behaviors to children. We posit that children's attention to such correlations plays a role in shaping the content of stereotypes and, in turn, prejudice (Fig. 1., bottom right oval feeding DSP). Studies providing empirical data relevant to the role of explicit and implicit links in the formation of stereotype content are summarized in Table 1.

The veridical presence of correlations between social categories and some attributes has led some psychologists to claim that stereotypes are accurate generalizations (see Lee, Jussim, & McCauley, 1995). We agree that the detection of group–attribute correlations plays a role in stereotyping, but we view as incomplete approaches holding that stereotypes are *merely* the reflections of true category–attribute relations or that children learn stereotypes *primarily* through environmental models (e.g., via mechanisms described by social-learning theory). Both approaches fail to account for the fact that children and adults typically develop stereotypic views and prejudices concerning groups that are meaningless (and thus uncorrelated with any observable traits or behaviors). Furthermore, such approaches fail to acknowledge that individuals show systematic biases (e.g., illusory correlations) when processing information about social groups (Brewer & Brown, 1998; Martin et al., 2002). In addition, virtually limitless category-to-attribute correlations are available to the child. It seems unlikely that a child could calculate the correlations between (a) each possible social group within an environment and (b) the traits, roles, and activities that co-vary with each of those groups. We think it unlikely, for example, that children calculate the relation between a person's height and the likelihood of being a nurse, between hair color and the likelihood of being gentle, or between religion and the likelihood of using an ironing board. Yet, most children detect the correlation between gender and each of these characteristics, and thus some statistical learning of group-to-attribute relations appears to occur. We argue (as do researchers who study infants' and young children's attention to statistical information in the service of language learning) that some processes must narrow the scope of the problem so that children's attention is directed toward only a subset of possible correlations. DIT suggests such processes, outlining the factors that serve to make some (but not other) attributes the basis for children's social categorization.

IMPLICATIONS

The approach reviewed here implies that certain social policies will affect stereotyping and prejudice formation among children. Specifically, DIT predicts that the psychological salience of particular social groups for children will increase to the extent that societies (a) exaggerate the perceptual discriminability of groups, (b) foster numeric imbalance across multiple contexts, (c) call attention to groups by labeling them or by explicitly and routinely using group membership as a basis for some action, and (d) present conditions (like segregation) that implicitly convey the importance of group membership.

Importantly, most of the factors that serve to make social groups psychologically salient are under social control. Laws, for example, explicitly constrain adults' use of social categories to label children in some ways (e.g., federal law forbids routinely labeling children's race in classrooms) and might be extended to others (e.g., forbidding routine labeling of gender). Laws likewise affect the implicit use of social categories (e.g., by allowing vs. prohibiting single-sex and single-race schools). Once categorization along some particular dimension occurs, stereotyping and prejudice are likely to follow. When groups are labeled, treated, or sorted differently, children come to conceptualize groups as different in meaningful ways and to show preferential bias toward their own in-group. Children are also likely to internalize the stereotypic beliefs explicitly communicated in their environment and to detect covariations between social groups and attributes that would have otherwise gone unnoticed.

Additional research is needed to add to the empirical base for DIT shown in Table 1 and reviewed elsewhere (Bigler & Liben, 2006) and to test means for countering stereotypes and prejudices that have already developed. For example, whereas DIT suggests minimizing attention to group categories to avoid the formation of stereotypes, it might be necessary to actively draw children's attention to groups and to relevant cognitive processes (e.g., reconstructive memory; illusory correlations) when helping children to overcome stereotypes they already harbor. Our hope is that DIT will prove useful not only for understanding the emergence and evolution of stereotypes and prejudices long reported in the social-psychological literature (Brewer & Brown, 1998) but also for developing policies that will reduce their early emergence and their myriad negative consequences.

Recommended Reading

Aboud, F.E. (2005). (See References)
Bigler, R.S., & Liben, L.S. (2006). (See References)
Martin, C.L., Ruble, D.N., & Szkrybalo, J. (2002). (See References)

Note

1. Address correspondence to Rebecca S. Bigler, Department of Psychology, 1 University Station A8000, University of Texas at Austin, Austin, TX 78712; e-mail: bigler@psy.utexas.edu.

References

Aboud, F.E. (2005). The development of prejudice in childhood and adolescence. In J.F. Dovidio, P. Glick, & L.A. Rudman (Eds.), *On the nature of prejudice: Fifty years after Allport* (pp. 310–326). New York: Blackwell.

Bigler, R.S. (1995). The role of classification skill in moderating environmental influences on children's gender stereotyping: A study of the functional use of gender in the classroom. *Child Development, 66,* 1072–1087.

Bigler, R.S. (2004, January). The role of segregation in the formation of children's intergroup attitudes. In S. Levy (Chair), *Integrating developmental and social psychological research on prejudice processes.* Symposium conducted at the 5th annual meeting of the Society for Personality and Social Psychology, Austin, TX.

Bigler, R.S., Brown, C.S., & Markell, M. (2001). When groups are not created equal: Effects of group status on the formation of intergroup attitudes in children. *Child Development, 72,* 1151–1162.

Bigler, R.S., Jones, L.C., & Lobliner, D.B. (1997). Social categorization and the formation of intergroup attitudes in children. *Child Development, 68*, 530–543.

Bigler, R.S., & Liben, L.S. (1992). Cognitive mechanisms in children's gender stereotyping: Theoretical and educational implications of a cognitive-based intervention. *Child Development, 63*, 1351–1363.

Bigler, R.S., & Liben, L.S. (2006). A developmental intergroup theory of social stereotypes and prejudice. In R.V. Kail (Ed.), *Advances in child development and behavior* (Vol. 34, pp. 39–89). San Diego: Elsevier.

Brewer, M.B., & Brown, R.J. (1998). Intergroup relations. In D.T. Gilbert, S.T. Fiske, & G. Lindsey (Eds.), *The handbook of social psychology* (Vol. 2, 4th ed., pp. 554–594). New York: McGraw-Hill.

Brown, C.S., & Bigler, R.S. (2002). Effects of minority status in the classroom on children's intergroup attitudes. *Journal of Experimental Child Psychology, 83*, 77–110.

Gelman, S.A. (2003). *The essential child.* New York: Oxford University Press.

Lee, Y.T., Jussim, L.J., & McCauley, C.R. (Eds.). (1995). *Stereotype accuracy: Toward appreciating group differences.* Washington, DC: American Psychological Association.

Liben, L.S., & Signorella, M.L. (1980). Gender-related schemata and constructive memory in children. *Child Development, 51*, 11–18.

Martin, C.L., Ruble, D.N., & Szkrybalo, J. (2002). Cognitive theories of early gender role development. *Psychological Bulletin, 128*, 903–933.

Mervis, C., & Rosch, E. (1981). Categorization of natural objects. *Annual Review of Psychology, 32*, 89–115.

Patterson, M.M. (2007). *Negotiating (non) normality: Effects of consistency between views of one's self and one's social group.* Unpublished doctoral dissertation, University of Texas at Austin.

Patterson, M.M., & Bigler, R.S. (2006). Preschool children's attention to environmental messages about groups: Social categorization and the origins of intergroup bias. *Child Development, 77*, 847–860.

Pettigrew, T.F., & Tropp, L.R. (2000). Does intergroup contact reduce prejudice?: Recent meta-analytic findings. In S. Oskamp (Ed.), *Reducing prejudice and discrimination* (pp. 93–114). Mahwah, New Jersey: Erlbaum.

Rutland, A. (1999). The development of national prejudice, in-group favouritism and self-stereotypes in British children. *British Journal of Social Psychology, 38*, 55–70.

Tajfel, H., & Turner, J.C. (1986). The social identity theory of intergroup behaviour. In S. Worchel & W.G. Austin (Eds.), *Psychology of intergroup relations* (pp. 7–24). Chicago: Nelson.

Turner, J.C., Hogg, M.A., Oakes, P.J., Reicher, S.D., & Wetherell, M.S. (1987). *Rediscovering the social group: A self-categorization theory.* Oxford: Blackwell.

This article has been reprinted as it originally appeared in *Current Directions in Psychological Science*. Citation information for this article as originally published appears above.

Children's Social and Moral Reasoning About Exclusion

Melanie Killen[1]
University of Maryland

Abstract

Developmental research on social and moral reasoning about exclusion has utilized a social-domain theory, in contrast to a global stage theory, to investigate children's evaluations of gender- and race-based peer exclusion. The social-domain model postulates that moral, social-conventional, and personal reasoning coexist in children's evaluations of inclusion and exclusion, and that the priority given to these forms of judgments varies by the age of the child, the context, and the target of exclusion. Findings from developmental intergroup research studies disconfirm a general-stage-model approach to morality in the child, and provide empirical data on the developmental origins and emergence of intergroup attitudes regarding prejudice, bias, and exclusion.

Keywords

social reasoning; exclusion; intergroup attitudes; moral judgment

How early do individuals become capable of moral reasoning? What is the evidence for morality in the child? Over the past two decades, research on children's moral judgment has changed dramatically, providing new theories and methods for analysis. In brief, the change has been away from a global stage model toward domain-specific models of development. According to Kohlberg's foundational stage model of moral development (Kohlberg, 1984), which followed Piaget's research on moral judgment (Piaget, 1932), children justify acts as right or wrong first on the basis of consequences to the self (preconventional), then in terms of group norms (conventional), and finally in terms of a justice perspective in which individual principles of how to treat one another are understood (postconventional). This approach involved assessing an individual's general scheme (organizing principle) for evaluating social problems and dilemmas across a range of contexts.

By the mid-1980s, however, studies of contextual variation in judgments provided extensive evidence contesting broad stages (Smetana, 2006; Turiel, 1998). For example, young children's evaluations of transgressions and social events reflect considerations of the self, the group, and justice; these considerations do not emerge hierarchically (respectively) but simultaneously in development, each with its own separate developmental trajectory (e.g., self-knowledge, group knowledge, and moral knowledge). Thus, multiple forms of reasoning are applied to the evaluations of social dilemmas and interactions. Social judgments do not reflect one broad template or stage, such as Kohlberg's preconventional stage to characterize childhood morality. Instead, children use different forms of reasoning, moral, conventional, and psychological, simultaneously when evaluating transgressions and social events.

One area of recent empirical inquiry pertains to social and moral evaluations of decisions to exclude others, particularly on the basis of group membership (such as gender, race, or ethnicity), referred to as *intergroup exclusion*. What makes this form of exclusion a particularly compelling topic for investigation from a moral viewpoint is that it reflects, on the one hand, prejudice, discrimination, stereotyping, and bias about groups, and, on the other hand, judgments about fairness, equality, and rights (Killen, Lee-Kim, McGlothlin, & Stangor, 2002). Conceptually, these judgments are diametrically opposed; prejudice violates moral principles of fairness, discrimination violates equality, and stereotyping restricts individual rights. Do both forms of reasoning exist within the child? What do children do when confronted with an exclusion decision that involves moral considerations of fairness and equal treatment, on the one hand, and stereotypic and social-conventional expectations, on the other?

A social-domain model proposes that morality includes fairness, justice, rights, and others' welfare (e.g., when a victim is involved; "It wouldn't be fair to exclude him from the game"); social-conventional concerns involve conventions, etiquette, and customs that promote effective group functioning (e.g., when disorder in the group occurs; "If you let someone new in the group they won't know how it works or what it's about and it will be disruptive"); and psychological issues pertain to autonomy, individual prerogatives, and identity (e.g., acts that are not regulated but affect only the self; "It's her decision who she wants to be friends with"). Social-domain-theory approaches to moral reasoning, along with social-psychological theories about intergroup attitudes, provide a new approach to understanding social exclusion.

Social exclusion is a pervasive aspect of social life, ranging from everyday events (e.g., exclusion from birthday parties, sports teams, social organizations) to large-scale social tragedies (e.g., exclusion based on religion and ethnicity resulting in genocide). These forms of interindividual and intergroup exclusion create conflict, tension, and, in extreme cases, chronic suffering. In the child's world, exclusion has been studied most often in the context of interindividual, rather than intergroup, conflict. Research on peer rejection and victimization, for example, has focused on individual differences and the social deficits that contribute to being a bully (lack of social competence) or a victim (wariness, shyness, fearfulness; Rubin, Bukowski, & Parker, 1998). The findings indicate that the long-term consequences for children and adults who experience pervasive exclusion are negative, resulting in depression, anxiety, and loneliness.

DEVELOPMENTAL APPROACHES

Recently, developmental researchers have investigated children's evaluations of intergroup exclusion (e.g., "You're an X and we don't want Xs in our group"). Decisions to exclude others involve a range of reasons, from group norms and stereotypic expectations to moral assessments about the fairness of exclusion. Much of what is known about group norms has been documented by social psychologists, who have conducted extensive studies on intergroup relationships. The findings indicate that social categorization frequently leads to intergroup bias and that explicit and implicit attitudes about others based on group membership contribute to prejudicial and discriminatory attitudes and behavior (Dovidio, Glick, & Rudman, 2005). Few researchers, however, have examined the developmental trajectory of exclusion from a moral-reasoning perspective.

Social-domain theory has provided a taxonomy for examining the forms of reasoning—moral, social-conventional, and psychological—that are brought to bear on intergroup exclusion decisions. One way that a social-domain model differs from the traditional stage model of moral reasoning, as formulated by Kohlberg in the late 1960s, is that the former provides a theory and a methodology for examining how individuals use different forms of reasons when evaluating everyday phenomena.

SOCIAL REASONING ABOUT EXCLUSION

One of the goals of social-domain research is to identify the conditions under which children give priority to different forms of reasons when evaluating social decisions, events, and interactions. What are the major empirical findings on intergroup exclusion decisions by children? Most centrally, children do not use one scheme ("stage") to evaluate all morally relevant intergroup problems and scenarios; moreover, although some types of decisions are age related, others are not. In a study with children in the 1st, 4th, and 7th grades, the vast majority of students (95%) judged it wrong to exclude a peer from a group solely because of gender or race (e.g., a ballet club excludes a boy because he's a boy; a baseball club excludes a girl because she's a girl), and based their judgment on moral reasons, such as that such exclusion would be unfair and discriminatory (Killen & Stangor, 2001); there were no age-related differences, contrary to what a stage-model approach would predict.

Introducing complexity, however, revealed variation in judgments and justifications. As shown in Figure 1, in an equal-qualifications condition ("What if there was only room for one more to join the club, and a girl and a boy both were equally qualified, who should the group pick?"), most children used moral reasons ("You should pick the person who doesn't usually get a chance to be in the club because they're both equally good at it"); but in an unequal-qualification condition ("What if X was more qualified, who should the group pick?"), age-related increases in the use of social-conventional reasons ("The group won't work well if you pick the person who is not very good at it") were found. Young adolescents weighed individual merits and considered the functioning of the club or team. Qualifications (e.g., good at ballet or baseball) were considered to be more salient considerations than preserving the "equal opportunity" dimensions (e.g., picking a girl for baseball who has not had a chance to play).

In fact, how children interpret their group's ingroup and out-group norms (conventions) appears to be related to prejudice and bias (moral transgressions; Abrams, Rutland, Cameron, & Ferrell, in press). Abrams et al. (in press) showed that children's view of whether exclusion is legitimate or wrong was contingent on whether they viewed an individual as supporting or rejecting an ingroup-identity norm. In other related developmental intergroup research, children's lay theories (conventional knowledge) about what it means to work in a group, and whether effort or intrinsic ability is what counts, have been shown

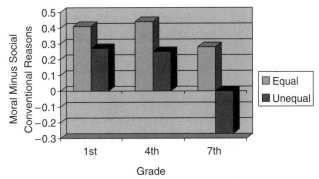

Fig. 1. Proportion of moral minus social-conventional reasons given by 1st, 4th, and 7th graders for peer-exclusion judgments based on gender or race. In one condition (equal), participants stated which of two children should be excluded from an after-school club with only one available opening when a stereotypical and nonstereotypical applicant both were equally qualified. In the other (unequal) condition, participants stated which child should be excluded if the child who fit the stereotype for that activity was also more qualified. After-school clubs were baseball/ballet and basketball/math, reflecting gender- and race-associated stereotypes, respectively. Reprinted from Killen & Stangor (2001).

to be significantly related to whether they view the denial of allocation of resources as fair or unfair (moral decision making); focusing on intrinsic ability in contrast to effort results in condoning prejudicial treatment (Levy, Chiu, & Hong, 2006). Moreover, adolescents' perceptions of the social status of membership in peer cliques (conventional knowledge) determine whether they view exclusion (e.g., excluding a "goth" from the cheerleading squad) as fair or legitimate (Horn, 2003). These findings demonstrate the nuanced ways in which children make judgments about groups and how group knowledge and group norms bear directly on moral judgments about exclusion and inclusion.

Research on intergroup contact in childhood provides information regarding how social experience influences the manifestation of children's stereotypes and conventional reasoning to justify exclusion. Intergroup-contact theory states that under certain conditions, contact with members of outgroups decreases prejudice (Pettigrew & Tropp, 2005). In a developmental study with participants enrolled in 13 public schools ($N = 685$) of varying ethnic diversity (see Fig. 2), European American students enrolled in heterogeneous schools were more likely to use explicit stereotypes to explain why interracial interactions make their peers uncomfortable, and were less likely to use moral reasons to evaluate peer exclusion, than were European Americans enrolled in homogeneous schools (Killen, Richardson, Kelly, Crystal, & Ruck, 2006). Children's positive experiences with students who are different from themselves, under certain conditions, facilitate moral reasoning about intergroup exclusion and suppress stereotypic expectations as a reason for an exclusion decision.

These findings support a domain-model view of social and moral judgment and challenge stage theory, which proposes that children are limited in their ability to make moral judgments by a general-processing scheme for assimilating information (their "stage"). From a stage view, one would expect children to use

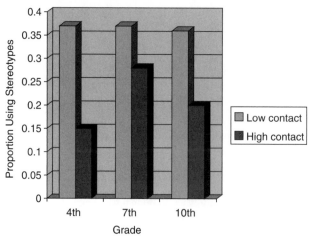

Fig. 2. Proportion of European American students who explicitly used stereotypes to explain what it is about interracial interactions that makes their peers uncomfortable, as a function of positive intergroup contact. Positive intergroup contact included cross-race friendship in classrooms, schools, and neighborhoods (based on data reported in Killen et al., 2006).

conventional or stereotypic (group-expectations) reasons, and expect older children to use moral reasons. Instead, researchers now find that children's reasoning varies by the context and a balance of priorities.

Context has many variables, and determining it involves investigating the role of the target of exclusion as well as participant variables (age, gender, race/ethnicity) on exclusion decisions. Regarding the target of exclusion, a series of findings reveals that gender exclusion is viewed as more legitimate than exclusion based on ethnicity, with more social-conventional reasons and stereotypic expectations used to support the former than the latter (Killen et al., 2002). As shown in Figure 3, children used fewer moral reasons to evaluate exclusion in a peer-group music context with a gender target ("What if the boys' music club will not let a girl join?") than with a race target ("What if the white students in a music club will not let a black student join?"). A significant proportion of students used social-conventional reasons, such as: "A girl/black student likes different music, so she/he won't fit in with the group." Not surprisingly, though, European American females, and minority participants (both males and females), were more likely to reject these forms of exclusion and to use moral reasons than were European American males. This inclusive orientation may be due to the perspective, empathy, and reciprocity that result from experiencing prior exclusion. Thus, these findings support social-domain-theory propositions that the target of exclusion is influential on evaluations of exclusion, and that specific types of peer experiences may contribute to judgments that exclusion is wrong.

Children reject atypical peers based on stigmatized group identity (Nesdale & Brown, 2004). This finding further indicates that peer experience with exclusion is an important variable for investigation. Nesdale and Brown propose that children who experience extensive exclusion may be at risk for demonstrating prejudicial behavior toward others, and for perpetuating a cycle of negative

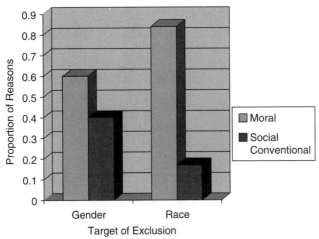

Fig. 3. Proportion of moral and social-conventional reasons for gender and racial targets of exclusion in peer-group contexts. Peer-group contexts referred to after-school music clubs that excluded a target child from joining the club due to his or her gender or race. Reasons were moral (unfairness) or social-conventional (group functioning; based on data from Killen, Lee-Kim, McGlothlin, & Stangor, 2002).

intergroup attitudes. At the same time, however, adolescents are cognizant of the wrongfulness of discrimination regarding stigmatized peers (Verkuyten & Thijs, 2002).

Although stereotypes and conventions are powerful forces that legitimize exclusion, there is also extensive evidence of how adolescents explain the wrongfulness of discrimination in terms of social justice. Social-reasoning categories provide evidence for the types of norms that children use to justify or reject exclusion decisions and for the conditions that promote children's change from a priority on morality to group functioning, which may, at times, occur at the expense of fairness.

NEW DIRECTIONS

Adults frequently use traditions and customs to justify exclusion. Tiger Woods' initial response to playing at the Augusta (Georgia) National Golf Club (host of the legendary Masters Tournament), which excludes women, was "That's just the way it is" (Brown, 2002)—categorized as social-conventional reasoning. More recently, Woods has stated, "Is it unfair? Yes. Do I want to see a female member? Yes" ("Woods Thinks Masters Debate Deserves a Private Meeting," 2005)—categorized as moral reasoning. Yet, he refuses to give up his participation in the event: "They're asking me to give up an opportunity to win the Masters three straight years" (Smith, 2003)—personal priority over the wrongfulness of exclusion. These quotes, which do not reflect coded responses from an in-depth systematic interview, nonetheless, reveal how an individual can give different priorities to exclusion decisions and how these priorities change depending on the context (Killen, Sinno, & Margie, in press). Social-conventional or personal reasons do not necessarily reflect a developmentally "primitive" response (as put forth by stage theory).

Are children moral? Yes, children demonstrate spontaneous and elaborated reasons for why it is wrong to exclude others based on group membership, referring to fairness, equality, and rights. Do children have stereotypes about others? Yes; how these stereotypes enter into moral decision making requires an in-depth analysis of how children weigh competing considerations, such as group functioning, traditions, customs, and cultural norms, when evaluating exclusion. What changes as children age is how these considerations are weighed, the contexts that become salient for children and adolescents, and the ability to determine when morality should take priority in a given situation.

What is not well known is how children's intergroup biases (those that are not explicit) influence their judgments about exclusion; what it is about intergroup contact that contributes to children's variation in reliance on stereotypes to evaluate exclusion; and how early intergroup attitudes influence children's awareness of justice, fairness, and equality. Given that stereotypes are very hard to change in adulthood, interventions need to be conducted in childhood. Understanding when children resort to stereotypic expectations is crucial information for creating effective interventions. Developmental findings on social reasoning about exclusion provide a new approach for addressing these complex issues in childhood and adulthood and for creating programs to reduce prejudice.

Recommended Reading

Aboud, F.E., & Amato, M. (2001). Developmental and socialization influences on inter-group bias. In R. Brown & S. Gaertner (Eds.), *Blackwell handbook of social psychology: Intergroup relations* (pp. 65–85). Oxford, England: Blackwell.

Gaertner, S.L., & Dovidio, J.F. (2000). *Reducing intergroup bias: The common ingroup identity model*. New York: Psychology Press.

Killen, M., Margie, N.G., & Sinno, S. (2006). Morality in the context of intergroup relationships. In M. Killen & J. Smetana (Eds.), *Handbook of moral development* (pp. 155–183). Mahwah, NJ: LEA.

Rutland, A. (2004). The development and self-regulation of intergroup attitudes in children. In M. Bennett & F. Sani (Eds.), *The development of the social self* (pp. 247–265). East Sussex, England: Psychology Press.

Turiel, E. (2002). *Culture and morality*. Cambridge, England: Cambridge University Press.

Acknowledgments—The author would like to thank Judith G. Smetana, Stefanie Sinno, and Cameron Richardson, for helpful comments on earlier drafts of this manuscript, and the graduate students in the Social and Moral Development Laboratory for collaborative and insightful contributions to the research reported in this paper. The research described in this manuscript was supported, in part, by grants from the National Institute of Child Health and Human Development (1R01HD04121-01) and the National Science Foundation (#BCS0346717).

Note

1. Address correspondence to Melanie Killen, 3304 Benjamin Building, Department of Human Development, University of Maryland, College Park, MD 20742-1131; e-mail: mkillen@umd.edu.

References

Abrams, D., Rutland, A., Cameron, L., & Ferrell, A. (in press). Older but wilier: Ingroup accountability and the development of subjective group dynamics. *Developmental Psychology*.

Brown, J. (2002, August 16). Should Woods carry the black man's burden? *The Christian Science Monitor* [electronic version]. Retrieved January 5, 2007, from http://www.csmonitor.com/2002/0816/p01s01-ussc.html

Dovidio, J.F., Glick, P., & Rudman, L. (Eds.). (2005). *Reflecting on the nature of prejudice: Fifty years after Allport*. Malden, MA: Blackwell.

Horn, S. (2003). Adolescents' reasoning about exclusion from social groups. *Developmental Psychology*, 39, 11–84.

Killen, M., Lee-Kim, J., McGlothlin, H., & Stangor, C. (2002). How children and adolescents evaluate gender and racial exclusion. *Monographs for the Society for Research in Child Development* (Serial No. 271, Vol. 67, No. 4). Oxford, England: Blackwell.

Killen, M., Richardson, C., Kelly, M.C., Crystal, D., & Ruck, M. (2006, May). *European-American students' evaluations of interracial social exchanges in relation to the ethnic diversity of school environments*. Paper presented at the annual convention of the Association for Psychological Science, New York City.

Killen, M., Sinno, S., & Margie, N. (in press). Children's experiences and judgments about group exclusion and inclusion. In R. Kail (Ed.), *Advances in child psychology*. New York: Elsevier.

Killen, M., & Stangor, C. (2001). Children's social reasoning about inclusion and exclusion in gender and race peer group contexts. *Child Development*, 72, 174–186.

Kohlberg, L. (1984). *Essays on moral development: Vol. 2. The psychology of moral development—The nature and validity of moral stages*. San Francisco: Harper & Row.

Levy, S.R., Chiu, C.Y., & Hong, Y.Y. (2006). Lay theories and intergroup relations. *Group Processes and Intergroup Relations*, 9, 5–24.

Nesdale, D., & Brown, K. (2004). Children's attitudes towards an atypical member of an ethnic ingroup. *International Journal of Behavioral Development*, 28, 328–335.

Pettigrew, T.F., & Tropp, L.R. (2005). Allport's intergroup contact hypothesis: Its history and influence. In J.F. Dovidio, P. Glick, & L. Rudman (Eds.), *Reflecting on the nature of prejudice: Fifty years after Allport* (pp. 262–277). Malden, MA: Blackwell.

Piaget, J. (1932). *The moral judgment of the child*. New York: Free Press.

Rubin, K.H., Bukowski, W., & Parker, J. (1998). Peer interactions, relationships and groups. In W. Damon (Ed.), *Handbook of child psychology: Vol. 3. Social, emotional, and personality development* (5th ed., pp. 619–700). New York: Wiley.

Smetana, J.G. (2006). Social domain theory: Consistencies and variations in children's moral and social judgments. In M. Killen & J.G. Smetana (Eds.), *Handbook of moral development* (pp. 119–154). Mahwah, NJ: Erlbaum.

Smith, T. (2003, February 20). A Master's challenge. *Online NewsHour*. Retrieved July 16, 2006, from http://www.pbs.org/newshour/bb/sports/jan-june03/golf_2-20.html

Turiel, E. (1998). The development of morality. In W. Damon (Ed.), *Handbook of child psychology: Vol. 3. Social, emotional, and personality development* (5th ed., pp. 863–932). New York: Wiley.

Verkuyten, M., & Thijs, J. (2002). Racist victimization among children in the Netherlands: The effect of ethnic group and school. *Ethnic and Racial Studies*, 25, 310–331.

Woods thinks Masters debate deserves a private meeting. (2005, February 14). *USA Today* [electronic version]. Retrieved January 10, 2007, from http://www.usatoday.com/sports/golf/2002-10-16-woodsmasters_x.htm

Peer Victimization in School: Exploring the Ethnic Context

Sandra Graham[1]

Department of Education, University of California, Los Angeles

Abstract

This article provides an overview of recent research on peer victimization in school that highlights the role of the ethnic context—specifically, classrooms' and schools' ethnic composition. Two important findings emerge from this research. First, greater ethnic diversity in classrooms and schools reduces students' feelings of victimization and vulnerability, because there is more balance of power among different ethnic groups. Second, in nondiverse classrooms where one ethnic group enjoys a numerical majority, victimized students who are members of the ethnic group that is in the majority may be particularly vulnerable to self-blaming attributions. The usefulness of attribution theory as a conceptual framework and ethnicity as a context variable in studies of peer victimization are discussed.

Keywords

peer victimization; attributions; ethnicity; ethnic diversity

A generation ago, if children and adolescents had been asked what they worried most about at school, they probably would have said passing their exams and being promoted to the next grade. Today, students' school concerns often revolve around safety, including the specter of peer victimization, as much as around achievement. Survey data indicate that anywhere from 40 to 80% of school-aged youth report that they personally have experienced victimization from peers, ranging from relatively minor instances of verbal abuse and intimidation to more serious forms of harassment, including assault, property damage, and theft (e.g., Nansel et al., 2001). Peer victimization is now recognized as a major public health concern, as the perpetrators of such abuse are perceived by many students as quite aggressive and the targets of their abuse report feeling quite vulnerable.

WHAT IS PEER VICTIMIZATION?

Peer victimization, also known as bullying or peer harassment (researchers tend to use these terms interchangeably), is defined as physical, verbal, or psychological abuse that takes place in and around school, especially in places where adult supervision is minimal. The critical features that distinguish victimization from simple conflict between peers are the intention to cause harm and an imbalance of power between perpetrator and victim (Olweus, 1993). Hitting, name calling, intimidating gestures, racial slurs, spreading of rumors, and exclusion from the group by powerful others are all examples of behaviors that constitute peer victimization. This definition of peer victimization does not include the more lethal sorts of peer-directed hostilities such as those seen in widely publicized school shootings. Although some of those shootings may have been precipitated by a history of peer abuse, they remain rare events. My focus here is on more typical and widespread types of peer harassment that affect the lives of many youth.

Research on the consequences of peer victimization confirms why it is a public health concern: A growing literature has documented that victims tend to have low self-esteem and to feel more lonely, anxious, and depressed than their nonvictimized peers do (see Juvonen & Graham, 2001). Victims also are disliked by their peers, particularly during the middle-school years. In general, early adolescents appear unsympathetic toward victims, who are often perceived to be responsible for their plight. Although studies linking victim status to academic achievement are fewer, there is evidence that victimization is associated with negative attitudes toward school or with poor performance as early as kindergarten and extending into the adolescent years (e.g., Schwartz, Gorman, Nakamoto, & Tobln, 2005). It is not difficult to imagine the chronic victim who becomes so anxious about going to school that she or he tries to avoid it at all costs.

THE ETHNIC CONTEXT OF PEER VICTIMIZATION

Most research on peer victimization has been conducted at the level of the individual. A common strategy involves first identifying students classified by peers as victims, as well as other behavior subtypes such as bullies and bully/victims, and then examining how those classifications map onto particular adjustment difficulties (e.g., Juvonen, Graham, & Schuster, 2003; Perry, Kusel, & Perry, 1988). Largely missing from that research is a focus on context, or the broader sociocultural milieu in which victimization unfolds. Contexts are the physical and social settings in which individuals develop, and some contextual factors include peer groups, ethnic groups, and classrooms. A good deal of peer-victimization research is conducted in urban schools where multiple ethnic groups are represented, but very little of that research has examined ethnicity-related context variables. This is disappointing because the factors that exacerbate or protect against peer victimization are likely influenced by such context factors as the ethnic composition of schools and neighborhoods, as well as the social and ethnic identities that are most significant to youth.

In our research, we have attempted to bring the ethnic context to the study of peer victimization. Figure 1 shows our conceptual model. We examine peer victimization from a social-cognitive perspective, which focuses on an individual's thoughts, perceptions, and interpretations of victimization as determinants of subsequent behavior. We are particularly interested in youth who make self-blaming attributions for victimization and how such attributions relate to specific adjustment outcomes. Attributions are answers to "why" questions: Why did I get picked on? Why doesn't anyone like me? (See Weiner, 1986.) We also examine the ways in which attributional processes are shaped by the ethnic context, specifically the ethnic composition of classrooms and schools. We do this in two ways. First, we investigate the ethnic context as an antecedent to both peer victimization and to related adjustment outcomes (paths a and b in Fig. 1). Second, we examine the ethnic context as a moderator of the relations between both victimization and adjustment (path c) and between victimization and self-blame (path d). Our model underscores the importance of causal beliefs as a theoretical

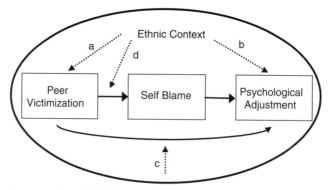

Fig. 1. Conceptual model of the relations between peer victimization, self-blame attributions, and psychological adjustment as moderated (paths a, b, c, and d) by the ethnic composition of schools and classrooms.

framework and of ethnicity as a central context variable for understanding the dynamics of peer victimization.

Ethnicity and the Antecedents of Peer Victimization

How might the ethnic context shed light on the factors that can increase or decrease perceived victimization and vulnerability? We hypothesized that greater diversity would lessen experiences with victimization and feelings of vulnerability because in diverse settings students belong to one of many ethnic groups who share a balance of power. We based this hypothesis on the definition of peer victimization as conflict that involves an imbalance of power between perpetrator and victim. Asymmetric power relations take many forms, as when stronger youth harass weaker classmates or when older students pick on younger peers. At the group level, an imbalance of power can also exist when members of majority ethnic groups (more powerful in the numerical sense) harass members of minority ethnic groups (less powerful in the numerical sense). When multiple ethnic groups are present and represented evenly, the balance of power is less likely to be tipped in favor of one ethnic group over another.

We examined how victimization and feelings of vulnerability vary as a function of school and classroom ethnic diversity (Juvonen, Nishina, & Graham, 2006). A large sample of 2,000 sixth-grade students was recruited from 99 classrooms in 11 different middle schools in metropolitan Los Angeles. The students self-identified as Latino (46%), African American (29%), Asian American (9%), Caucasian (9%), or multiethnic (7%). The middle schools that these students attended were carefully selected to vary in ethnicity such that five schools were predominantly Latino (more than 50%), three were predominantly African American, and three were ethnically diverse, with no single ethnic group constituting a 50% majority. Students reported on experiences with victimization and indicators of vulnerability using well-validated rating scales.

Ethnic diversity in the 99 classrooms and 11 schools was measured with an instrument adapted from the ethology literature, known as Simpson's index

(Simpson, 1949); it is a measure that captures both the number of different groups in a setting and the relative representation of each group. With scores ranging from 0 to approximately 1, Simpson's index was used to calculate the probability that any two students randomly selected from the same classroom or school will be from a different ethnic group. Higher scores reflected greater diversity (i.e., more ethnic groups that are relatively evenly represented, or a higher probability that two randomly selected students will be from different ethnic groups).

Figure 2 shows how students' self-reported victimization and feelings of vulnerability in the spring of sixth grade varied as a function of classroom diversity (the data on school-level diversity were almost identical). Plotted in the figure are the slopes predicting levels of vulnerability at high and low levels of classroom diversity. As diversity increased, self-reported victimization and loneliness decreased, whereas self-worth and perceived school safety increased. Thus, when there was a shared balance of power, students felt less vulnerable at school. Although a few studies in the literature have examined peer victimization in different ethnic groups (e.g., Hanish & Guerra, 2000), to my knowledge this is the first study to document the buffering effects of greater ethnic diversity.

Ethnicity and the Consequences of Peer Harassment

In the next set of analyses, we examined how the ethnic context influences the consequences of peer victimization (paths c and d in Fig. 1). Juvonen et al. (2006) revealed that as ethnic diversity decreased, students felt more vulnerable. In nondiverse contexts there are both a majority ethnic group and one or more minority ethnic groups. Is one group more vulnerable to the consequences of peer harassment than the other? It seems reasonable to think that members of

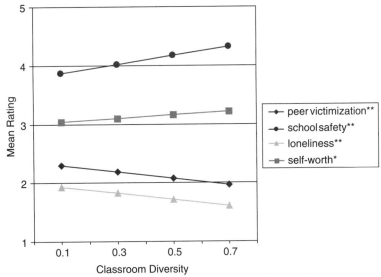

Fig. 2. Effects of classroom-level diversity on ratings of self-reported peer victimization, loneliness, self-worth, and perceived safety during spring of sixth grade (*$p < .05$, **$p < .001$; data from Juvonen, Nishina, & Graham, 2006).

the numerical-minority ethnic groups would be more vulnerable. That would be consistent with conventional wisdom, the way in which we think about an imbalance of power, and the reality that minority-group victims may have fewer same-ethnicity friends to either ward off potential harassers or buffer the consequences of victimization.

Yet, consider what it must be like to be both a victim and a member of a numerical-majority group. Having a reputation as a victim when one's ethnic group holds the numerical balance of power might be especially debilitating because that person deviates from what is perceived as normative for his or her group. Social psychologists have used the term *social misfit* to describe the negative outcomes of an individual whose problem social behavior deviates from group norms (Wright, Giammarino, & Parad, 1986).

Guided by the social-misfit analysis, we developed a two-part hypothesis. First we proposed that the relations between victim reputation and psychological adjustment would be stronger for students in our sample who were members of the ethnic majority group (path c in Fig. 1). That hypothesis was supported (Bellmore, Witkow, Graham, & Juvonen, 2004). As the number of same-ethnicity peers in one's classroom increased, the relations between victim status and the outcomes of social anxiety and loneliness increased.

In the second part of our hypothesis we turned to attributions as mediators of the relations between victimization and adjustment. When someone is a member of the majority ethnic group, repeated encounters with peer harassment, or even an isolated yet particularly painful experience, might lead that victim to ask, "Why me?" In the absence of disconfirming evidence, such an individual might come to blame him- or herself—concluding, for example, that "I'm the kind of kid who deserves to be picked on." Self-blame can then lead to many negative outcomes, including low self-esteem and depression. In the literature on causal explanations for adult rape (another form of victimization), attributions that imply personal deservingness—called characterological self-blame—are especially detrimental (Janoff-Bulman, 1979). From an attributional perspective, characterological self-blame is internal and therefore reflects on the self; it is stable and therefore leads to an expectation that harassment will be chronic; and it is uncontrollable, suggesting an inability to prevent future harassment. Attributions for social failure to internal, stable, and uncontrollable causes lead individuals to feel both hopeless and helpless. Several researchers have documented that individuals who make characterological self-attributions for negative outcomes cope more poorly, feel worse about themselves, and are more depressed than are individuals who attribute outcomes to their own actions (as opposed to character) (see Anderson, Miller, Riger, Dill, & Sedikides, 1994).

In earlier research we documented that victims of harassment were more likely than were nonvictims to endorse characterological self-blame and that they also felt more lonely and anxious at school (Graham & Juvonen, 1998). In the present multiethnic sample, we examined the mediating role of self-blame attributions and the possibility that relations between victim reputation, self-blame, and maladjustment would be moderated by classroom ethnic composition. We hypothesized that victims whose behavior deviated from local norms (i.e., victim status when one's group holds the numerical balance of power) would be particularly vulnerable to self-blaming attributions ("It must be me"). As the number of same-ethnicity peers increases in one's social milieu, external attributions that protect self-esteem become less plausible. On the other hand, being a victim and a member of the minority group should facilitate external attributions to the prejudice of others ("It could be them"). For minority ethnic-group members, we therefore expected weak relations between victim status, self-blaming tendencies, and adjustment. Finally, in ethnically diverse contexts, with a greater balance of power, we expected the most attributional ambiguity ("It might be me, but it could be them").

We identified groups of students who were members of the majority ethnic group in their classroom, who were members of a minority group, or who were in diverse classrooms with no majority group. Separately in each group, structural-equation modeling was performed to test relations between victimization, self-blame, and the maladjustment outcomes of depression and low self-esteem (Graham, Bellmore, Nishina, & Juvonen, 2006). As predicted, the strongest evidence for the relation between victim status and self-blame was documented for students who were members of the majority ethnic group, the weakest evidence was found for minority-group members, and students who were in ethnically diverse classrooms fell between these extremes.

CONCLUSION

The research presented here suggests that ethnicity is an important context variable for understanding the experiences of students who are victimized by their peers. Our sample included Latino, African American, Asian American, Caucasian, and multiracial students. Yet ethnic-group membershp per se was less relevant than ethnicity within a particular school context. No one ethnic group is more or less at risk for being the target of peer abuse. Rather, a more critical variable is whether an ethnic group does or does not hold the numerical balance of power. If one's ethnic group is the numerical majority that holds that balance of power, then one's construals about the causes of victimization are more likely to implicate the self. Being both a victim and a member of the ethnic majority group has its own unique vulnerability.

In contrast, ethnic diversity in context—where no one group holds the numerical balance of power—may have particular psychological benefits. We propose that ethnic diversity creates enough attributional ambiguity to ward off self-blaming tendencies while allowing for attributions that have fewer psychological costs. Attributional ambiguity has a somewhat different meaning in social-psychology research on stigma. Such research highlights the threats to self-esteem when individuals stigmatized due to the prejudice of others are unsure about whether to attribute negative outcomes to that prejudice or to their own personal shortcomings (e.g., Major, Quinton, & McCoy, 2002). But in social contexts where multiple social cues are present and multiple causal appraisals of social predicaments are possible, attributional ambiguity can be adaptive if it allows the perceiver to draw from a larger repertoire of causal schemes.

Although I focus on an attributional explanation, there surely are other factors that can explain the positive effects of classroom ethnic diversity. For example, perhaps teachers in more diverse classrooms do something different (e.g., addressing equity issues or promoting more cultural awareness) than teachers in nondiverse classrooms do. Or it could be that diversity fosters strong ethnic identity, which then acts as a buffer against general feelings of vulnerability. No doubt there are many other psychological benefits of multiethnic school environments, just as there are some contexts in which being a part of the ethnic-majority group has self-enhancing functions. These are questions for the future. For now, I hope that the conceptual analysis and research presented here will stimulate new ways to think about ethnicity in context, ethnic diversity, and coping with peer victimization. With creative ways to measure ethnic diversity, today's multiethnic urban schools provide ideal settings for studying the social-cognitive mediators and contextual moderators of the linkages between victimization and adjustment.

Recommended Reading

Juvonen, J., & Graham, S. (Eds.). (2001). (See References)
Olweus, D. (1993). (See References)
Sanders, C., & Phye, G. (Eds.). (2004). *Bullying: Implications for the classroom*. San Diego, CA: Elsevier.

Note

1. Address correspondence to Sandra Graham, Department of Education, University of California, Los Angeles, CA; e-mail: shgraham@ucla.edu.

References

Anderson, C., Miller, R., Riger, A., Dill, J., & Sedikides, C. (1994). Behavioral and characterological attributional styles as predictors of depression and loneliness: Review, refinement, and test. *Journal of Personality and Social Psychology, 66*, 549–558.

Bellmore, A., Witkow, M., Graham, S., & Juvonen, J. (2004). Beyond the individual: The impact of ethnic diversity and behavioral norms on victims' adjustment. *Developmental Psychology, 40*, 1159–1172.

Graham, S., Bellmore, A., Nishina, A., & Juvonen, J. (2006). Ethnic context and attributions for victimization. Manuscript submitted for publication.

Graham, S., & Juvonen, J. (1998). Self-blame and peer victimization in middle school: An attributional analysis. *Developmental Psychology, 34*, 587–599.

Hanish, L.D., & Guerra, N.G. (2000). The roles of ethnicity and school context in predicting children's victimization by peers. *American Journal of Community Psychology, 28*, 201–223.

Janoff-Bulman, R. (1979). Characterological and behavioral self-blame: Inquiries into depression and rape. *Journal of Personality and Social Psychology, 37*, 1798–1809.

Juvonen, J., & Graham, S. (Eds.). (2001). *Peer harassment in school: The plight of the vulnerable and the victimized*. New York: Guilford Press.

Juvonen, J., Graham, S., & Schuster, M. (2003). Bullying among young adolescents: The strong, the weak, and the troubled. *Pediatrics, 112*, 1231–1237.

Juvonen, J., Nishina, A., & Graham, S. (2006). Ethnic diversity and perceptions of safety in urban middle schools. *Psychological Science, 17*, 393–400.

Major, B., Quinton, W., & McCoy, S. (2002). Antecedents and consequences of attributions to discrimination: Theoretical and empirical advances. In M. Zanna (Ed.), *Advances in experimental social psychology* (Vol. 34, pp. 251–330). San Diego, CA: Academic Press.

Nansel, T., Overpeck, M., Pilla, R., Ruan, W., Simons-Morton, B., & Scheidt, P. (2001). Bullying behaviors among U.S. youth: Prevalence and association with psychosocial adjustment. *JAMA: The Journal of the American Medical Association, 285*, 2094–2100.

Olweus, D. (1993). *Bullying at school*. Malden, MA: Blackwell Publishers.

Perry, D., Kusel, S., & Perry, L. (1988). Victims of peer aggression. *Developmental Psychology, 24*, 807–814.

Schwartz, D., Gorman, A., Nakamoto, J., & Tobin, R. (2005). Victimization in the peer group and children's academic functioning. *Journal of Educational Psychology, 97*, 425–435.

Simpson, E. (1949). Measurement of diversity. *Nature, 163*, 688.

Weiner, B. (1986). *An attributional theory of motivation and emotion*. New York: Springer.

Wright, J., Giammarino, M., & Parad, H. (1986). Social status in small groups: Individual-group similarity and the "social misfit." *Journal of Personality and Social Psychology, 50*, 523–536.

This article has been reprinted as it originally appeared in *Current Directions in Psychological Science*. Citation information for this article as originally published appears above.

Understanding Popularity in the Peer System

Antonius H.N. Cillessen[1]
University of Connecticut

Amanda J. Rose
University of Missouri-Columbia

Abstract

Much research has focused on youth who are rejected by peers; who engage in negative behavior, including aggression; and who are at risk for adjustment problems. Recently, researchers have become increasingly interested in high-status youth. A distinction is made between two groups of high-status youth: those who are genuinely well liked by their peers and engage in predominantly prosocial behaviors and those who are seen as popular by their peers but are not necessarily well liked. The latter group of youth is well known, socially central, and emulated, but displays a mixed profile of prosocial as well as aggressive and manipulative behaviors. Research now needs to address the distinctive characteristics of these two groups and their developmental precursors and consequences. Of particular interest are high-status and socially powerful aggressors and their impact on their peers. The heterogeneity of high-status youth complicates the understanding of the social dynamics of the peer group, but will lead to new and important insights into the developmental significance of peer relationships.

Keywords

peer relations; popularity; social status

Developmental psychologists continue to be interested in the social structure and dynamics of the peer group in childhood and adolescence. Peer status is an important construct in their research. In the past, much of this research has been driven by a concern for children and adolescents with low social status, who operate at the fringe of the peer system and may be categorized as rejected. As a result, much has been learned about the origins of peer rejection and its effects on development (Asher & Coie, 1990). More recently, researchers have become increasingly interested in peer-group members with high social status. Interestingly, high-status children and adolescents do not form a uniform group.

For example, consider the profiles of two eighth graders, Tim and Jason. Tim is well liked by his peers. He is genuinely nice to others and helps out when needed. Tim is athletic but does not use his physical abilities to aggress against others. In fact, Tim tends to avoid even verbal confrontations when possible, preferring instead to find prosocial ways of solving conflicts. Compared with Tim, Jason is better known by his classmates but he is not necessarily well liked. Even peers who do not know him personally know who he is. Many of Jason's classmates imitate his style of dress and taste in music and would like to be better friends with him so they could be part of the in-crowd. Jason can be very nice to other kids but can also in-timidate them when provoked or angry, or can manipulate social situations to his advantage.

Developmental psychologists know a fair amount about youth like Tim. Youth who are well liked by others are categorized by peer-relations researchers as *sociometrically popular*. Sociometrically popular youth generally display high levels of prosocial and cooperative behavior and low levels of aggression (Rubin, Bukowski, & Parker, 1998). But although developmentalists would refer to Tim as sociometrically popular, he is not the type of person most youth would consider one of their "popular" peers. They think of popular peers as those who, like Jason, are well known, socially central, and emulated (Adler & Adler, 1998). In recent years, developmentalists have begun to study more seriously youth like Jason, referring to them as *perceived popular*, rather than sociometrically popular. Although evidence suggests that perceived-popular youth have aggressive traits in addition to prosocial ones, youth aspire to be popular like Jason more than they aspire to be like Tim (Adler & Adler, 1998). Accordingly, it is important to consider seriously the meaning and function of these divergent forms of popularity.

In this article, we consider how perceived-popular youth are similar to and different from sociometrically popular youth. Specifically, we discuss: (a) the conceptualization and measurement of sociometric and perceived popularity, (b) the social behavior of sociometrically and perceived-popular youth, and (c) the adjustment outcomes for the two groups. We conclude by outlining important directions for future research.

SOCIOMETRIC VERSUS PERCEIVED POPULARITY

Traditionally, the study of peer relations has focused on sociometric status, how well liked (or rejected) youth are by their peers (Asher & Coie, 1990; Coie & Cillessen, 1993). Several decades of research have provided data on the behavioral and adjustment correlates of sociometric status (Kupersmidt & Dodge, 2004). This research provides a crucial foundation for understanding peer relations.

Recently, researchers have begun to examine perceived popularity as a unique but equally important dimension. Educational sociologists have long recognized the social power (influence over others) of perceived-popular youth as evidenced by qualitative descriptions of them by their peers (Adler & Adler, 1998; Eder, 1985). Only in the past 5 to 10 years have researchers begun to study perceived popularity with quantitative methods.

Sociometric popularity is usually assessed with a peer-nomination procedure, in which participants are asked to name the peers in their grade who they like most and like least. Nominations for each question are counted and adjusted for grade size so that the data are comparable across grades (Coie, Dodge, & Coppotelli, 1982). Sociometric popularity for each person is represented with a score on a continuous scale (social preference) calculated by using the number of liked-most nominations minus the number of liked-least nominations he or she received. Alternatively, rather than using such scores, researchers may employ a categorical approach and identify sociometrically popular youth as those with many liked-most and few liked-least nominations.

In early qualitative research, educational sociologists using ethnographic methods identified perceived-popular youth by simply observing which classmates were referred to as popular by their peers (Adler & Adler, 1998; Eder, 1985). In recent quantitative studies, however, perceived popularity has been derived from peer nominations (i.e., participants name who they see as most popular and who they see as least popular; Cillessen & Mayeux, 2004; LaFontana & Cillessen, 2002; Parkhurst & Hopmeyer, 1998; Rose, Swenson, & Waller, 2004). Scores on a continuous scale of perceived popularity have been derived from the number of most-popular nominations or the number of most-popular minus least-popular nominations. In other studies, researchers have taken a categorical approach and identified youth with high perceived popularity as those with many most-popular nominations and few least-popular nominations. Interestingly, in neither the original ethnographic research nor the recent quantitative studies did researchers provide participants with an a priori definition of popularity; rather, they relied on the participants' intuitive understanding of the concept. Recently, researchers have begun to map the meanings children and adolescents ascribe to "popularity," again without providing an a priori definition (e.g., LaFontana & Cillessen, 2002). Findings from these studies show that children and adolescents associate a mixture of prosocial and antisocial traits and behaviors with perceived popularity.

Although there is overlap between sociometric and perceived popularity, the constructs are not redundant (LaFontana & Cillessen, 2002; Rose et al., 2004). Consider one study that employed a categorical approach to identify sociometrically popular and perceived-popular youth (Parkhurst & Hopmeyer, 1998). Only 36% of sociometrically popular students were also perceived popular, and only 29% of perceived-popular students were also sociometrically popular. There is enough distinction between the two constructs to determine similarities as well as differences between the characteristics of sociometrically popular and perceived-popular youth.

BEHAVIORAL PROFILES

Research on the behavioral profiles of sociometrically and perceived-popular youth has revealed similarities and differences. Both kinds of youth are found to be prosocial and cooperative. However, whereas sociometrically popular youth score very low on aggression, perceived popularity is positively associated with aggression (see Rubin et al., 1998, for a review of the behavioral profiles of sociometrically popular youth).

In quantitative studies on how perceived popularity correlates with behavior, researchers have typically measured overt and relational aggression separately. Overt aggression refers to physical assaults and direct verbal abuse. Relational aggression is aimed at damaging relationships and includes behaviors such as ignoring or excluding a person and spreading rumors (Crick & Grotpeter, 1995). Both overt and relational aggression are related to perceived popularity. For example, Parkhurst and Hopmeyer (1998) found that youth who were perceived popular but not sociometrically popular were overtly aggressive. Rodkin, Farmer, Pearl, and Van Acker (2000) empirically discriminated a subgroup of "model" popular youth with high scores for affiliative (e.g., friendly) behaviors and low scores for overt aggression from a subgroup of "tough" popular youth with high scores for overt aggression and average scores for affiliative behavior. Studies in which both overt and relational aggression were assessed and in which perceived popularity was measured as a continuous variable demonstrated positive associations of both forms of aggression with perceived popularity (LaFontana & Cillessen, 2002; Rose et al., 2004).

Why would presumably aversive aggressive behaviors be associated with high status as indicated by perceived popularity? It may be that some children or adolescents use aggression in certain situations (e.g., when publicly provoked) or against certain people (e.g., competitors for social status) strategically to achieve or maintain perceived popularity. For example, perceived-popular youth may use overt or relational aggression to intimidate and deter competitors or other youth who in some way threaten their social standing. Consistent with this idea, a study by Vaillancourt, Hymel, and McDougall (2003) revealed an association between bullying and perceived popularity. Moreover, perceived-popular youth use a strategic combination of both aggressive and prosocial behaviors to manipulate peers in ways that result in high status (Hawley, 2003).

Recent longitudinal research supports the hypothesis that some youth deliberately act aggressively to enhance their perceived popularity. This research also suggests an especially important association between relational aggression and perceived popularity. In a 5-year longitudinal study (Cillessen & Mayeux, 2004), relational aggression was found to be more strongly related to later perceived popularity than was overt aggression. Similarly, another study (Rose et al., 2004) found that relational aggression was more strongly related to perceived popularity 6 months later than was overt aggression. Overt aggression may be related to perceived popularity because youth can display dominance through overtly aggressive acts. However, relational aggression may be especially effective for managing social power. For example, by selectively excluding others, youth may influence who is in the popular crowd and keep out those who threaten their social status. Engaging in other relationally aggressive behaviors, such as spreading rumors, affords one a degree of anonymity and therefore the opportunity to strategically hurt other people while hiding the appearance of being mean.

Research further indicates that the relation between aggression and perceived popularity may vary by age and gender. In our research, we found positive associations between overt and relational aggression and perceived popularity in 12- to 15-year-old adolescents (grades 6–9), but not in 9- to 11-year-old children (grades 3–5). This shift coincided with the transition from elementary school to middle school and may have been due to the fact that the social skills required to act aggressively in ways that lead to high status are complex and develop with age (LaFontana & Cillessen, 2002; Rose et al., 2004).

We also found that the link between relational aggression and perceived popularity was stronger for girls than for boys (Cillessen & Mayeux, 2004; Rose et al., 2004). Figure 1 illustrates this finding for data collected in eighth grade (Cillessen & Mayeux, 2004), but the pattern was similar across grades six through nine. As can be seen in Figure 1, relational aggression was positively associated with perceived popularity for both boys and girls but was a particularly strong predictor of high status for girls.

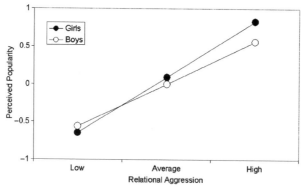

Fig. 1. Perceived popularity of girls and boys who exhibit low, average, and high levels of relational aggression (Cillessen & Mayeux, 2004).

ADJUSTMENT OUTCOMES

An important reason for studying peer relations is that experiences with peers may be predictive of personal adjustment. Accordingly, much research has addressed how sociometric status correlates with adjustment, and the research consistently indicates that sociometric popularity is predictive of positive adjustment both concurrently and in the future (Rubin et al., 1998). For example, sociometrically popular youth tend to be well adjusted emotionally and to have high-quality friendships.

Considerably less is known about the adjustment of perceived-popular youth. Previous research on status and behavior in the peer group leads to opposing expectations. On the one hand, because aggression is associated with behavior problems, one would expect similar behavior problems for popular youth who are aggressive. On the other hand, because high status in the peer group is associated with being well adjusted, one would expect that perceived popularity, even if achieved through aggressive means, is associated with positive adjustment. The limited evidence available at this time seems to favor the second expectation—that perceived popularity has immediate rewards (Hawley, 2003) without concurrent negative consequences (Rodkin et al., 2000). Hawley's (2003) research indicates that a mixture of prosocial behavior and coercive or aggressive behavior makes youth effective at getting what they want in social contexts. And the tough popular youth identified by Rodkin and his colleagues (2000) did not demonstrate elevated symptoms, such as depression or anxiety. The contradictory expectations may be reconciled if perceived-popular and aggressive youth experience benefits in the immediate social context of the adolescent peer group, but pay a price in terms of their long-term adjustment beyond adolescence.

Thus, we hypothesize that for perceived-popular youth, short-term advantages may be combined with long-term disadvantages. Establishing whether this is true will require long-term follow-up studies of such youth. Just as there are tough and model high-status subgroups (Rodkin et al., 2000), there may be two diverging developmental paths that popular youth follow into young adulthood. In one path, perceived-popular youth may continue to be influential and serve in leadership roles in later peer groups. In the other, they may no longer be socially central and successful when they move into new social contexts that have different reward structures and different criteria for social prominence. Which of these two pathways an individual follows may depend on whether he or she is able to strike the optimal, delicate balance between prosocial and Machiavellian behaviors, to gain both social preference as well as influence in new groups. Discovering how this balance may be achieved developmentally and how it may affect what pathway is followed in later life is an exciting avenue for future research.

CONCLUSIONS

Decades of research on sociometric popularity have produced consistent and important findings with potential practical application. Recent research suggests that the complex construct of perceived popularity needs to be incorporated into this research. Given all that is known about the negative developmental consequences of aggression, researchers need to learn why aggression sometimes leads to high status in the form of perceived popularity. Moreover, it will be important to learn whether aggressive perceived-popular youth are on a positive or negative developmental trajectory. Although they seem to benefit in the short term in the immediate social context of the peer group, the longer-term outcomes associated with their status and behavior are not yet known.

Researchers also must learn about the impact of perceived-popular aggressors on the development and adjustment of their peers. Of particular concern are youth who are victimized by them. The negative consequences of victimization may be exacerbated when the aggressor is socially central and powerful and therefore can easily engage other people in the victimization. Furthermore, perceived-popular youth may influence the development of antisocial behavior among their peers. Because perceived-popular youth are emulated, their antisocial or risky behaviors may disperse through the peer group especially quickly. Clearly, the function and impact of popularity in the peer context are complex; learning more about these processes will be challenging, but will yield important new insights into the social dynamics of peer groups across the life span.

Recommended Reading

Adler, P.A., & Adler, P. (1998). (See References)
Asher, S.R., & Coie, J.D. (1990). (See References)
Kupersmidt, J.B., & Dodge, K.A. (Eds.). (2004). (See References)

Note

1. Address correspondence to Antonius H.N. Cillessen, Department of Psychology, University of Connecticut, 406 Babbidge Rd., U-1020, Storrs, CT 06269-1020; e-mail: antonius.cillessen@uconn.edu.

References

Adler, P.A., & Adler, P. (1998). *Peer power: Preadolescent culture and identity*. New Brunswick, NJ: Rutgers University Press.
Asher, S.R., & Coie, J.D. (1990). *Peer rejection in childhood*. New York: Cambridge University Press.

Cillessen, A.H.N., & Mayeux, L. (2004). From censure to reinforcement: Developmental changes in the association between aggression and social status. *Child Development, 75*, 147–163.

Coie, J.D., & Cillessen, A.H.N. (1993). Peer rejection: Origins and effects on children's development. *Current Directions in Psychological Science, 2*, 89–92.

Coie, J.D., Dodge, K.A., & Coppotelli, H. (1982). Dimensions and types of social status: A cross-age perspective. *Developmental Psychology, 18*, 557–570.

Crick, N.R., & Grotpeter, J.K. (1995). Relational aggression, gender, and social-psychological adjustment. *Child Development, 66*, 710–722.

Eder, D. (1985). The cycle of popularity: Interpersonal relations among female adolescents. *Sociology of Education, 58*, 154–165.

Hawley, P.H. (2003). Prosocial and coercive configurations of resource control in early adolescence: A case for the well-adapted Machiavellian. *Merrill-Palmer Quarterly, 49*, 279–309.

Kupersmidt, J.B., & Dodge, K.A. (Eds.). (2004). *Children's peer relations: From development to intervention to policy.* Washington, DC: American Psychological Association.

LaFontana, K.M., & Cillessen, A.H.N. (2002). Children's stereotypes of popular and unpopular peers: A multi-method assessment. *Developmental Psychology, 38*, 635–647.

Parkhurst, J.T., & Hopmeyer, A.G. (1998). Sociometric popularity and peer-perceived popularity: Two distinct dimensions of peer status. *Journal of Early Adolescence, 18*, 125–144.

Rodkin, P.C., Farmer, T.W., Pearl, R., & Van Acker, R. (2000). Heterogeneity of popular boys: Antisocial and prosocial configurations. *Developmental Psychology, 36*, 14–24.

Rose, A.J., Swenson, L.P., & Waller, E.M. (2004). Overt and relational aggression and perceived popularity: Developmental differences in concurrent and prospective relations. *Developmental Psychology, 40*, 378–387.

Rubin, K.H., Bukowski, W.M., & Parker, J.G. (1998). Peer interactions, relationships, and groups. In W. Damon (Series Ed.) & N. Eisenberg (Vol. Ed.), *Handbook of child psychology: Vol. 3. Social, emotional, and personality development* (5th ed., pp. 619–700). New York: Wiley.

Vaillancourt, T., Hymel, S., & McDougall, P. (2003). Bullying is power: Implications for school-based intervention strategies. In M.J. Elias & J.E. Zins (Eds.), *Bullying, peer harassment, and victimization in the schools: The next generation of prevention* (pp. 157–176). New York: Haworth Press.

Section 5: Critical Thinking Questions

1. Some school districts have recently established single-sex science or math classes within otherwise co-educational schools. Drawing from the articles by Martin and Ruble and by Bigler and Liben, what are some possible consequences? Now suppose a boy wants to join the "girls" science class in one of these schools. Based on your reading of the article by Killen, what arguments might you expect to hear from (a) children and (b) teachers for or against his being allowed to join the class? What position would you take on this matter?

2. The articles by Cillessen and Rose and by Graham both focus on peer relations. They differ, however, in their substantive focus (focusing on popularity vs. victimization, respectively) and in their level of analysis (focusing primarily on the level of the individual vs. the social context, respectively). How might each of these programs of work inform the other? Would you expect that findings concerning popularity would be different if they were studied in contexts that differ with respect to ethnic diversity? Would contexts that exaggerate social group differences (e.g., those outlined by Bigler & Liben) be likely to affect the patterns of popularity and victimization?

This article has been reprinted as it originally appeared in *Current Directions in Psychological Science*. Citation information for this article as originally published appears above.

Section 6: Cultural Contexts

Earlier sections have made clear that developmental outcomes are influenced by the immediate groups with which the individual interacts (family and social groups) and, in passing, have demonstrated effects of the broader environment as well. The articles in the current section focus explicitly on the role of culture, ranging from thinking about culture in the broadest sense of human culture (contrasting humans and chimpanzees), to culture in the sense of national culture (contrasting Western and East Asian culture), and culture in the narrower sense of sub-groups within a community (contrasting cultures of poverty and affluence within the United States).

In the first article, Michael Tomasello begins with yet another reminder about the nature-nurture debate by contrasting biological versus cultural theories to explain development. He considers the notion of human culture at the broad level by asking if and how *human* culture differs from the social structure of other species. Specifically, he contrasts the ways human infants and chimpanzees differ in how they learn from others. Tomasello reviews evidence showing that only human learning is affected by understanding others' intentionality, and explores the consequences for individuals and the culture more generally.

Mary Gauvain also takes a broad view of culture. Among other points, she offers many specific examples of ways in which the tools and artifacts available in a particular culture (e.g., the availability of an abacus vs. Roman numerals vs. Arabic notation) provide very different environments in which individual children develop. As she correctly reminds us, it is useful to consider historical change and cross-cultural contexts to help avoid the assumption that the local, contemporary circumstances define the conditions in which all individuals develop.

In the third article, Denise Park and Angela Gutchess address issues at the intersection of culture and biology by studying cognitive development over a large portion of the lifespan (from young adulthood through old age). They begin by describing some of the same observations about cognitive aging reported by Salthouse (see section III), distinguishing between cognitive hardware or mechanics (e.g., speed, working memory) and software or acquired knowledge (e.g., vocabulary). They then review empirical work on cognitive functioning of individuals from Western and East Asian cultures, concluding that culture has relatively little impact on cognitive mechanics, but considerable impact on knowledge-based structures.

The remaining two articles examine culture at a finer-grained level of analysis. Nancy Hill and Lorraine Taylor discuss how children's school achievement may be affected by the family's school involvement, and how that involvement, in turn, varies across cultural, economic, and community contexts. They review work establishing the positive effects of family involvement with schools, enumerate factors that predict greater levels of involvement (e.g., higher levels of parental education, shared ethnic and cultural backgrounds between families and teachers), and offer suggestions for interventions to enhance involvement and promote better child outcomes.

Suniya Luthar and Shawn Latendresse focus on a sub-culture typically assumed to be at low risk for developmental outcomes—children from affluent homes. The idea of vulnerability in this population is startling given that risk is more typically associated with limited financial or educational resources. Yet, the work reviewed by Luthar and Latendresse leads to the conclusion that affluent, suburban students show a variety of problems (e.g., high levels of depression and drug use). After reviewing some of the factors that appear to be responsible for these outcome (e.g., high pressure for achievement, isolation from adults), they discuss data showing evidence for continuing problems later in life, and offer some suggestions for interventions.

Culture and Cognitive Development

Michael Tomasello[1]
*Max Planck Institute for Evolutionary Anthropology,
Leipzig, Germany*

Abstract

Human beings are biologically adapted for culture in ways that other primates are
not. The difference can be clearly seen when the social learning skills of humans and
their nearest primate relatives are systematically compared. The human adaptation
for culture begins to make itself manifest in human ontogeny at around 1 year of age
as human infants come to understand other persons as intentional agents like the
self and so engage in joint attentional interactions with them. This understanding
then enables young children (a) to employ some uniquely powerful forms of cultural
learning to acquire the accumulated wisdom of their cultures, especially as embodied in language, and also (b) to comprehend their worlds in some uniquely powerful
ways involving perspectivally based symbolic representations.

Keywords

culture; cognition; human evolution; language; joint attention

Until fairly recently, the study of children's cognitive development was dominated
by the theory of Jean Piaget. Piaget's theory was detailed, elaborate, comprehensive, and, in many important respects, wrong. In attempting to fill the theoretical
vacuum created by Piaget's demise, developmental psychologists have sorted
themselves into two main groups. In the first group are those theorists who emphasize biology. These neonativists believe that organic evolution has provided human
beings with some specific domains of knowledge of the world and its workings and
that this knowledge is best characterized as "innate." Such domains include, for
example, mathematics, language, biology, and psychology.

In the other group are theorists who have focused on the cultural dimension
of human cognitive development. These cultural psychologists begin with the
fact that human children grow into cognitively competent adults in the context
of a structured social world full of material and symbolic artifacts such as tools
and language, structured social interactions such as rituals and games, and cultural institutions such as families and religions. The claim is that the cultural
context is not just a facilitator or motivator for cognitive development, but rather
a unique "ontogenetic niche" (i.e., a unique context for development) that actually structures human cognition in fundamental ways.

There are many thoughtful scientists in each of these theoretical camps. This
suggests the possibility that each has identified some aspects of the overall theory
that will be needed to go beyond Piaget and incorporate adequately both the cultural and the biological dimensions of human cognitive development. What is
needed to achieve this aim, in my opinion, is (a) an evolutionary approach to the
human capacity for culture and (b) an ontogenetic approach to human cognitive
development in the context of culture.

CHIMPANZEE AND HUMAN CULTURE

It is widely agreed among behavioral biologists that the best examples of animal culture come from chimpanzees. For example, different chimpanzee communities have been documented to have different tool-use traditions, such as termite-fishing, ant-fishing, ant-dipping, nut-cracking, and leaf-sponging (Tomasello & Call, 1997). Some of these community differences are due to the different local ecologies of different groups of chimpanzees. The individuals of each group learn to solve the problems presented by their local environment using the resources available in that environment.

But experimental studies have shown that there is more to it than this; chimpanzees can learn things from observing others using tools. What they learn, however, is less than might be expected. They learn the effects on the environment that can be produced with a particular tool; they do not actually learn to copy another chimpanzee's behavioral strategies. For example, in one study, chimpanzees were presented with a rakelike tool and an out-of-reach object. The tool could be used in either of two ways to obtain the object. One group of chimpanzees observed one way of using the tool, and another group observed the other way. However, the demonstration observed had no effect on which method or methods the chimpanzees used to obtain the object. This kind of learning is called emulation learning. In contrast, when human children were given this same task, they much more often imitatively learned the precise technique demonstrated for them (see Tomasello, 1996, for a review). Studies of chimpanzee gestural communication have found similar results. Young chimpanzees ritualize signals with group mates over repeated encounters in which they essentially shape one another's behavior. They do not learn the signals of group mates via imitation (Tomasello et al., 1997).

Chimpanzees and other nonhuman animals may thus engage in some forms of cultural transmission, defined very broadly as the nongenetic transfer of information, but they do not do this by means of imitative learning if this is defined more narrowly as the reproduction of another individual's actual behavioral strategy toward a goal. In contrast, human beings learn from conspecifics by perceiving their goals and then attempting to reproduce the strategies the other persons use in attempting to achieve those goals—truly cultural learning, as opposed to merely social learning (Tomasello, Kruger, & Ratner, 1993).

This small difference in learning process leads to a huge difference in cultural evolution; specifically, only cultural learning leads to cumulative cultural evolution in which the culture produces artifacts—both material artifacts, such as tools, and symbolic artifacts, such as language and Arabic numerals—that accumulate modifications over historical time. Thus, one person invents something, other persons learn it and then modify and improve it, and then this new and improved version is learned by a new generation—and so on across generations. Imitative learning is a key to this process because it enables individuals to acquire the uses of artifacts and other practices of their social groups relatively faithfully, and this relatively exact learning then serves as a kind of ratchet—keeping the practice in place in the social group (perhaps for many generations) until some creative innovation comes along. Each human child, in using these artifacts to mediate its interactions with the world, thus grows up in the context of something like the accumulated wisdom of its entire social group, past and present.

HUMAN CULTURAL LEARNING

The human adaptation for cultural learning is best seen ontogenetically and in the context of infants' other social and cognitive activities. The key transition occurs at 9 to 12 months of age, as infants begin to engage in interactions that are triadic in the sense that they involve the referential triangle of child, adult, and some outside entity to which they are both attending. Thus, infants at this age begin to flexibly and reliably look where adults are looking (gaze following), use adults as emotional reference points (social referencing), and act on objects in the way adults are acting on them (imitative learning)—in short, 1-year-olds begin to "tune in" to the attention and behavior of adults toward outside entities. At this same age, infants also begin to use communicative gestures to direct adult attention and behavior to outside entities in which *they* are interested—in short, to get the adult to "tune in" to them. Most often, the term joint attention has been used to characterize this whole complex of triadic social skills and interactions, and it represents a revolution in the way infants understand other persons. There is evidence that infants can begin to engage in joint attentional interactions only when they understand other persons as intentional agents like themselves, that is, as persons who have behavioral and perceptual goals and make active choices among the means for attaining those goals (Carpenter, Nagell, & Tomasello, 1998). (I understand attention to be intentional focusing on one aspect of experience to the exclusion of others.)

This social-cognitive revolution at 1 year of age sets the stage for the 2nd year of life, in which infants begin to imitatively learn the use of all kinds of tools, artifacts, and symbols. For example, in a study by Meltzoff (1988), 14-month-old children observed an adult bend at the waist and touch his head to a panel, thus turning on a light. They followed suit. Infants engaged in this unusual and awkward behavior even though it would have been easier and more natural for them simply to push the panel with their hand. One interpretation of this behavior is that the infants understood that (a) the adult had the goal of illuminating the light and then chose one means for doing so, from among other possible means, and (b) if they had the same goal, they could choose the same means. Cultural learning of this type thus relies fundamentally on infants' tendency to identify with adults, and on their ability to distinguish in the actions of others the underlying goal and the different means that might be used to achieve it. This interpretation is supported by Meltzoff's (1995) more recent finding that 18-month-old children also imitatively learn actions that an adult intends to perform, even if she is unsuccessful in doing so. Similarly, my colleagues and I (Carpenter, Akhtar, & Tomasello, 1998) found that 16-month-old infants imitatively learned from a complex behavioral sequence only those behaviors that appeared intentional, ignoring those that appeared accidental. Young children do not just mimic the limb movements of other persons; rather, they attempt to reproduce other persons' intended, goal-directed actions in the world.

Although it is not obvious at first glance, something like this same imitative learning process must happen if children are to learn the symbolic conventions of their native language. In some recent experiments, we have found that children learn words in situations in which they must work fairly hard to discern the adult's communicative intentions. For example, one study involved an adult playing a "finding game" with children. The adult had each child find four different objects in four different hiding places, one of which was a very distinctive toy barn. Once the child had learned which objects went with which places, the adult announced her intention to "find the gazzer." She then went to the toy barn, but it turned out to be "locked." She then frowned at the barn and proceeded to extract other objects from the other hiding places. Later, the children demonstrated that they had learned "gazzer" as the name of the object locked in the barn. What is significant about this finding is that the children knew which one was the gazzer even though they never saw the target object after they heard the new word; they had to infer from the adult's behavior (trying to get into the barn and frowning when it was impossible) which object she wanted, without even seeing the object (see Tomasello, in press, for a review).

This kind of learning can be referred to as cultural learning because the child is not just learning things *from* other persons but is learning things *through* them—in the sense that he or she must know something of the adult's perspective on a situation in order to learn the same intentionally communicative act (Tomasello et al., 1993). The adult in the study just described is not just moving and picking up objects randomly, she is searching for an object, and the child must know this in order to make enough sense of her behavior to connect the new word to its intended referent. An organism can engage in cultural learning of this type only when it understands others as intentional agents like the self who have a perspective on the world that can be entered into, directed, and shared. Indeed, a strong argument can be made that children can understand a symbolic convention in the first place only if they understand their communicative partner as an intentional agent with whom one may share attention—because a linguistic symbol is nothing other than a marker for an intersubjectively shared understanding of a situation (Tomasello, in press). Thus, children with autism do not understand other persons as intentional agents, or they do so to only an imperfect degree, and so (a) they are very poor at the imitative learning of intentional actions in general, (b) only half of them ever learn any language at all, and (c) those who do learn some language are very poor in word-learning situations such as those just described (Hobson, 1993).

It is important to emphasize as well that when children learn linguistic symbols, what they are learning is a whole panoply of ways to manipulate the attention of other persons, sometimes on a single entity, on the basis of such things as

- generality (*thing, furniture, chair, desk chair*),
- perspective (*chase-flee, buy-sell, come-go, borrow-lend*), and
- function (*father, lawyer, man, American; coast, shore, beach*).

And there are many other perspectives that arise in grammatical combinations of various sorts (*She smashed the vase* vs. *The vase was smashed*). Consequently, as children internalize a linguistic symbol—as they learn the human perspective embodied in that symbol—they not only cognitively represent the perceptual or motoric aspects of a situation, but also cognitively represent one way, among other ways of which they are also aware, that the current situation may be attentionally construed by "us," the users of the symbol. The perspectival nature of linguistic symbols thus represents a clear break with straightforward perceptual or sensory-motor cognitive representations, and indeed this perspectivity is what gives linguistic symbols their awesome cognitive power (Tomasello, 1999). It even allows children to learn linguistic means for conceptualizing objects as actions (*He porched the newspaper*), actions as objects (*Skiing is fun*), and many other metaphorical construals (*Love is a journey*).

CULTURAL COGNITION

The biological origin of human culture is an adaptation that occurred at some point in human evolution—probably quite recently, in the past 150,000 years, with the rise of modern humans. It was not an everyday adaptation, however, because it did not just change one relatively isolated characteristic, it changed the process of human evolution. It did this most immediately by changing the nature of human social cognition, which in turn changed the nature of human cultural transmission, which in turn led to a series of cascading sociological and psychological events in historical and ontogenetic time. The new form of social cognition that started the entire process was the understanding of other persons as intentional agents like the self, and the new process of cultural transmission was the various forms of cultural learning, the first and most important of which was imitative learning (the others are instructed learning and collaborative learning). These new forms of cultural learning created the possibility of a kind of ratchet effect in which human beings not only pooled their cognitive resources contemporaneously, but also built on one another's cognitive inventions over time. This new form of cultural evolution thus created artifacts and social practices with a "history." The most important artifact in this connection is language, the acquisition of which leads to some new forms of perspectivally based (i.e., symbolic) cognitive representation. Modern human cognition is thus a result not just of processes of biological evolution, but also of cultural processes that human biological evolution made possible in both cultural-historical time and ontogenetic time.

Recommended Reading

Boesch, C., & Tomasello, M. (1998). Chimpanzee and human culture. *Current Anthropology, 39*, 591–604.
Carpenter, M., Nagell, K., & Tomasello, M. (1998). (See References)
Tomasello, M. (1999). (See References)
Tomasello, M., & Call, J. (1997). (See References)
Tomasello, M., Kruger, A., & Ratner, H. (1993). (See References)

Note

1. Address correspondence to Michael Tomasello, Max Planck Institute for Evolutionary Anthropology, Inselstrasse 22, D-04103 Leipzig, Germany; e-mail: tomas@eva.mpg.de.

References

Carpenter, M., Akhtar, N ., & Tomasello, M. (1998). 14- through 18-month-old infants differentially imitate intentional and accidental actions. *Infant Behavior and Development, 21*, 315–330.

Carpenter, M., Nagell, K., & Tomasello, M. (1998). Social cognition, joint attention, and communicative competence from 9 to 15 months of age. *Monographs of the Society for Research in Child Development, 63*(4, Serial No. 255).

Hobson, P. (1993). *Autism and the development of mind*. Hillsdale, NJ: Erlbaum.

Meltzoff, A. (1988). Infant imitation and memory: Nine-month olds in immediate and deferred tests. *Child Development, 59*, 217–225.

Meltzoff, A. (1995). Understanding the intentions of others: Re-enactment of intended acts by 18-month-old children. *Developmental Psychology, 31*, 838–850.

Tomasello, M. (1996). Do apes ape? In J. Galef & C. Heyes (Eds.), *Social learning in animals: The roots of culture* (pp. 319–346). New York: Academic Press.

Tomasello, M. (1999). *The cultural origins of human cognition*. Cambridge, MA: Harvard University Press.

Tomasello, M. (in press). Perceiving intentions and learning words in the second year of life. In M. Bowerman & S . Levinson (Eds.),*Language acquisition and conceptual development*. New York: Cambridge University Press.

Tomasello, M., & Call, J. (1997). *Primate cognition*. New York: Oxford University Press.

Tomasello, M., Call, J., Warren, J., Frost, T ., Carpenter, M., & Nagell, K. (1997). The ontogeny of chimpanzee gestural signals: A comparison across groups and generations. *Evolution of Communication, 1*, 223–253.

Tomasello, M., Kruger, A., & Ratner, H. (1993). Cultural learning. *Behavioral and Brain Sciences, 16*, 495–552.

Cognitive Development in Social and Cultural Context

Mary Gauvain[1]
Department of Psychology, University of California at Riverside, Riverside, California

Abstract

The development of thinking is discussed from a sociocultural perspective. Three features of the social and cultural context that play important roles in organizing and directing cognitive development are presented and illustrated empirically: (a) activity goals and values of the culture, (b) material and symbolic tools for satisfying cultural goals and values, and (c) higher level structures that instantiate cultural goals and values in everyday practices. The article concludes with a discussion of the utility of this approach for advancing understanding of human intellectual growth.

Keywords

cognitive development; sociocultural influences; sociohistorical approach

In all societies throughout the world, most children grow up to be competent members of their communities. This impressive phenomenon—and indeed it is impressive—relies on some inherent human ability to develop intellectual and social skills adapted to the circumstances in which growth occurs. It also relies on social and cultural practices that support and maintain desired patterns of development. This article focuses on two questions pertaining to this process. First, how do children develop the skills and knowledge to become competent members of their community? Second, how are cultures uniquely suited to support and lead this development? To address these questions, I discuss culturally devised ways for supporting the development and maintenance of valued cultural skills. Several areas of research are foundational to the ideas presented here.

The first influence is a cultural-practice view of cognition (Chaiklin & Lave, 1996), which includes research on situated learning, everyday cognition, and practical intelligence. This work takes as a starting point the idea that people learn to think in specific contexts in which human activity is directed toward practical goals. An important contribution of this work is attention to the coordination between the thinker and the actions performed. The main limitation for present purposes is that it concentrates on learning rather than development. A second influence is the sociohistorical tradition (Cole, 1996), which emphasizes the role of material, symbolic, and social resources in organizing and supporting mental growth. The primary contribution of this approach is attention to the opportunities and constraints for cognitive development provided by the cultural community in which growth occurs. A practical limitation is that this idea, to date, has been broad in conception, touching on many aspects of psychological development. An organizational framework that links this approach more systematically to contemporary domains of research is needed for further examination and incorporation into the field. A final influence is the concept of the *developmental niche* (Super & Harkness, 1986), which characterizes the psychological structure of the human ecosystem that guides children's development. The central idea is that it is not only the organism that provides structure and direction to development; rather, culture also possesses structure and direction, and it is through the conjoining of these two organized systems that human development unfolds. Super and Harkness proposed three subsystems of the developmental niche, physical and social settings, customs of child care, and psychology of the caregiver. These subsystems concentrate on social development. In this review, I extend this basic framework to the study of cognitive development.

THREE COGNITIVE SUBSYSTEMS
OF THE DEVELOPMENTAL NICHE

Three subsystems of the developmental niche that connect cognitive development to culture are the activity goals and values of the culture and its members; historical means for satisfying cultural goals and values, especially the material and symbolic tools that support thinking and its development; and higher level structures that instantiate cultural goals and values in everyday practice and through which children become participants in the intellectual life of their community. These subsystems are hierarchically organized, from the microanalytic level (i.e., the level of individual psychological activity) to the broader social circumstances of development. A key point is the range of human experience represented: Culture penetrates human intellectual functioning and its development at many levels, and it does so through organized individual and social practices.

Activity Goals and Values of the Culture

Human behavior and thinking occur within meaningful contexts as people conduct purposeful, goal-directed activities (Vygotsky, 1978). The developmental implication is that children learn about and practice thinking in the course of participating in goal-directed activities—activities defined and organized by the cultural community in which development occurs. Much psychological research has focused on the organized, goal-directed nature of human activity (e.g., Duncker's classic studies of functional fixedness[2] and Bartlett's studies of memory), so this basic idea is not new. However, a cultural psychological approach offers two unique contributions: (a) an emphasis on the connection between activity structures (the means and goals that define human action) and the cultural practices from which they stem and (b) an examination of the relations among activity structures, cultural practices, and cognitive growth.

Research on children's everyday mathematics illustrates this linkage. Studies of the mathematical skills of Brazilian children who sell candy in the street (Carraher, Carraher, & Schliemann, 1985) indicate that mental activity reflects the practices that individuals engage in, that these practices are defined by cultural convention and routine, and that mathematical activities are handled differently, and more successfully, when the goal of the calculation is meaningful than when it is not. Another example is found in how intelligent behavior changes following social reorganization. Inkeles and Smith (1974) observed industrialization in non-Western communities and found that one behavioral change was greater concern with time and planning activities in advance. The point is not that Westerners plan and non-Westerners do not. What occurred was a reorganization of cultural practices that, in turn, led to the reorganization of a cognitive behavior, planning.

The main point is that activities and the goals that guide them are expressions of culture. Focusing on the cultural context of human activity may advance understanding of how the human mind is organized over the course of development to fit with the requirements and opportunities of the culture. Incidentally, this point may offer insight into the issue of transfer or generalization of cognitive skills across different task contexts, a topic that has vexed psychologists for generations. Psychologists have often sought transfer by focusing on isomorphic tasks (i.e., tasks that are very similar in structure). However, the key psychological linkage supporting transfer may not be task properties per se, but may instead be the meaning and goals of an activity and how a culture has devised ways, such as problem-solving routines, to achieve these goals and connect human action over time and space.

Material and Symbolic Tools

Material and symbolic tools, or artifacts (Cole, 1996), are developed and used by cultural communities to support mental activity. Such tools not only enhance thinking but also transform it, and in so doing, they channel cognitive development in unique ways. Involvement with more experienced cultural members, who demonstrate and convey the use of these tools, is a critical part of this process. Through the use of such "tools for thinking," a person's mental functioning acquires an organized link to sociohistorically formulated means of thinking transmitted through these tools.

Research on the use of particular cultural tools and the development of mathematical thinking illustrates this point. Children who are skilled at using the abacus employ a "mental abacus" when calculating solutions in their heads (Hatano, Miyake, & Binks, 1977), and this skill enhances mental calculation. Historical examination lends further insight into this process (Swetz, 1987). Late in the 12th century, a book by Leonardo of Pisa, who was also known as Fibonacci, introduced Hindu-Arabic notation and described the commercial applications of this system. This idea was picked up by Italian merchants in the next century and led to changes in conventions of calculating. At the time, Roman numerals were used, and large calculations were executed on the counting board, a form of abacus. These boards were very large, hard to transport, and difficult to use. Extensive training was needed to reach competence, and only a few people could do the calculations or check them for correctness. Hindu-Arabic numerals were entirely different. Far less equipment was needed to calculate with this system—ink and paper sufficed. This equipment was easy to transport, and, more important, it was easy to teach and learn. In a brief period of time, the long-established form of calculation was replaced. Although the Hindu-Arabic system limited the need for mental calculation, it helped lay the foundation for further developments in mathematics, especially in areas like number theory, in that calculations can be represented on paper and reexamined for patterns and structure (Swetz, 1987).

How does this historical case relate to the findings about skilled abacus users? Think again about mental calculation, a cognitive process that research indicates is aided by skill with the abacus. What this history tells us is that the shift from Roman to Hindu-Arabic numerals made mental calculation largely obsolete, as well as less valued, because calculating on paper allowed people to demonstrate their solution steps. It appears that differential skill of people who do and do not use the abacus may have origins in the notation shift introduced in the 13th and 14th centuries. The mathematical skills of experts are consistent with the requirements of the apparatus and the practice their notation systems afford.

The main point is that cultural tools and the thinking they support are not independent but merged. To describe thinking by concentrating on one and not the other is to ignore part of the problem-solving process. Too often in psychological research when tools of thinking are described, they are treated as entities outside the head, and therefore not part of, or at least not central to, the cognitive process being investigated. However, such thinking tools, both material and symbolic, are constituent elements of cognition and its development. The historical example suggests that many of the concepts considered fundamental to human cognition in the domains in which artifacts play important roles have not always been in place, at least not in the way they are conceptualized today. Certain tools of thought came into being at various points during human history, and these influenced thinking in extraordinary ways. These historical "changes of mind" may be illuminating for scholars interested in cognitive development. Although historical analysis is of limited use to psychologists for many reasons, such cases may be helpful for demonstrating an organized link among artifacts, social processes, and the mind that is often difficult to see in the more local, contemporary circumstances in which psychologists usually do their research.

Higher Level Structures and Practices

Organized social practices or conventions allow people to share their knowledge with one another. These structures help connect members of a community to each other and to a shared system of meaning. Examples of the connection between cognitive development and cultural ways of organizing and communicating knowledge exist in the developmental literature. Research on scripts, which are "outlines" of common, recurrent events (Nelson & Gruendel, 1981), treats the acquisition of culturally organized knowledge as a critical developmental achievement. Research on the development of other pragmatic conventions, such as skill at describing large-scale space (Gauvain & Rogoff, 1989) as if one is being taken on an imagined walk through it (a "mental tour"), also suggests that one important aspect of development is the increasing alignment of knowledge with the conventions of the community in which development occurs.

An intriguing question is whether these conventional forms influence the process of thinking and its development. There is far less data on this question. However, an interesting series of studies by Levinson (1996) in an Australian

Aboriginal community, the Guugu Yimithirr, is relevant. To describe spatial location, the language used in this community does not rely on relativistic terms, like left and right, but on absolute or fixed directional terms, like north, south, windward, and upstream. How do these speakers encode spatial information? In one study, objects were positioned on a table in a windowless, nondescript room. Each participant studied these placements, was then taken to a similar room that was oriented differently, and asked to place the same set of objects on a table so as to duplicate the placements in the first room. Participants placed the items in ways that respected the cardinal directions of the original placements (i.e., an object placed on the north side of the table was placed on the north, even though this would mean that it would be on the "other side" of an object to an observer using relative position as a guide). Although these results do not specify the cognitive processes underlying this behavior, they suggest that performance on tasks involving spatial cognition involves the coordination of visual and linguistic encoding in ways related to practices of the cultural community.

Another set of higher level structures related to the development of thinking appears in practices of social interaction. In recent years, there has been extensive research on the influence of social interaction on cognitive development, with much of this work based on Vygotsky's (1978) notion of the zone of proximal development, which is defined as the distance between an individual's attained level of development and the individual's potential level of development that may be reached by guidance and support from others (see Rogoff, 1990). Results from this research support the claim that intelligence, especially in the early years, develops largely through social experiences. For example, when Tessler and Nelson (1994) tested the recall of 3- to 3½-year-old children about a visit they took to a museum with their mothers, none of the children recalled any information that they had seen in the museum but not discussed with their mothers. Dyadic interaction with adults or peers is only one form of social exchange that may determine young children's opportunities for cognitive development in social context. Parents also influence children's learning via the practical routines they adopt to organize children's behaviors and by regulating the composition of children's social groups. Beyond the family and peer group, cognitive development is influenced by children's participation in more formal social institutions, especially school, and by opportunities to observe more competent cultural members as they engage in cognitive activities, a process Lave and Wenger (1991) call legitimate peripheral participation.

The point is that cognitive development occurs in and emerges from social situations. Conventions for organizing and conveying knowledge, as well as social practices within which knowledge is displayed and communicated, are an inherent aspect of thinking. For research to advance, these social systems need to be connected in a principled way to the developmental processes they help organize, as well as to the cultural system of meaning and practice they represent.

CONCLUSIONS

In summary, a sociocultural view of cognitive development enhances understanding of this psychological process. Dimensions of culture are realized in human action, and it is possible to specify and study these dimensions in relation to psychological development. They can bring the social and cultural character of intellectual development into relief. Understanding culture and cognitive development can be advanced via research designed for this purpose as well as by reexamining findings extant in the literature.

All this said, many hard questions remain. One concerns how to understand and describe individual skill that emerges in and is displayed in social situations. Psychologists have yet to devise a language for describing thinking that is not entirely in the head of the child or is only partially in place (i.e., evident only in some circumstances). Haith (1997) pointed out that many of the cognitive skills that children develop are defined in dichotomous terms. Consider mental representations. Representations are typically understood as something that a person either has or does not have (i.e., as states of understanding rather than as processes), and rarely as something that is partially or incompletely achieved. Such conceptualization may suffice in describing the mature thinker, though this is an open question. But it is surely inadequate for describing the development of knowledge that appears in the form of "partial understanding," such as that located in social performance. Thus, in order to incorporate the notion of partial or socially contextualized intellectual accomplishments into an understanding of cognitive development, we need a different conceptualization of many cognitive skills.

The analysis of culture in all aspects of psychological functioning is likely to increase dramatically in the next decade. How psychologists, especially those interested in intellectual development, will address this concern is unclear. Perhaps by developing conceptual frameworks, such as the one presented here, in which social and cultural systems of interacting and supporting psychological functions are an inextricable part of human behavior and development, this task may be eased.

Recommended Reading

Cole, M. (1996). (See References)

Gauvain, M. (1995). Thinking in niches: Sociocultural influences on cognitive development. *Human Development, 38*, 25–45.

Goodnow, J.J. (1990). The socialisation of cognition. In J.W. Stigler, R.A. Shweder, & G. Herdt (Eds.), *Cultural psychology* (pp. 259–286). New York: Cambridge University Press.

Nelson, K. (1990). *Language in cognitive development: The emergence of the meditated mind*. Cambridge, England: Cambridge University Press.

Rogoff, B. (1998). Cognition as a collaborative process. In W. Damon (Series Ed.) & D. Kuhn & R.S Siegler (Vol. Eds.), *Handbook of child psychology: Vol. 2. Cognition, perception, and language* (pp. 679–744). New York: John Wiley and Sons.

Notes

1. Address correspondence to Mary Gauvain, Department of Psychology, University of California at Riverside, Riverside, CA 92521; e-mail: mary.gauvain@ucr.edu.

2. Functional fixedness is a problem-solving phenomenon in which people have difficulty seeing alternate uses for common objects.

References

Carraher, T.N., Carraher, D.W., & Schliemann, A.D. (1985). Mathematics in the streets and in schools. *British Journal of Developmental Psychology, 3*, 21–29.

Chaiklin, S., & Lave, J. (1996). *Understanding practice: Perspectives on activity and context.* Cambridge, England: Cambridge University Press.

Cole, M. (1996). *Cultural psychology.* Cambridge, MA: Harvard University Press.

Gauvain, M., & Rogoff, B. (1989). Ways of speaking about space: The development of children's skill at communicating spatial knowledge. *Cognitive Development, 4*, 295–307.

Haith, M.M. (1997, April). *Who put the cog in infant cognition? Is rich interpretation too costly?* Paper presented at the biennial meeting of the Society for Research in Child Development, Washington, DC.

Hatano, G., Miyake, Y., & Binks, M. (1977). Performance of expert abacus operators. *Cognition, 9*, 47–55.

Inkeles, A., & Smith, D.H. (1974). *Becoming modern.* Cambridge, MA: Harvard University Press.

Lave, J., & Wenger, E. (1991). *Situated learning: Legitimate peripheral participation.* New York: Cambridge University Press.

Levinson, S.C. (1996). Frames of reference and Molyneux's question: Crosslinguistic evidence. In P. Bloom, M.A. Peterson, L. Nadel, & M.F. Garrett (Eds.), *Language and space* (pp. 109–169). Cambridge, MA: MIT Press.

Nelson, K., & Gruendel, J. (1981). Generalized event representations: Basic building blocks of cognitive development. In M.E. Lamb & A.L. Brown (Eds.), *Advances in developmental psychology* (Vol. 1, pp. 131–158). Hillsdale, NJ: Erlbaum.

Rogoff, B. (1990). *Apprenticeship in thinking.* New York: Oxford University Press.

Super, C.M., & Harkness, S. (1986). The developmental niche: A conceptualization at the interface of child and culture. *International Journal of Behavioral Development, 9*, 545–569.

Swetz, F.J. (1987). *Capitalism and arithmetic.* La Salle, IL: Open Court.

Tessler, M., & Nelson, K. (1994). Making memories: The influence of joint encoding on later recall. *Consciousness and Cognition, 3*, 307–326.

Vygotsky, L.S. (1978). *Mind in society.* Cambridge, MA: Harvard University Press.

This article has been reprinted as it originally appeared in *Current Directions in Psychological Science*. Citation information for this article as originally published appears above.

The Cognitive Neuroscience of Aging and Culture

Denise Park[1]
University of Illinois at Urbana-Champaign

Angela Gutchess
Harvard University, and The Athinoula A. Martinos Center for Biomedical Imaging

Abstract

Research into the cognitive neuroscience of aging has revealed exciting and unexpected changes to the brain over the lifespan. However, studies have mostly been conducted on Western populations, raising doubts about the universality of age-related changes. Cross-cultural investigation of aging provides a window into the stability of changes with age due to neurobiology, as well as into the flexibility of aging due to life experiences that impact cognition. Behavioral findings suggest that different cultures process distinct aspects of information and employ diverse information-processing strategies. The study of aging allows us to identify those age-related neural changes that persist across cultures as well as the changes that are driven by culture-specific life experiences.

Keywords

cognition; aging; culture; cognitive neuro-science

There is compelling evidence for differences in cognitive function as a result of culture (Nisbett & Masuda, 2003). Behavioral evidence suggests that, because of cultural norms that focus on relationships and group function, East Asians develop a bias to monitor their environment more than Westerners do, resulting in greater attention to context (such as a picture's background) and more holistic encoding of stimuli. In contrast to East Asians, the individualistic society of Westerners produces a bias to attend more to focal objects and to engage in more analytic information processing (reviewed by Nisbett & Masuda, 2003).

In the present paper, we examine what is known and what can be learned about cognitive processes and human development from a joint exploration of culture and aging variables, and we show how neuroscience approaches to this issue can be particularly informative. The joint examination of cultural differences in a lifespan sample of adults permits an assessment of the interplay of experience (through culture) with neurobiology (through aging) in sculpting the neurocognitive system. Neuro-imaging data indicate that the aging brain is different from the young adult brain, with the former continuously changing and adapting to its diminished efficiency (Reuter-Lorenz & Lustig, 2005). When aged brains show broad similarities across cultures in terms of neural recruitment patterns and structural integrity, we can be almost certain that these changes, relative to young brains, represent biological aging. If older adults, however, exhibit differences in neural circuitry and activation as a function of culture, this is likely because of experience and gives us a window into the plasticity of the aging neurocognitive system. Relatively little is known, behaviorally or neurally, about cultural differences in cognitive aging. The extant data involves contrasts between Western and East Asian cultures, and thus we limit our discussion to these cultures.

BEHAVIORAL EVIDENCE FOR DIFFERENCES IN COGNITIVE PROCESSES AS A FUNCTION OF AGE AND CULTURE

When one examines behavioral data on cognitive aging, the picture is one of decreased efficiency in basic cognitive processes such as speed, working memory, and long-term memory, although knowledge remains preserved or even grows (see Fig. 1). A framework for understanding the joint impact of culture and aging on cognition was proposed by Park, Nisbett, and Hedden (1999), taking into account these different cognitive domains. Park et al. (1999) propose that it is important to consider the distinction (discussed by Baltes, 1987) between basic cognitive hardware or *mechanics*—such as speed, working memory, and inhibition—and acquired knowledge (described as software or cognitive *pragmatics*) in understanding the impact of culture on cognitive aging. Park et al. (1999) suggest that when young adults evidence cultural differences in cognitive pragmatics, the differences will magnify with age, because they are based on acquired knowledge and older adults have more experience with the culture than younger adults do. Conversely, differences in basic processes (mechanics) that occur in young people will be minimized with age, as age-related decreases in capacity will operate to limit flexibility in mental operations, resulting in more similarity across

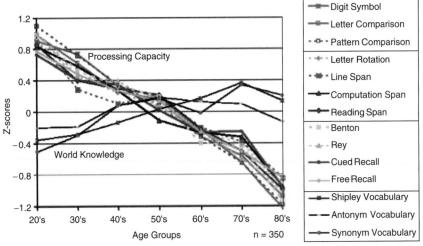

Fig. 1. The aging mind, showing regular decreases in various measures of processing capacity (including speed of processing, working memory, and long-term memory measures) but maintenance, or perhaps even augmentation, of knowledge of the world (as measured by vocabulary tests) over the lifespan. Adapted from "Models of visuospatial and verbal memory across the adult life span," by D.C. Park, G. Lautenschlager, T. Hedden, N.S. Davidson, A. Smith, and P.K. Smith, 2002, *Psychology & Aging, 17*, p. 305. Copyright 2002 by the American Psychological Association. Adapted with permission.

cultures with age. Research on old and young Chinese and Americans have provided some support for this model. For example, Hedden et al. (2002) studied backward digit span, which assesses participants' ability to manipulate a series of numbers in working memory and to repeat the numbers back in the reverse order in which they were originally presented. For this cognitive mechanic, the researchers found larger culture differences in young people than in old people. In contrast, Gutchess, Yoon, et al. (in press) examined the use of strategies for categorical clustering in a memory task (a strategy largely based on world knowledge) and found larger culture differences in old people than in young people.

Although cultural differences in cognition do exist, the behavioral evidence to date suggests that the impact of aging on cognitive mechanics is much greater than the impact of culture. Park et al. (1999) conducted a large study of young and old Chinese and Americans, and collected multiple measures of speed and working memory. They developed separate structural models for each of the four groups and found larger differences in the structural models due to age than due to culture. Similarly, in a study of source memory, in which subjects recalled the identity of speakers presenting facts in a video, no differences in source memory were observed as a function of culture, but large age differences were reported (Chua, Chen, & Park, in press). Likewise, elderly adults of both cultures recalled similar numbers of words in a free-recall task and recalled significantly fewer words than young people of both cultures did, even though American elderly evidenced greater use of a categorical clustering strategy (Gutchess, Yoon et al., in press).

The relatively modest impact of culture and the strong effects of age on cognitive mechanics suggest that biological aging primarily drives age-related differences in resource-demanding, strategic functions. In contrast to these findings, the impact of culture, relative to age, on knowledge-based structures shows almost a complete reversal, with culture assuming a much larger role than age. In a recent study, Yoon et al. (2004) provided young and old Chinese and young and old Americans with the names of 105 categories. Subjects provided five exemplars for each category, providing a careful mapping of category structure as a function of age and culture. The results indicated that there were only 13 categories that were culturally equivalent across both age groups. Category exemplars were far more similar across age groups within a culture. Thus, in the development of knowledge structures, culture is much more important than age, suggesting that discriminating between types of cognitive processes is critical to understanding the impact of culture on cognitive aging. (Complete norms for categories, as well as for picture naming, which have been used in other studies, are available online at http://agingmind.cns.uiuc.edu/ourresearch_cfdb.html.)

PATTERNS OF NEUROCOGNITIVE AGING

Neuroimaging techniques have added to our understanding of the aging mind. Consistent with behavioral data showing decreases in cognitive function (see Fig. 1), structural brain imaging reveals that the frontal cortex and, to a lesser extent, the medial temporal cortex exhibit significant loss of volume with age. In the face of declines in many cognitive systems, one might expect that neural activation would systematically decrease, paralleling the behavioral changes. Functional neuroimaging, however, has revealed that the aging brain is a dynamic system and that when young and old adults perform the same task, (a) neural activation is distributed across more brain sites and structures in old adults compared to young adults, (b) older adults frequently engage the same region in two hemispheres for tasks in which younger adults activate only one hemisphere, and (c) sometimes older adults show greater activation than young adults in the identical neural regions (Reuter-Lorenz & Lustig, 2005). Advances in neuroimaging have been largely responsible for views suggesting that the aging brain has residual plasticity, or cognitive reserve that can be utilized to reorganize neural circuitry to respond to the challenge of neurobiological aging.

Coincident with evidence that the brain responds to the challenge of neuro-biological aging by reorganizing are neuro-imaging findings suggesting that neural structures may develop or change in response to sustained exposure to stimuli or repetitive events. For example, merely 3 months of juggling training increased grey matter, relative to the brains of nonjugglers (Draganski et al., 2004)—increases that were maintained 3 months later without additional juggling practice.

DEVELOPING A COGNITIVE NEUROSCIENCE OF CULTURE AND AGING

Evidence that experience affects neural functions and structures leads logically to the notion that differences in cultural values and customs could affect development of neural activation patterns, as well as create differences in the size of various neural structures (Park & Gutchess, 2002). In the first exploration of cultural differences in neural function, we hypothesized that East Asians and Westerners would differentially engage neural hardware in the ventral visual cortex that is specialized for processing different elements of a scene. Using functional magnetic resonance imaging (fMRI), we found that Americans showed more engagement of object-processing areas in the ventral visual cortex than did Chinese (Gutchess, Welsh, Bod-uroglu, & Park, in press). This pattern is consistent with behavioral evidence that Westerners show a bias to process object information whereas East Asians preferentially process background information (Nisbett & Masuda, 2003). In a later fMRI study, we presented young and old Singaporeans of Chinese descent with complex pictorial scenes and examined how specialized areas within the ventral visual cortex adapted to repetition of different elements of the scene. We found that the old Singaporean adults showed less activation than young adults did in object-processing areas (the lateral occipital complex), but old and young adults engaged background processing structures (the parahippocampus) equally (Chee et al., 2006). We then tested a matching group of young and old Americans to determine whether, as our cultural theories would predict, old Sing-aporeans showed less activation of object-processing structures than old Americans did. Preliminary results suggest that young Singaporeans and Americans showed relatively similar engagement of all of these specialized structures, but old Singaporeans showed a larger object-processing deficit than old Americans did, suggesting that cultural differences in neural response magnified over the lifespan. These data, combined with behavioral data revealing that East Asians show more eye fixations on backgrounds than on objects (Chua, Boland, & Nisbett, 2005), suggest that after a lifetime of culturally biased information processing the neural circuitry for looking at scenes may be sculpted in a culturally biased way.

We should note that cross-cultural neuroimaging research has many unique challenges. We are sensitive to the possibility that we could find cultural differences in neural activation due to data collection from different magnets (one in the United States and one in Singapore). To address this concern, we have conducted exhaustive studies of differences in signals between magnets by scanning the same individuals on the same task in both Singapore and the United States, and we have found compelling preliminary evidence for replicability across magnets. On a number of important dimensions, the difference in neural signal from an individual tested on identical model magnets at both sites is no greater than the difference in the signal from an individual tested twice using the same magnet. This finding provides clear evidence that we may appropriately attribute signal differences to actual differences in subjects tested rather than to hardware.

We also recognize that culture is more remote from the individual than most other variables psychologists study. This distal nature of culture, combined with possible genetic differences between samples, as well as differences in education, diet, and other variables, can make it difficult to definitively argue that differences observed in neural activation are due to cultural beliefs and practices. These problems can be minimized when cultural brain research is guided by specific behavioral hypotheses (e.g., that East Asians show less activation of object areas), so that the research is confirmatory rather than exploratory. We have also found that working in an area of the brain (the ventral visual cortex) in which highly specific functions have been isolated in young Western adults has enhanced the precision of cultural hypotheses and interpretation of findings. Cross-cultural research focused on activations in the frontal cortex will prove to be more challenging, as this is a highly flexible and strategic area of the brain, with more variability between subjects in activation patterns.

Despite these concerns, the cultural neuroscience of aging has great potential for separating the relative contributions of experience and biology to the process of aging. Cultural neuroscience work may hold the key to the "use it or lose it" hypothesis of cognitive aging—that is, that neurocognitive health is maintained by sustained intellectual engagement across the lifespan. If we can find some structures that are systematically engaged more by Asians compared to Westerners, we might expect that these structures will maintain volume and function across the lifespan better in the culture that uses them more. Similarly, if certain patterns of neural recruitment (such as bilateral engagement of the frontal cortex) are shown to be universal with age across cultures, we can be relatively certain that such recruitment patterns are a result of biological aging rather than experience.

SUMMARY

Through both behavioral and neuroimaging cross-cultural studies, we can learn much about the interplay between biology and environment as it affects cognitive aging. Our knowledge about cognitive aging (and even about cognition in general) is almost entirely limited to Western samples. At present, our research suggests that many cognitive processes decline similarly across cultures, revealing the universality of cognitive aging. At the same time, however, it appears that culture modulates neurocognitive aging, as demonstrated by the differences in activation of object-processing areas in old adults from Asian versus Western cultures. The study of culture, cognition, and aging can answer questions, not only about modifiability of neurocognitive processes across the lifespan but also about the nature of social-cognitive function in late adulthood. For example, representations of self differ across cultures (Markus & Kitayama, 1991), and fMRI allows us to examine the neural circuitry underlying such differences and how it evolves with age. Our understanding of stability and flexibility regarding self in late adulthood could also be greatly expanded by examining the neurocognitive processes that occur in old and young bicultural individuals when they switch from one cultural frame to another. Another critically important question is whether culturally determined neural differences observed in aging brains become hardwired (e.g., structural changes occur and circuitry is automatically engaged) or merely reflect neural circuitry associated with strategy differences that can readily be controlled by individuals with appropriate instructions. Most important, the emergence of a cultural psychology of aging will inform us about the plasticity of the neurocognitive system, as well as about biological imperatives associated with cognitive aging that are unchanged by any cultural context.

Recommended Reading

Li, S.-C. (2003). Biocultural orchestration of developmental plasticity across levels: The interplay of biology and culture in shaping the mind and behavior across the life span. *Psychological Bulletin, 129*, 171–194.

Nisbett, R.E. (2003). *The geography of thought: How Asians and Westerners think differently . . . and why*. New York: The Free Press.

Nisbett, R.E., Peng, K., Choi, I. & Norenzayan, A. (2001). Culture and systems of thought: Holistic versus analytic cognition. *Psychological Review, 108*, 291–310.

Park, D.C., Nisbett, R., & Hedden, T. (1999). (See References)

Acknowledgments—Funding from the National Institute on Aging (Grant R01 AG015047) supported preparation of this article.

Note

1. Address correspondence to Denise Park, 405 N. Mathews, The Beckman Institute, The University of Illinois at Urbana-Champaign, Urbana, IL 61801; e-mail: denisep@uiuc.edu.

References

Baltes, P.B. (1987). Theoretical propositions of life-span developmental psychology: On the dynamics between growth and decline. *Developmental Psychology, 23*, 611–626.

Chee, M.W.L., Goh, J.O.S., Venkatraman, V., Tan, J.C., Gutchess, A., Sutton, B., Hebrank, A., Leshikar, E., & Park, D. (2006). Age-related changes in object processing and contextual binding revealed using fMR adaptation. *Journal of Cognitive Neuroscience, 18*, 495–507.

Chua, H.F., Boland, J.E., & Nisbett, R.E. (2005). Cultural variation in eye movements during scene perception. *Proceedings of the National Academy of Sciences, USA, 102*, 12629–12633.

Chua, H.F., Chen, W., & Park, D.C. (in press). Source memory, aging, and culture. *Gerontology*.

Draganski, B., Gaser, C., Busch, V., Schuierer, G., Bogdahn, U., & May, A. (2004). Changes in grey matter induced by training. *Nature, 427*, 311–312.

Gutchess, A.H., Welsh, R.C., Boduroglu, A., & Park, D.C. (in press). Cultural differences in neural function associated with object processing. *Cognitive, Affective, and Behavioral Neuroscience.*

Gutchess, A.H., Yoon, C., Luo, T., Feinberg, F., Hedden, T., Jing, Q., Nisbett, R.E., & Park, D.C. (in press). Categorical organization in free recall across culture and age. *Gerontology.*

Hedden, T., Park, D.C., Nisbett, R., Ji, L.-J., Jing, Q., & Jiao, S. (2002). Cultural variation in verbal versus spatial neuro-psychological function across the life span. *Neuropsychology, 16*, 65–73.

Markus, H.R., & Kitayama, S. (1991). Culture and the self: Implications for cognition, emotion, & motivation. *Psychological Review, 98*, 224–253.

Nisbett, R.E., & Masuda, T. (2003). Culture and point of view. *Proceedings of the National Academy of Sciences, USA, 100*, 11163–11170.

Park, D.C., & Gutchess, A.H. (2002). Aging, cognition, and culture: A neuroscientific perspective. *Neuroscience and Biobehavioral Reviews, 26*, 859–867.

Park, D.C., Lautenschlager, G., Hedden, T., Davidson, N.S., Smith, A.D., & Smith, P.K. (2002). Models of visuospatial and verbal memory across the adult life span. *Psychology & Aging, 17*, 299–320.

Park, D.C., Nisbett, R., & Hedden, T. (1999). Aging, culture, and cognition. *Journals of Gerontology Series B: Psychological Sciences and Social Sciences, 54*, P75–P84.

Reuter-Lorenz, P.A., & Lustig, C. (2005). Brain aging: Reorganizing discoveries about the aging mind. *Current Opinion in Neurobiology, 15*, 245–251.

Yoon, C., Feinberg, F., Hu, P., Gutchess, A.H., Hedden, T., Chen, H., Jing, Q., Cui, Y., & Park, D.C. (2004). Category norms as a function of culture and age: Comparisons of item responses to 105 categories by American and Chinese adults. *Psychology and Aging, 19*, 379–393.

Parental School Involvement and Children's Academic Achievement: Pragmatics and Issues

Nancy E. Hill[1]
Duke University

Lorraine C. Taylor
University of North Carolina

Abstract

Developing collaborations between families and schools to promote academic success has a long-standing basis in research and is the focus of numerous programs and policies. We outline some of the mechanisms through which parental school involvement affects achievement and identify how patterns and amounts of involvement vary across cultural, economic, and community contexts and across developmental levels. We propose next steps for research, focusing on the importance of considering students' developmental stages, the context in which involvement takes place, and the multiple perspectives through which involvement may be assessed. Finally, we discuss enhancing involvement in diverse situations.

Keywords

parental involvement; academic achievement; family-school partnerships

Families and schools have worked together since the beginning of formalized schooling. However, the nature of the collaboration has evolved over the years (Epstein & Sanders, 2002). Initially, families maintained a high degree of control over schooling by controlling hiring of teachers and apprenticeships in family businesses. By the middle of the 20th century, there was strict role separation between families and schools. Schools were responsible for academic topics, and families were responsible for moral, cultural, and religious education. In addition, family and school responsibilities for education were sequential. That is, families were responsible for preparing their children with the necessary skills in the early years, and schools took over from there with little input from families. However, today, in the context of greater accountability and demands for children's achievement, schools and families have formed partnerships and share the responsibilities for children's education. Parental school involvement is largely defined as consisting of the following activities: volunteering at school, communicating with teachers and other school personnel, assisting in academic activities at home, and attending school events, meetings of parent-teacher associations (PTAs), and parent-teacher conferences.

It is well established that parental school involvement has a positive influence on school-related outcomes for children. Consistently, cross-sectional (e.g., Grolnick & Slowiaczek, 1994) and longitudinal (e.g., Miedel & Reynolds, 1999) studies have demonstrated an association between higher levels of parental school involvement and greater academic success for children and adolescents. For young children, parental school involvement is associated with early school success, including academic and language skills and social competence (Grolnick & Slowiaczek, 1994; Hill, 2001; Hill & Craft, 2003). Head Start, the nation's largest intervention program for at-risk children, emphasizes the importance of parental involvement as a critical feature of children's early academic development because parental involvement promotes positive academic experiences for children and has positive effects on parents' self-development and parenting skills.

Most of the literature focuses on parental school involvement in elementary schools. Parental school involvement is thought to decrease as children move to middle and high school, in part because parents may believe that they cannot assist with more challenging high school subjects and because adolescents are becoming autonomous (Eccles & Harold, 1996). However, few parents stop caring about or monitoring the academic progress of their children of high school age, and parental involvement remains an important predictor of school outcomes through adolescence. For example, one study demonstrated that parental school involvement was associated with adolescents' achievement and future aspirations across middle and high school (Hill et al., in press). Moreover, although direct helping with homework declines in adolescence, parental school involvement during middle and high school is associated with an increase in the amount of time students spend on homework and with an increase in the percentage of homework completed (Epstein & Sanders, 2002).

HOW DOES PARENTAL SCHOOL INVOLVEMENT MAKE A DIFFERENCE?

There are two major mechanisms by which parental school involvement promotes achievement. The first is by increasing social capital. That is, parental school involvement increases parents' skills and information (i.e., social capital), which makes them better equipped to assist their children in their school-related activities. As parents establish relationships with school personnel, they learn important information about the school's expectations for behavior and homework; they also learn how to help with homework and how to augment children's learning at home (Lareau, 1996). When parents are involved in their children's schooling, they meet other parents who provide information and insight on school policies and practices, as well as extracurricular activities. Parents learn from other parents which teachers are the best and how difficult situations have been handled successfully. In addition, when parents and teachers interact, teachers learn about parents' expectations for their children and their children's teachers. Baker and Stevenson (1986) found that compared with parents who were not involved, involved parents developed more complex strategies for working with schools and their children to promote achievement.

Social control is a second mechanism through which parental school involvement promotes achievement. Social control occurs when families and schools work together to build a consensus about appropriate behavior that can be effectively communicated to children at both home and school (McNeal, 1999). Parents' coming to know one another and agree on goals—both behavioral and academic—serves as a form of social constraint that reduces problem behaviors.

When children and their peers receive similar messages about appropriate behavior across settings and from different sources, the messages become clear and salient, reducing confusion about expectations. Moreover, when families do not agree with each other or with schools about appropriate behavior, the authority and effectiveness of teachers, parents, or other adults may be undermined. Through both social capital and social control, children receive messages about the importance of schooling, and these messages increase children's competence, motivation to learn, and engagement in school (Grolnick & Slowiaczek, 1994).

FAMILY AND SCHOOL CHARACTERISTICS THAT INFLUENCE PARENTAL SCHOOL INVOLVEMENT

Parent-school relationships do not occur in isolation, but in community and cultural contexts. One of the biggest challenges schools have today is the increasing diversity among students (Lichter, 1996). Demographic characteristics, such as socioeconomic status, ethnicity, and cultural background, and other parental characteristics are systematically associated with parental school involvement. Overall, parents from higher socioeconomic backgrounds are more likely to be involved in schooling than parents of lower socioeconomic status. A higher education level of parents is positively associated with a greater tendency for them to advocate for their children's placement in honors courses and actively manage their children's education (Baker & Stevenson, 1986). In contrast, parents from lower socioeconomic backgrounds face many more barriers to involvement, including nonflexible work schedules, lack of resources, transportation problems, and stress due to residing in disadvantaged neighborhoods. Finally, because parents in lower-socioeconomic families often have fewer years of education themselves and potentially harbor more negative experiences with schools, they often feel ill equipped to question the teacher or school (Lareau, 1996). It is unfortunate that parents with children who would most benefit from parental involvement often find it most difficult to become and remain involved.

Involvement in school sometimes varies across ethnic or cultural backgrounds as well. Often, teachers who are different culturally from their students are less likely to know the students and parents than are teachers who come from similar cultural backgrounds; culturally different teachers are also more likely to believe that students and parents are disinterested or uninvolved in schooling (Epstein & Dauber, 1991). One study found that teachers believed that those parents who volunteered at school valued education more than other parents, and this belief about parents' values was in turn associated with the teachers' ratings of students' academic skills and achievement (Hill & Craft, 2003). Parental school involvement seems to function differently or serve different purposes in different ethnic and cultural groups. For example, African American parents often are more involved in school-related activities at home than at school, whereas Euro-American parents often are more involved in the actual school setting than at home (Eccles & Harold, 1996). This tendency to be more involved at home than at school may be especially true for ethnic minorities whose primary language is not English. Among African American kindergartners, parental involvement at school is associated with enhanced academic skills, perhaps reflecting the role of social capital (Hill & Craft, 2003), and the influence of parental involvement in schooling on achievement is stronger for African Americans than Euro-Americans among adolescents (Hill et al., in press).

Apart from demographic factors, parents' psychological state influences parental school involvement. Depression or anxiety present barriers to involvement in schooling. Studies consistently show that mothers who are depressed tend to be less involved than nondepressed mothers in preparing young children for school and also exhibit lower levels of involvement over the early years of school.

Self-perceptions also affect parents' school involvement. Negative feelings about themselves may hinder parents from making connections with their children's schools. Parents' confidence in their own intellectual abilities is the most salient predictor of their school involvement (Eccles & Harold, 1996). A factor that may be especially important in this regard is the experience of poverty. Poverty exerts direct effects on parents' mental health and self-perceptions through increased stress resulting from the struggle to make ends meet. Poverty also has indirect effects on children's early school outcomes because its adverse effects on parents are in turn associated with lower parental involvement in school.

Parents' own experiences as students shape their involvement in their children's schooling. As a parent prepares a child to start school, the parent's memories of his or her own school experiences are likely to become reactivated and may influence how the parent interprets and directs the child's school experiences (Taylor, Clayton, & Rowley, in press). Memories of supportive school experiences are likely to enhance parents' involvement and comfort interacting with their children's school.

In addition to characteristics of the parent and family, the school's context and policies influence parental school involvement. Teachers' encouragement of such involvement is associated with greater competence among parents in their interactions with their children and more parental involvement in academic activities at home (Epstein & Dauber, 1991). There is increasing recognition of the importance of promoting *schools'* readiness for children (Pianta, Cox, Taylor, & Early, 1999). "Ready schools" (Pianta et al., 1999) reach out to families, building relationships between families and the school setting before the first day of school. The success of teachers' and schools' efforts to encourage parental school involvement suggests that parents want and will respond to information about assisting their children. For example, LaParo, Kraft-Sayre, and Pianta (2003) found that the vast majority of families were willing to participate in school-initiated kindergarten-transition activities. These practices were associated with greater involvement across subsequent school years, underscoring the importance of school-based activities that encourage family-school links.

KEY ISSUES FOR RESEARCH

The most significant advances in the research on parental school involvement have arisen from the recognition that context is important and there are multiple dimensions to parental school involvement. Whether parental school involvement occurs because a child is having problems in school or because of ongoing positive dialogue between parents and school makes a difference in how involvement influences children's academic outcomes (Hill, 2001). For example, a parent who volunteers in the classroom to learn more about the teacher's expectations for students and a parent who volunteers in the classroom to monitor the teacher's behavior toward her child are both involved in the school, but only the latter parent is likely to create distrust that may impact the children's attitudes toward the school and the teacher.

Parental school involvement does not reflect just one set of activities. Such diverse activities as volunteering in the classroom, communicating with the teacher, participating in academic-related activities at home, communicating the positive value of education, and participating in the parent-teacher relationship are all included in parental school involvement, and each is related to school performance (Epstein & Sanders, 2002; Hill & Craft, 2003). Research on parental school involvement is taking these diverse factors into account.

Despite the recent advances in conceptualizing and studying parental school involvement, there are still challenges. First, the multidimensional nature of parental school involvement has led to a lack of agreement about definitions and to measurement inconsistencies, making it difficult to compare findings across studies. In addition, whereas research typically examines the relations between types of parental involvement and achievement, the types of parental involvement may influence each other. For example, a high-quality parent-teacher relationship may strengthen the positive impact of a parent's home involvement on achievement. And volunteering at school may lead to an increase in the communicated value of education or change the way parents become involved at home. Issues concerning the reciprocal relations among different types of involvement have yet to be addressed.

The second research challenge is integrating various perspectives. Whom should we survey when assessing parental school involvement? Parents? Teachers? Students? Is one perspective more accurate than another perspective? In fact, multiple perspectives are important for understanding parental school involvement. Although few studies have examined the influence of different perspectives on our understanding of parental school involvement, some studies found that teachers', children's, and parents' reports of parental school involvement were only moderately correlated, but each was related to achievement, suggesting that each perspective is unique and important (Hill et al., in press). The vast majority of research on parental school involvement, like parenting research, in based on mothers' involvement. What are the roles of fathers and other relatives? Does involvement of other family members vary according to demographic background?

Some research suggests that teachers' or parents' perspectives may be biased. Teachers often evaluate African American and low-income families more negatively than Euro-American and higher-income families (Epstein & Dauber, 1991). Moreover, teachers who are not particularly supportive of parental school involvement may tend to prejudge minority or low-income parents (Epstein & Dauber, 1991). Such stereotyping often results in substandard treatment of students and of parents when they do become involved.

Much of our knowledge about parental school involvement is based on research in elementary schools. Parental school involvement declines as children grow up, and middle and high schools are less likely than elementary schools to encourage involvement (Eccles & Harold, 1996). Despite this decline, parental school involvement remains associated with academic outcomes in adolescence (Epstein & Sanders, 2002; Hill et al., in press). Thus, the third research challenge is to take into consideration developmental changes in parental school involvement. Parental school involvement may be different for a 7th-grade student selecting course tracks or 11th-grade student selecting colleges than for a 1st-grade student learning to read. Current measures of parental school involvement do not reflect these developmental variations. In fact, parents' involvement in schooling may not decline during middle and high school; rather, the research may show declining involvement only because the nature of involvement changes in ways that are not reflected in our measures.

FROM RESEARCH TO PRACTICE

Evidence strongly supports the potential benefits of policies and programs to increase parental school involvement across the school years and even before children start school. Most parents want information about how to best support their children's education, but teachers have little time or resources to devote to promoting parental school involvement, and some parents are simply "hard to reach." How do we help teachers facilitate parental school involvement? Most teacher training programs do not include courses on how to effectively involve parents. Linking research on parental school involvement to teacher training programs may go far to support family-school collaborations.

When parents cannot become involved, how can schools compensate for the loss of the benefits of involvement? Understanding the mechanisms through which involvement promotes academic achievement would point to logical targets for intervention. For example, if parental school involvement promotes achievement through its effects on the completion and accuracy of homework, then providing homework monitors after school might be an appropriate intervention strategy.

Impoverished families are less likely to be involved in schooling than wealthier families, and schools in impoverished communities are less likely to promote parental school involvement than schools in wealthier communities. Consequently, the children who would benefit most from involvement are those who are least likely to receive it unless a special effort is made. Promoting parental school involvement entails more in disadvantaged schools than in wealthier schools. Compared with more advantaged parents, parents in impoverished communities often need much more information about how to promote achievement in their children, are overcoming more of their own negative school experiences, and have less social capital. Thus, programs and policies designed to promote parental school involvement in advantaged districts may be ineffective in promoting parental school involvement in high-risk or disadvantaged communities. Understanding each community's unique barriers and resources is important for establishing and maintaining effective collaborations between families and schools.

Recommended Reading

Booth, A., & Dunn, J.F. (Eds.). (1996). *Family-school links: How do they affect educational outcomes?* Mahwah, NJ: Erlbaum.
Epstein, J.L., & Sanders, M.G. (2002). (See References)

National PTA. (2000). *Building successful partnerships: A guide for developing parent and family involvement programs.* Bloomfield, IN: National Education Service.

Note

1. Address correspondence to Nancy E. Hill, Department of Psychology, Duke University, Box 90085, Durham, NC 27708-0085; e-mail: nancy@duke.edu.

References

Baker, D.P., & Stevenson, D.L. (1986). Mothers' strategies for children's school achievement: Managing the transition to high school. *Sociology of Education, 59,* 156–166.

Eccles, J.S., & Harold, R.D. (1996). Family involvement in children's and adolescents' schooling. In A. Booth & J.F. Dunn (Eds.), *Family-school links: How do they affect educational outcomes?* (pp. 3–34). Mahwah, NJ: Erlbaum.

Epstein, J.L., & Dauber, S.L. (1991). School programs and teacher practices of parent involvement in inner-city elementary and middle schools. *The Elementary School Journal, 91,* 289–305.

Epstein, J.L., & Sanders, M.G. (2002). Family, school, and community partnerships. In M.H. Bornstein (Ed.), *Handbook of parenting: Vol. 5. Practical issues in parenting* (pp. 407–437). Mahwah, NJ: Erlbaum.

Grolnick, W.S., & Slowiaczek, M.L. (1994). Parents' involvement in children's schooling: A multidimensional conceptualization and motivation model. *Child Development, 65,* 237–252.

Hill, N.E. (2001). Parenting and academic socialization as they relate to school readiness: The role of ethnicity and family income. *Journal of Educational Psychology, 93,* 686–697.

Hill, N.E., Castellino, D.R., Lansford, J.E., Nowlin, P., Dodge, K.A., Bates, J., & Pettit, G. (in press). Parent-academic involvement as related to school behavior, achievement, and aspirations: Demographic variations across adolescence. *Child Development.*

Hill, N.E., & Craft, S.A. (2003). Parent-school involvement and school performance: Mediated pathways among socioeconomically comparable African-American and Euro-American families. *Journal of Educational Psychology, 95,* 74–83.

LaParo, K.M., Kraft-Sayre, M., & Pianta, R.C. (2003). Preschool to kindergarten transition activities: Involvement and satisfaction of families and teachers. *Journal of Research in Childhood Education, 17*(2), 147–158.

Lareau, A. (1996). Assessing parent involvement in schooling: A critical analysis. In A. Booth & J.F. Dunn (Eds.), *Family-school links: How do they affect educational outcomes?* (pp. 57–64). Mahwah, NJ: Erlbaum.

Lichter, D.T. (1996). Family diversity, intellectual inequality, and academic achievement among American children. In A. Booth & J.F. Dunn (Eds.), *Family-school links: How do they affect educational outcomes?* (pp. 265–273). Mahwah, NJ: Erlbaum.

McNeal, R.B., Jr. (1999). Parental involvement as social capital: Differential effectiveness on science achievement, truancy, and dropping out. *Social Forces, 78,* 117–144.

Miedel, W.T., & Reynolds, A.J. (1999). Parent involvement in early intervention for disadvantaged children: Does it matter? *Journal of School Psychology, 37,* 370–402.

Pianta, R.C., Cox, M.J., Taylor, L.C., & Early, D.M. (1999). Kindergarten teachers' practices related to the transition into school: Results of a national survey. *Elementary School Journal, 100,* 71–86.

Taylor, L.C., Clayton, J.D., & Rowley, S.J. (in press). Academic socialization: Understanding parental influences on children's school-related development in the early years. *Review of General Psychology.*

This article has been reprinted as it originally appeared in *Current Directions in Psychological Science.* Citation information for this article as originally published appears above.

Children of the Affluent: Challenges to Well-Being

Suniya S. Luthar[1] and Shawn J. Latendresse
Teachers College, Columbia University

Abstract

Growing up in the culture of affluence can connote various psychosocial risks. Studies have shown that upper-class children can manifest elevated disturbance in several areas—such as substance use, anxiety, and depression—and that two sets of factors seem to be implicated, that is, excessive pressures to achieve and isolation from parents (both literal and emotional). Whereas stereotypically, affluent youth and poor youth are respectively thought of as being at "low risk" and "high risk," comparative studies have revealed more similarities than differences in their adjustment patterns and socialization processes. In the years ahead, psychologists must correct the long-standing neglect of a group of youngsters treated, thus far, as not needing their attention. Family wealth does not automatically confer either wisdom in parenting or equanimity of spirit; whereas children rendered atypical by virtue of their parents' wealth are undoubtedly privileged in many respects, there is also, clearly, the potential for some nontrivial threats to their psychological well-being.

Keywords

affluence; risk; contextual influences; socioeconomic status

Children of upper-class, highly educated parents are generally assumed to be at "low risk," but recent evidence suggests that they can face several unacknowledged pressures. In this article, we describe programmatic research relevant to this issue. We begin by characterizing the samples of youth we have studied across suburban communities in the Northeast. We then provide an overview of findings of problems in various spheres of adjustment and discuss associated implications for research, practice, and policy.

RESEARCH INVOLVING UPPER-CLASS SAMPLES

Since the late 1990s, our group has accumulated data on three cohorts of youth from high-income communities; characteristics of these cohorts are summarized in Table 1. The first, which we refer to as Cohort I, consisted of 264 tenth graders attending a suburban high school serving three contiguous towns.[2] These students were followed annually through their senior year, and as sophomores, we contrasted them with 224 tenth graders in an inner-city school.

Cohort II encompassed 302 middle school students from another high-income town, whom we studied when they were in the sixth and seventh grades (Luthar & Becker, 2002). Cohort III, subsequently recruited from the same community as Cohort II, incorporated all children attending the sixth grade during the 1998–1999 academic year, and these students were then followed annually (11th-grade assessments had been completed at the time of writing this report). In parallel, we obtained annual assessments of an inner-city middle school sample,

Table 1. *Characteristics of the samples*

Source and sample	N	Minority ethnicity in sample (%)	Eligible for free or reduced lunch in school (%)	Median annual family income in region (census)	Adults with graduate or professional degrees in region (%; census)
Luthar & D'Avanzo (1999)					
Suburban Cohort I: 10th graders followed through high school	264	18	1	$80,000–$102,000	24–37
Comparison sample: inner-city 10th graders	224	87	86	$35,000	5
Luthar & Becker (2002)					
Suburban Cohort II: 6th and 7th graders	302	8	3	$120,000	33
Luthar & Latendresse (in press)					
Suburban Cohort III: 6th graders followed annually through high school (ongoing)	314	7	3	$125,000	33
Comparison sample: inner-city 6th graders followed through 8th grade	300	80	79	$27,000	6

enabling further comparisons of youngsters from widely disparate sociodemographic settings.

EVIDENCE OF ADJUSTMENT DISTURBANCES

The first set of questions addressed with Cohort I was focused on substance use and related problems (Luthar & D'Avanzo, 1999), and descriptive analyses showed many signs of trouble among the suburban students. These youngsters reported significantly higher use of cigarettes, alcohol, marijuana, and hard drugs than did their inner-city counterparts, and also showed elevations in comparison with national norms. Suburban teens also reported significantly higher anxiety and somewhat higher depression than did inner-city youth. In comparison with normative samples, girls in the suburbs were three times more likely to report clinically significant levels of depression.

Also disturbing were findings on correlates of substance use. Among affluent (but not inner-city) youth, substance use was linked with depression and anxiety, suggesting efforts to self-medicate; this "negative affect" type of substance use tends to be sustained over time, rather than remitting soon after the teen years. In addition, among suburban boys (but not other subgroups in the study), popularity with classmates was linked with high substance use, suggesting that the peer group may endorse and even encourage substance use among affluent teenage boys.

In Cohort II, we saw no evidence of disturbance among the sixth graders, but among the seventh graders, some problems were beginning to emerge (Luthar & Becker, 2002). Among the older girls, for example, rates of clinically significant depressive symptoms were twice as high as those in normative samples. Whereas no boys in the sixth grade had used alcohol or marijuana, 7% of seventh-grade boys reported having drunk alcohol until intoxicated or using marijuana about once a month. Finally, results supported the earlier findings on correlates of substance use, which had significant links with depression and anxiety in this middle school sample, and with peer popularity among the seventh-grade boys.

In Cohort III, as well, preliminary data showed that suburban sixth graders scored below national norms on depression and anxiety, and also had lower scores than inner-city comparison youth. Once again, however, some signs of trouble began to emerge by the seventh grade, with popular students, for example, reporting significantly higher levels of substance use than others (Luthar & Sexton, 2004). We are currently examining different developmental pathways to problems and to well-being from pre- through midadolescence.

WHY MIGHT "PRIVILEGED" YOUTH BE TROUBLED?

In exploring pathways to maladjustment in affluent suburbia, we considered two sets of potential antecedents in our study of Cohort II. The first encompassed *achievement pressures*. Statistical analyses showed, in fact, that children with very high perfectionist strivings—those who saw achievement failures as personal failures—had relatively high depression, anxiety, and substance use, as did those who indicated that their parents overemphasized their accomplishments, valuing them disproportionately more than their personal character (Luthar & Becker, 2002).

The second potential antecedent was *isolation from adults*, both literal and emotional. Among upper-middle-class families, secondary school students are often left home alone for several hours each week, with many parents believing that this promotes self-sufficiency. Similarly, suburban children's needs for emotional closeness may often suffer as the demands of professional parents' careers erode relaxed "family time" and youngsters are shuttled between various after-school activities. Again, results showed that both literal and emotional isolation were linked to distress as well as substance use.

We next sought to explore family functioning in greater depth among sixth graders in Cohort III and, simultaneously, their inner-city counterparts. A common assumption is that parents are more accessible to high- than to low-income youth, but our data showed otherwise (Luthar & Latendresse, in press). We considered children's perceptions of seven aspects of parenting, and average ratings on four of these dimensions were similar for the two sets of students: felt closeness to mothers, felt closeness to fathers, parental values emphasizing integrity, and regularity of eating dinner with parents. Inner-city students did fare more poorly than suburban students on two of the remaining three dimensions—parental criticism and lack of after-school supervision—but at the same time, they did significantly better than suburban students on the last dimension, parental expectations.

Results also revealed the surprising unique significance of children's eating dinner with at least one parent on most nights. Even after the other six parenting dimensions (including emotional closeness both to mothers and to fathers) were taken into account, this simple family routine was linked not only to children's self-reported adjustment, but also to their performance at school. Striking, too, were the similarities of links involving family dining among families ostensibly easily able to arrange for shared leisure time and those who had to cope with the sundry exigencies of everyday life in poverty.

Subsequent analyses with Cohort III students and their inner-city counterparts when they were in the seventh grade revealed similarities in peer-group influences as well (Luthar & Sexton, 2004). Early adolescents at both socioeconomic extremes showed admiration for classmates who openly flouted authority. In the suburban context, high peer status was linked with overt displays of low academic effort, disobedience at school, aggressiveness among girls, and substance use among boys, and in the urban context, high peer status was associated with aggression and substance use among both boys and girls. Also noteworthy were startlingly strong links between physical attractiveness and peer popularity among affluent girls. This variable alone explained more than half the variation in their popularity scores, suggesting particularly high emphasis on physical appearance among this subgroup of girls (the links between attractiveness and popularity were substantially weaker among inner-city girls and among both groups of boys). All in all, the substantive message was that affluent adolescents, just like their inner-city counterparts, valued some peer attributes that could potentially compromise overall competence or well-being.

DOES REBELLION AMONG AFFLUENT TEENS REALLY "MATTER"?

All adolescents might be drawn to overt forms of rebellion, but it is quite plausible that wealthy youth, unlike their poor counterparts, can dabble in drug use or delinquency without any substantive damage to their life prospects, given various safety nets (i.e., concerned adults and access to high-quality treatment services). To examine this possibility, we returned to our high school Cohort I data, as older teens reflect more variability on such forms of behavioral deviance than middle school students do. Once again, our findings showed that youth at the socioeconomic extremes were more similar than different (Luthar & Ansary, in press). In both settings, we found a distinct subgroup of teens who manifested multiple behavior problems—substance use, delinquency, poor interest in academics—and had school grades that were significantly lower than the average. Although the findings on urban adolescents were unsurprising in light of prior empirical evidence, the results on affluent youth were noteworthy in indicating that, despite the resources ostensibly available to them, nearly 1 of every 10 teenagers in this cohort exhibited high levels of behavior disturbances across multiple domains, and concurrently experienced significant risk for poor grades during the sophomore year of high school.

We also examined substance use among this subgroup of suburban sophomores annually through the remainder of high school (McMahon & Luthar, 2004). Twenty percent of these students showed persistently high substance use across time. Furthermore, across all three assessments, this group also showed relatively high levels of depression and physiologically manifest anxiety (e.g., nausea, difficulty breathing), as well as poor grades and negative teacher ratings. For as many as one in five of these affluent youth, therefore, high substance use, coexisting with depression, anxiety, and both behavioral and academic problems, was sustained up to the age of 18 years.

IMPLICATIONS FOR INTERVENTIONS

All is not necessarily well among children of the affluent. Across three suburban cohorts, a nontrivial proportion of youth reported diverse adjustment problems, and disconnectedness in families and pressured lifestyles constituted discernible challenges (for parallel evidence among adult samples, see Csikszentmihalyi, 1999; Kasser, 2002; Myers, 2000).

Why do affluent youth have these problems—despite all the mental health services ostensibly available? One possibility is that although high-income parents are generally willing to place overtly troubled youth in psychotherapy or on medication, they are less eager to delve into the less "conspicuous" problems in their children, in themselves, or in family processes more generally. Research has shown, for example, that parents in general tend to be aware when their children are depressed, but tend not to seek professional help unless symptoms include those that inconvenience adults, such as disobedience or asthma (Puura et al., 1998).

Upper-class parents can be particularly reluctant to seek help for the less visible problems because of privacy concerns, as well as embarrassment. Affluent adults are often very concerned about keeping family troubles private; this is not surprising, as misfortunes of the wealthy tend to evoke a malicious pleasure in people who are less well-off (a phenomenon called *schaden-freude*; see Feather & Sherman, 2002). Upper-class parents also can feel more compelled than most to maintain a veneer of well-being, feeling that "those at the top are supposed to be better able to handle their problems than those further down the scale" (Wolfe & Fodor, 1996, p. 80).

Then there are realities of everyday lives that impede change. In the subculture of affluent suburbia, overscheduled days are often the norm for young people, with high school students participating in numerous activities, which can then be logged on college applications. The careers of many parents, similarly, do in fact demand long work hours: Job sharing and flexible hours are not an option for chief executive officers or university presidents. At the same time, these careers do bring many personal rewards, including the gratification of mastering substantial professional challenges, and of providing well for stellar educations and leisure activities for the next generation. Few people would blithely repudiate such rewards.

Also relevant is practitioners' perseverance—or lack thereof—in pursuing nascent signs of trouble. School psychologists, for example, often hesitate to express concerns to high-income parents, anticipating resistance and sometimes even threats of lawsuits. Consequently (and paradoxically), wealthy youth can end up having less access to school-based counseling services than do students who are less well-off (Pollak & Schaffer, 1985). Clinicians may also minimize problems they see among the wealthy. The same symptoms are more often viewed as signs of mental illness among the poor than among the affluent; by corollary, the rich are more often dismissed as "not needing help" even when they report distress commensurate with that of others typically judged to be needing assistance (Luthar & Sexton, 2004).

Even if affluent youth do, in fact, receive high-quality psychiatric care, it should be emphasized that this is no substitute for strong attachments with parents. Decades of work on children's mental health policies have established that psychotherapy to address crystallized maladjustment is largely unproductive as long as the child's everyday life continues to present major challenges to adjustment (Knitzer, 2000).

In the future, an expedient first step toward addressing these issues would be to raise awareness of the potential costs of overscheduled, competitive lifestyles (Luthar & Sexton, 2004). This can be done effectively via books comprehensible to the lay public, such as those by Kasser (2002) and Myers (2000). Although obviously not panaceas, such dissemination efforts could begin to sensitize caregivers to risks in the context of affluence—risks that they (like developmental scientists) may have been only faintly aware of in the past.

Consideration of these issues is important not only for the families themselves, but also for society in general. Many children of highly educated, affluent parents will likely come to assume positions of influence in society, and their own equanimity of spirit may have far-reaching ramifications. Depression vastly impairs productivity. And people who are unhappy, with a fragile, meager sense of self, can be more acquisitive than philanthropic, focused more on gaining more for themselves than on improving the lot of others (Diener & Biswas-Diener, 2002).

CONCLUSIONS

Until the 1970s, developmental scientists had largely ignored children in poverty, and it is critical to correct the neglect of another group of youngsters heretofore invisible in psychological science: those in high-income families. Systematic research is needed on the generalizability of research results obtained thus far. Scientists need to establish, for instance, whether elevated distress or pressured lifestyles occur in wealthy metropolitan locations, and not just in suburban communities. It will also be important to determine whether these problems are discernible in nationally representative samples (assuming, of course, that high-income families are appropriately represented in them). Also critical are prospective studies that can indicate (a) whether problems such as depression or drug use generally represent temporary blips of adolescent angst among the wealthy or are early signs of continuing problems and, conversely, (b) if factors such as prolonged isolation and pressure within families do, in fact, set apart those teens who carry adolescent adjustment disturbances into adulthood. Finally, practitioners and parents must be alert to the risks potentially attached to wealth and status. The American dream spawns widespread beliefs that Ivy League educations and subsequently lucrative careers are critical for children's long-term happiness. In the sometimes single-minded pursuit of these goals, let us not lose sight of the possible costs to mental health and well-being of all concerned.

Recommended Reading

Csikszentmihalyi, M. (1999). (See References)
Kasser, T. (2002). (See References)
Luthar, S.S. (2003). The culture of affluence: Psychological costs of material wealth. *Child Development, 74,* 1581–1593.
Luthar, S.S., & Sexton, C. (2004). (See References)
Myers, D.G. (2000). (See References)

Acknowledgments—Preparation of this manuscript was supported by grants from the National Institutes of Health (RO1-DA10726, RO1-DA11498, RO1-DA14385), the William T. Grant Foundation, and the Spencer Foundation.

Notes

1. Address correspondence to Suniya S. Luthar, Teachers College, Columbia University, 525 West 120th St., Box 133, New York, NY 10027-6696.
2. We are currently examining effects of varying affluence across neighborhoods subsumed in wealthy townships.

References

Csikszentmihalyi, M. (1999). If we are so rich, why aren't we happy? *American Psychologist, 54,* 821–827.
Diener, E., & Biswas-Diener, R. (2002). Will money increase subjective well-being? *Social Indicators Research, 57,* 119–169.
Feather, N.T., & Sherman, R. (2002). Envy, resentment, Schaden-freude, and sympathy: Reactions to deserved and undeserved achievement and subsequent failure. *Personality and Social Psychology Bulletin, 28,* 953–961.
Kasser, T. (2002). *The high price of materialism.* Cambridge, MA: MIT Press.

Knitzer, J. (2000). Early childhood mental health services: A policy and systems development perspective. In J.P. Shonkoff & S.J. Meisels (Eds.), *Handbook of early childhood intervention* (2nd ed., pp. 416–438). New York: Cambridge University Press.

Luthar, S.S., & Ansary, N.S. (in press). Dimensions of adolescent rebellion: Risks for academic failure among high- and low-income youth. *Development and Psychopathology*.

Luthar, S.S., & Becker, B.E. (2002). Privileged but pressured: A study of affluent youth. *Child Development, 73*, 1593–1610.

Luthar, S.S., & D'Avanzo, K. (1999). Contextual factors in substance use: A study of suburban and inner-city adolescents. *Development and Psychopathology, 11*, 845–867.

Luthar, S.S., & Latendresse, S.J. (in press). Comparable "risks" at the SES extremes: Pre-adolescents' perceptions of parenting. *Development and Psychopathology*.

Luthar, S.S., & Sexton, C. (2004). The high price of affluence. In R.V. Kail (Ed.), *Advances in child development* (Vol. 32, pp. 126–162). San Diego, CA: Academic Press.

McMahon, T.J., & Luthar, S.S. (2004). *Substance use, psychopathology, and social competence: A longitudinal study of affluent, suburban, high school students.* Manuscript submitted for publication.

Myers, D.G. (2000). *The American paradox: Spiritual hunger in an age of plenty.* New Haven, CT: Yale University Press.

Pollak, J.M., & Schaffer, S. (1985). The mental health clinician in the affluent public school setting. *Clinical Social Work Journal, 13*, 341–355.

Puura, K., Almqvist, F., Tamminen, T., Piha, J., Kumpulainen, K., Raesaenen, E., Moilanen, I., & Koivisto, A.M. (1998). Children with symptoms of depression: What do adults see? *Journal of Child Psychology and Psychiatry and Allied Disciplines, 39*, 577–585.

Wolfe, J.L., & Fodor, I.G. (1996). The poverty of privilege: Therapy with women of the "upper classes." *Women & Therapy, 18*, 73–89.

Section 6: Critical Thinking Questions

1. One challenge that underlies the articles in this section is the degree to which investigations of cultural effects on development must rely on correlational designs that necessarily entail potentially important confounds. Select one or two articles and identify one or more potential confounds in each that make it difficult to determine if cultural effects being studied are in fact the factors responsible for observed outcomes. Have the investigators acknowledged the potential problems of their correlational designs? Can you suggest research designs that might be used to clarify results from this correlational research?

2. One point that emerges from the articles in this section is that developmental outcomes may differ as a consequence of dimensions that differ over cultures (e.g., a difference in individualistic vs. group orientation in Western vs. East Asian cultures; the availability of different mathematical tools across history and cultures). But it is not always necessary to travel to distant lands or to go back hundreds of years to see cultural contrasts. Consider the dramatic changes in technologies that have occurred in our own lifetimes. Pick one or two of these (e.g., cell phones, Global Positioning Systems [GPS], access to the Internet via handheld devices) and speculate about how each may be affecting some aspect of cognitive development (e.g., memory, spatial skills) and some aspect of social development (e.g., parent-child or peer relationships). How would these new technologies be viewed from an evolutionary, comparative perspective like the one taken by Tomasello?

This article has been reprinted as it originally appeared in *Current Directions in Psychological Science*. Citation information for this article as originally published appears above.